Essentials of
Polygraph and
Polygraph Testing

Essentials of
Polygraph and
Polygraph Testing

Nathan J. Gordon

CRC Press
Taylor & Francis Group
Boca Raton London New York

CRC Press is an imprint of the
Taylor & Francis Group, an **informa** business

CRC Press
Taylor & Francis Group
6000 Broken Sound Parkway NW, Suite 300
Boca Raton, FL 33487-2742

Printed on acid-free paper
Version Date: 20160825

International Standard Book Number-13: 978-1-4987-5771-3 (Hardback)

Library of Congress Cataloging-in-Publication Data

Names: Gordon, Nathan J., author.
Title: Essentials of polygraph and polygraph testing / Nathan J. Gordon, M.A.
Description: Boca Raton, FL : CRC Press, [2017]
Identifiers: LCCN 2016020930| ISBN 9781498757713 (hardback) | ISBN 1498757715 (hardback) | ISBN 9781315438627 (web pdf) | ISBN 1315438631 (web pdf)
Subjects: LCSH: Lie detectors and detection--United States.
Classification: LCC HV8078 .G67 2017 | DDC 363.25/4--dc23
LC record available at https://lccn.loc.gov/2016020930

Visit the Taylor & Francis Web site at
http://www.taylorandfrancis.com

and the CRC Press Web site at
http://www.crcpress.com

Printed and bound in the United States of America by Publishers Graphics,
LLC on sustainably sourced paper.

I dedicate this book to Cleve Backster. I believe he had the greatest influence on the polygraph profession, as well as on my own development. Along with the other "gods" of polygraph, they have set the foundation for me and others to build on.

Polygraph Examiner's Prayer

By William L. Fleisher

Thank you for blessing us with the knowledge

to recognize the truth and detect deception;

Always help us to remember that our skills have the power

to clear the innocent and capture the guilty;

Strengthen our conviction that each person before us is one of your children and should always be treated with respect and fairness regardless of the charges against them;

By your grace, allow us to reach inward for the strength

and insight with which we have been Blessed;

Never let us forget that ours is an honorable and noble profession and that our greatest challenge is not to identify the guilty,

but to clear the innocent;

Grant us to have the faith in our art, that under Your watchful eye, the guilty will always reveal themselves;

With these words we affirm our gratitude to You

for Your continued trust in us.

Bless us who are here to share, to learn and to seek the truth.

Contents

Preface

One only has to go to the early pages of the Holy Bible, in Genesis, to realize crime has existed from the very beginnings of our species, or, to any newspaper around the world today to realize it remains.

Criminal investigations, as we know it today, only began in eighteenth-century England, when massive changes in society were occurring due to the Agricultural and Industrial Revolutions. In 1750, Henry Fielding established a small group of volunteer, nonuniformed homeowners known as the "Bow Street Runners." These Londoners ran to the scenes of reported crimes and began investigations, thus becoming the first modern detective force. It wasn't until 1829, due to the efforts of Sir Robert Peel, that the English Parliament created the Metropolitan Police Force in London, with their headquarters eventually becoming known as "Scotland Yard."

The development of policing in the United States closely followed the development of policing in England. In the early colonies, policing took two forms. The watch system was composed of community volunteers whose primary duty was to warn of impending danger. Boston created a night watch in 1636, New York in 1658, and Philadelphia in 1700. Philadelphia created the first day watch in 1833. Augmenting the watch system was a system of constables, official law enforcement officers, usually paid by the fee system for warrants they served. It was not until the 1830s that the idea of a centralized municipal police department first emerged in the United States.

One of the leading law enforcement officials in the United States in the early 1900s was August Vollmer, Chief of Police, Berkeley, California. Due to his insight, the Berkeley California Police Department became the first police department in the world to develop and utilize a new investigative tool—the polygraph.

Polygraph takes the investigator where no other investigative tool can go—into the mind of the suspect. Today it is without question the "gold standard" for truth verification. Polygraph testing is used in all types of investigations, screening of applicants for almost every government and law enforcement agency in the United States and companies considered by the government to be of high importance to the public. Polygraph plays a major role in the intelligence community and in protecting our country. It is used to ensure community safety from offenders of serious crimes, such as sexual offenders, offenders of domestic violence, and offenders who have been convicted of driving under the influence. It is with great responsibility that the professional polygraph examiner applies his/her art in the search for truth.

The author intends to give a critical insight into the art of truth verification and hopefully share valuable information based on years of studying, applying, and teaching polygraph to those interested in the essentials of polygraph, as well as enhance the knowledge and skills of those who have entered into the profession of polygraph testing.

Acknowledgments

I thank the true pioneers of the polygraph profession. I have always called them the polygraph Gods: Leonarde Keeler, John E. Reid, Cleve Backster, and Richard O. Arther. From their sharing, teaching, and nurturing came excellent examiners who rose to great heights in our profession—examiners like Frank Horvath, Gordon Barland, Ron Decker, Stanley Abrams, Warren Holmes, Ed Gelb, Bob Brisintine, Eric Holden, Lynn Marcy, and Shirley Sturm, and a whole list of men and women that have spent their lives in the search for truth.

I am grateful to have had the opportunity to share pieces of my career and exchange experiences and ideas with my colleagues: Philip Cochetti, my first partner in polygraph; William Fleisher, who has been my partner for the past 20 years; Essam Gamaleldin; Tuvia Shurany; Jim Matte; and Ray Morgan.

Polygraph has given me the opportunity to lecture and meet people from around the world. I have lectured throughout the United States, Mexico, Hong Kong, Switzerland, Philippines, Colombia, Guatemala, Israel, South Africa, Nigeria, Saudi Arabia, Egypt, Turkey, Singapore, the United Arab Emirates, and Russia. I have shared my ideas with such prestigious groups as the CIA, FBI, Secret Service, and the staff at Camp David.

Special thanks to Gloria Alvarado, my office manager and my professional "right hand." She is the office boss that keeps me focused on the tasks at hand. I also thank our administrative assistant Kim Norton for helping proof this book, and Stacy Forchetti, Esq., for assisting in writing Chapter 11.

I would be remiss not to thank my wife Kathy, my daughters, and grandchildren. They have always supported my efforts and tolerated the many weeks each year I have spent away from home sharing my experiences and teaching those in pursuit of the profession.

Author

Nathan J. Gordon is director of the Academy for Scientific Investigative Training (www. polygraph-training.com), where he was the principal developer of the Integrated Zone Comparison Technique, Polygraph Verification Test, Horizontal Scoring System, the Academy's Algorithm for Manual Scoring, ASIT PolySuite Computerized Algorithm for Data Analysis, the Forensic Assessment Interview Technique, and the Integrated Interrogation Technique.

Gordon is an internationally recognized expert in the fields of forensic psychophysiology, forensic assessment, and interviewing and interrogation. He has lectured and conducted seminars on these subjects to thousands of law enforcement, intelligence, and private security officers throughout the United States, Africa, Europe, Latin America, and Asia. He has conducted lectures for such prestigious groups as the Central Intelligence Agency, the Federal Bureau of Investigation, the Secret Service, and the staff at Camp David.

Gordon is president of the International Society of Polygraph Examiners (www.isope.net), president of the Pennsylvania Polygraph Examiners' Association, former president of the American Polygraph Association, and a member of the board of directors of the Vidocq Society, a cold case pro bono homicide organization, where he was awarded the Vidocq Medal of Honor for assisting in the confession that led to the resolution of the 14-year-old cold case of Terri Brooks' homicide.

He has a master's degree in criminology, a baccalaureate degree in psychology, and an associate's degree in criminal justice. Gordon is also a member of the American Society of Industrial Security, ASTM International, the American Association of Police Polygraphists, Association for the Treatment of Sexual Abusers, and the American Academy of Forensic Sciences.

Polygraph History

1

All truths are easy to understand once they are discovered; the point is to discover them.

Galileo Galilei

In 2007, the American Polygraph Association (APA) under the direction of President Donald Krapohl introduced a standard of practice that stipulated that within 5 years (by January 1, 2012), all polygraph techniques being taught at accredited schools and used by field examiners must meet certain levels of criterion accuracy. A meta-analysis study was performed to identify those formats that qualified.[1] All techniques had to have at least two independent research studies showing its accuracy. Approved polygraph techniques had to have less than a 20% inconclusive rate. These techniques would then be classified into the following groups:

Evidentiary techniques	Any polygraph examination that was being conducted to be submitted to a judicial proceeding, which required a mean accuracy of 90% or above.
Paired testing techniques	Paired testing (also known as the "Marin Protocol") is a method of utilizing polygraph testing in situations in which two or more subjects assert contradictory accounts of a particular incident in such a way that at least one of the subjects must certainly be lying. The method utilizes two independent examiners with established accuracy and error rates to assess the veracity of at least two subjects in such circumstances. Paired testing requires a mean accuracy of 86% or above.
Investigative techniques	Defined as a polygraph examination, which is intended to supplement and/or assist an investigation and for which the examiner has not been informed and does not reasonably believe that the results of the examination will be tendered for admission as evidence in a court proceeding. Types of investigative examinations can include applicant testing, counterintelligence screening, community safety examinations (e.g., postconviction sex offender testing, domestic violence testing, intoxicated drivers on probation), as well as multiple-facet diagnostic testing.[2] The mean accuracy required for investigative examinations is 80% or above.[3]

The need to detect deception is hardly a twentieth-century phenomenon. Ever since small familial groups of humans banded together for mutual social benefit, or for protection of person and property, individuals whose practices deviated from the societal covenant have plagued humankind. The activities of these individuals, if not checked, could sometimes destroy the societal group as a whole.[4]

Given that, the search for a reliable means to identify the untrustworthy is as ancient as man. Some techniques were founded in superstition and/or the religious belief that a moral God would in some way reveal the truth and disallow immorality. Many of these attempts, in fact, had some psychological or physiological basis; other methods relied solely on fear of continued pain and torture.[4]

The earliest form of lie detection was the resolving of an issue through battle, which is called "trial by combat." Consider the problem of two primitive men who approach a fallen prey. Each believes he killed it and that it belongs to him; they refuse to compromise. As simplistic as it seems, each sees himself as making a truthful claim and the other as not. To decide the "truth," which actually means possession, they engage in combat. The ideal assumption is that the individual with truth on his side will prevail. However, the most cunning and skilled of the combatants usually was victorious and got to eat that night, while the other did not. Not a very fair way of determining truth!

The scenario changed very little by medieval times. It was the custom that knights engage in mortal combat to decide whose Lord had the right in any given controversy (Figure 1.1). While the practice was functionally the

Figure 1.1 It was thought that the knight representing the truth would be victorious due to "divine intervention."

same as trial by combat, the ethical premise was different. It was held that while the fighting skill of an individual was not related to his truth or lying, the knight representing the truth would be victorious due to "divine intervention," that is, that God would ensure the correct outcome.

The interesting thing about tests for truth is they rarely become extinct. So even today, in any major city around the world on any given weekend night, police are summoned to a local club or bar where two men are about to enter into "trial by combat" to determine who the young lady seated between them is really with.

The next development in the search for truth was "trial by ordeal.[5]" It was assumed once again that God would intervene on behalf of the innocent and would not allow any innocent individual to be harmed. While these attempts to detect truth appeared to be laden with religious beliefs, they were in fact based on practical observations of both psychological and physiological phenomena, which play an important role in the truth-finding processes.

For example, in China, in approximately 1000 BC, it was common practice to have an accused person chew a handful of dry crushed rice and then attempt to spit it out. If the rice became wet from saliva and therefore easy to spit out, the person was considered truthful. If the rice remained dry due to a lack of salivation in the mouth and did not stick together making it difficult for the suspect to spit out, then he was thought to be lying. However, the gods were not involved in this test as much as the salivary gland. As you can see, this test was based on the physiological phenomenon of inhibited salivary gland activity caused by fear or stress. The truthful individual had normal salivary gland activity, causing the rice to become wet and easy to spit out. The stressed or deceptive person had a dry mouth, and the rice in his or her mouth remained dry, making it difficult to spit out. It is unclear how the Chinese arrived at their test for truth. They either just observed that liars' mouths remained dry or had some understanding that the autonomic nervous system inhibits salivation and all digestive processes when an individual is under serious threat.

It is interesting that testing for a dry mouth was and continues to be found in a wide range of diverse and unrelated societies. The most severe version of these tests often consisted of putting some type of hot object on the tongue. If the person was truthful, the normal saliva in the mouth protected the tongue from being burnt. If the person was lying, the mouth became dry and the hot metal burned and blistered the unprotected tongue, as can be seen in Figure 1.2. Even today, in the Middle East, it is common in some geographical areas that the accused in minor cases can choose this traditional method to prove their innocence.

In various societies, truth tests were developed whose premises were psychological, not physiological. Trial by the "sacred ass[6]" is a classic psychological test that was practiced in India, around 500 BC. In this test, a donkey was

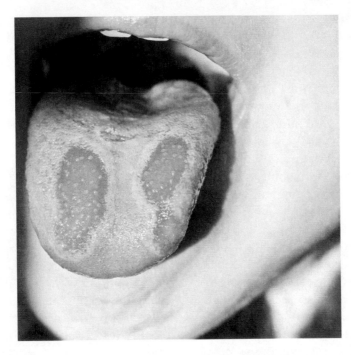

Figure 1.2 According to many cultures, if the person was lying, the mouth became dry and the hot metal burned and blistered the unprotected tongue.

staked out in the center of a pitch dark hut. The priests informed the suspect that inside the hut was a "sacred ass" that could differentiate between a truthful person and a liar when its tail was pulled. It did this by braying only when the guilty (lying) person pulled its tail. They were also told the animal would remain silent if an innocent (truthful) person pulled its tail.

Each suspect was sent into the hut alone with instructions to pull the tail of the "sacred ass." Unbeknownst to the suspects, the priests had covered the donkey's tail with lamp black, or soot. The truthful individuals, having nothing to fear, entered and pulled the tail. The donkey may or may not have brayed, but those who were innocent came out with soot all over their hands. The guilty party, on the other hand, would enter the hut and not risk pulling the donkey's tail and disclosing their guilt. He might promise it an apple or stroke the donkey's head, but he would not pull the tail. After all, he believed if he did not touch the tail of the "sacred ass," it would have no reason to bray and he would fool the priests into incorrectly identifying him as truthful. However, by not pulling the tail, it became a simple matter for the priests to properly identify him by his clean hands.

Society's next advancement in its search for truth was "trial by torture." The assumption was that an innocent suspect would withstand any amount of suffering to preserve his reputation and, in religious societies,

Figure 1.3 Three women executed as witches in Derneburg, Germany, in October 1555. Europeans began prosecuting suspected witches in the fourteenth century. Sixteenth-century woodcut with modern watercolor.

his immortal soul. In reality, given enough pain, any man might confess, and most torturers knew that. "The trial," in fact, became indistinguishable from the punishment itself and was justified in that the "truth seekers" found almost everyone guilty. "Trial by torture" was the method of justice during the infamous witch hunts and inquisitions in Europe (Figure 1.3).

These latter methods are of particular interest, since they did not have as their basis the seeking of truth. Rather, the method addressed a perceived threat from forces whose existence could not be proven. Thus, "trials by torture" were not always designed to find truth, but sometimes to justify and validate the prejudices and fears of the society and the claims of its leaders. Such "trials" were commonplace during the Middle Ages and the Renaissance and continue into more recent periods when people believed that witches or some other group (e.g., Jews, communists, reactionaries, homosexuals) threatened the social order.

During the infamous witch hunts in Europe, two of the ways an inquisitor attempted to prove a person was a witch were[7] (1) finding the "devil's mark" and (2) getting a confession. The devil's mark was an alleged spot on a witch's body that showed she had been attached to the devil (much like we have a navel where we were once attached to our mothers). Although the devil's mark was invisible, it could be found because it was a spot on the witch's body that would not bleed. Suspected witches were tied down and continuously pricked as the inquisitors searched for the spot. It is not known how many witches were discovered by finding the elusive mark; however, many "witches" confessed during the process. Unfortunately, "trial by torture" is still used today to solve "crimes" by confession, the solution of the crime being of greater importance than whether the suspect is actually guilty or innocent.

As civilized societies searched for a more just and credible way to separate the innocent from the guilty, "trial by torture" lost credibility and was replaced by "trial by jury." While the jury in its early form was not made up of one's peers, it is the origin of our judicial system in the United States, in which the "finder of fact," either a judge or a jury of peers, listens to evidence introduced by witnesses and makes a determination whether it is true or not. The finder of fact then decides the defendant's guilt or innocence based on some standard of proof.

The latter involves the subjective interpretation of the witnesses' credibility and/or expertise by the judge or jury and, among other things, is subject to manipulation by a clever liar as we have seen in numerous cases in recent history, as well as innocent people found guilty and later proved to have been wrongly convicted by scientific evidence, such as DNA. While the jury system proved more humane and more just, the finder of fact's inability to separate truth from deception in complex cases leaves it seriously flawed.

Many of the developments in truth verification were actually made through the exploration of physiology and anatomy. Erasistratus, a Greek physician, living around 300–250 BC, was the royal physician under Seleucus I Nicator of Syria. He is credited for his description of the valves of the heart and concluded that the heart functioned as a pump. He was one of the first scientists to distinguish between veins and arteries and believed that the arteries were full of air that carried the "animal spirit" called pneuma.

Erasistratus was credited with using the pulse to detect deception. The King's son, Antiochus, fell in love with his mother-in-law, but did not disclose his passion, and became sickly as he hid his emotion in silence. The physicians were quite unable to discover the cause and nature of his problem. When Erasistratus could not find anything physically wrong with Antiochus, he began to suspect that the problem may be mental rather than physical. The solution involved no instrumentation. His theory was confirmed when he observed Antiochus's pulse get stronger and quicker whenever the woman came near him.[8]

Claudius Galenus, a Greek physician, was born in the city of Pergamon and lived from AD 130 to 200. Known as Galen, he was the first person known to dissect animals in an attempt to get a better understanding of anatomy. He proved that arteries contained blood, and not some mystical life force, and theorized that emotions began in the mind and could be detected by physiological changes, such as sudden variations of the pulse. Galen was the first scholar to recognize that the heart was the principal part of the body involved in circulation. He discovered the correlation between the rhythm of the heart and the pulsation in the arteries, and that one could be judged by the other.

Andrea Vesalius, born in Brussels in 1514, laid the foundation of modern anatomy. He named every bone, muscle, and most of the blood vessels in the body. However, he did not know how the body functions.

In 1581, Galileo Galilei invented the "pulsilogium," or pulse watch. It was the first objective attempt to count the pulse rate. In 1610, he also invented the microscope.

In 1604, William Harvey, an Englishman, discovered that arteries moved blood away from the heart, while veins moved blood toward it. Harvey was a pupil of Fabricius of Acquapendente, who discovered the workings of valves in the veins. In 1621, Harvey explained that the heart pumped the same blood over and over again. He correctly theorized the workings of the circulatory system; that blood moved in a constant circle from the heart to the arteries, the arteries to the veins, veins to the heart, then from the heart to the lungs for oxygenation and back to the heart to again begin circulating to the body.

Marcello Malpighi, aided by Galilei's microscope, became the first scientist to actually observe circulation taking place. In 1661, while observing circulation in a frog, he discovered hairlike vessels connecting the arteries and veins. He named these small vessels capillaries, Latin for hairlike. The capillaries were also independently discovered by Anthony van Leeuwenhoek, of Holland, who observed them in the transparent tails of fish and eels while viewing them with a microscope.

In 1728, Lancisi, a Roman court physician, expressed his belief that emotions were mental explanations for physiological changes taking place in the body. A person begins crying and then intellectually decided what was happening. If he was at a funeral of a loved one, he interprets the change as sadness. If he opens the door and everyone is yelling "Surprise!" he interprets it as joy.

In 1773, Stephen Hales, an English physiologist and chemist, discovered blood pressure. Convinced that circulating blood must exert some type of force on the arteries, he tied a horse to a gate and clamped off an artery in the horse's leg. Cutting the artery open, he inserted one end of a brass pipe and placed the other end of the pipe into a glass tube. Releasing the clamp, blood spurted from the artery into the tube, reaching a height of nearly 9 ft.

Luigi Galvani published a paper in 1791, on "Animal Electricity." This phenomenon was later termed "Galvanism." Galvani inadvertently reached his concept of animal electricity when he noticed a muscular contraction in a frog's leg when a piece of electrical equipment was turned on. Alessandro Volta later demonstrated the actual cause of the muscle contraction and proved that Galvani had erred.

Intrigued by Hans Christian Oersted's discovery that there was a connection between electricity and magnetism, Andre Ampere published a paper on September 18, 1820, on an instrument he constructed to measure electrical currents. He named the instrument galvanometer, in honor of Luigi Galvani.

The accuracy of the galvanometer was improved by George Simon Ohm's addition of a torsion device in the 1800s. In 1843, Wilhelm Weber invented the "electrodynamometer," which measured the strength of an unknown electrical current by its interaction with a known current.

J.M. Poisville, a French medical doctor, invented a mercury manometer in the 1800s. It recorded pressure of vapors with floating pens. In 1856, Laivre made the first direct blood pressure measurement in a human.

In the early 1890s, Angelo Mosso, an Italian physiologist, studied the effect of fear on the cardiovascular and respiratory systems. Mosso (Figure 1.4) was particularly interested in measuring changes in the flow of blood in the circulatory system of the body. He developed a mechanical device known as the "scientific cradle," often called "Mosso's cradle." This device was nothing more than a balanced table-like platform and mounted on a fulcrum (Figure 1.5).[9]

Mosso theorized that during emotional stress, such as fear of being caught in a lie, blood rushed to the head. This, he believed, explained why

Figure 1.4 Photograph of Angelo Mosso. (From U.S. National Library of Medicine, History of Medicine Division, Bethesda, MD.)

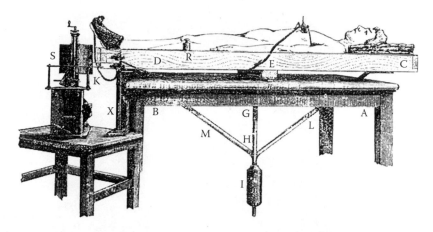

Figure 1.5 Mosso's "human circulation balance," used to measure cerebral activity during resting and cognitive states.

a person's face flushed during emotional states. He theorized this concentration of blood in the brain caused by fear would result in a slight shift in the subject's body weight and thus a corresponding measurable movement of the cradle. Mosso proposed that he would then analyze the lines drawn on the kymograph and determine the credibility of the witness. There is, however, no evidence that Mosso ever put his theory into practice. In all probability, the device was too crude and unreliable to make the kind of measurements that Mosso would have found useful.

In 1895, Cesare Lombroso (Figure 1.6), an instructor of Mosso,[10] applied the use of more precise instrumentation sensitive to changes in volumetric displacement to measure emotional changes and detect deception. Lombroso postulated:

> It is well known that any emotion that makes the heartbeat to quicken or become slower causes humans to blush or pale. These vasomotor phenomena are entirely beyond our control. If we plunge our hands into the volumetric tank invented by Francis Frank, the level of the liquid registered on the tube above will rise and fall at every pulsation. Besides these regular fluctuations, variations may be observed which correspond to every stimulation of the senses, every thought, and above all, every emotion.[11]

The "volumetric glove (Figure 1.7)," developed by Patrizi, was considered an improvement over the volumetric tank. The suspect put his hand in a sealed rubber glove filled with air. Changes in air pressure due to heart pulsations were then recorded on a Marey tympanum and on a revolving cylinder covered with smoked paper.

Figure 1.6 Photograph of Cesare Lombroso.

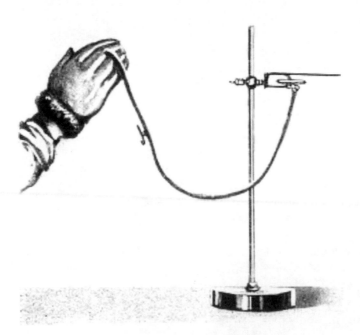

Figure 1.7 Professor M. L. Patrizi's volumetric glove.

Lombroso's daughter writes in the *Criminal Man:*

> My father sometimes made successful use of the plethysmograph to discover whether an accused person was guilty of the crime imputed to him, by mentioning it suddenly while his hands were in the plethysmograph or placing the photograph of the victim before his eyes.

Lombroso became the first person to use scientific instrumentation successfully in the detection of deception. He is considered the father of modern criminology.[12]

In 1897, Harold Sticker[13] became the first person to suggest the application of the galvanometer for detecting deception. Sticker, a psychologist, experimented on sweat gland secretion as a measure of psychological stress. In pursuit of his data, he was the first experimenter to apply Ampere's principle to measure physiological change. Sticker's research that galvanic activity was due to mental excitation was not original; it was an extension of research completed by Adamkiewicz,[13] who had already demonstrated that sweat gland activity was linked to the mental processes. Sticker simply applied the principle, theorizing that stress would lead to increases in the secretion of the sweat glands. He believed that changes in skin conductivity caused by sweating could be measured, that a galvanometer attached to a person would allow the observation of galvanic skin response (GSR) changes in the body's resistance to small charges of electricity, and that the GSR reflected changes in the subject's mental excitation. Sticker further suggested that the use of the GSR together with the showing of pictures, or asking of questions, would stimulate the emotional responses that could then be reliably measured physiologically.

In 1907, Otto Veraguth,[13] a Swiss neurologist, suggested the use of the GSR in conjunction with psychological word association tests. He proposed that the GSR be used as a diagnostic tool in assessing psychological disorders. He coined the term "psychogalvanic reflex." Following Veraguth's suggestion, such prominent psychologists as Jung and Peterson began using the GSR to detect emotional issues with their patients. By the 1950s, GSR instruments were available for detection of deception (Figure 1.8).

Hugo Munsterberg (Figure 1.9) first advanced the concept of applying scientific instrumentation to measure numerous physiological changes indicative of deception[13] in 1909. Munsterberg, a professor of law at Harvard University, was so concerned that perjury was destroying the integrity of the judicial system he devoted an entire chapter of his book, *On the Witness Stand*, recommending that physiological activity of a witness be monitored as testimony was given to ensure the witness was telling the truth. He also asserted that the simultaneous measurement of a broad range of physiological responses would be more reliable. Among the physiological parameters he suggested to be monitored were muscle contractions, eye movement,

Figure 1.8 1950s era of galvanic skin response instrument.

Figure 1.9 Photograph of Hugo Munsterberg.

Figure 1.10 Photograph of Vittorio Benussi.

breathing, cardiovascular activity, and changes in electrodermal activity (GSR). Following the publication of his book, a great deal of research began to appear concerning deception and physiological functions.

In 1914, early results of this research were reported. Vittorio Benussi[14] (Figure 1.10) published data on respiration changes that were correlated with conscious deception. Benussi measured the length of time it took the individual to complete the two different parts of a single breath, inhalation (breathing in) and exhalation (breathing out). His highly accurate research demonstrated that the inhalation–exhalation (I/E) ratio under normal conditions was approximately three units of inhalation to five units of exhalation (3:5). Following a conscious lie, he found the ratio changed to two units inhalation and to six units exhalation (2:6). Therefore, during deception, he reported the period of inhalation quickened and the period of exhalation became longer (Figure 1.11).

I:E Ratio normal (3:5)   Deception (2:6)

Figure 1.11 Inhalation–exhalation (I–E) ratio of 3:5 versus 2:6.

Figure 1.12 Harvard psychologist Dr. William Marston and creator of the comic book character Wonder Woman.

Meanwhile, other physiological research was proceeding. In 1917, a student of Munsterberg's, William Marston (Figure 1.12), published a research paper on the discontinuous method of measuring differences in systolic blood pressure readings to detect deception. Periodically, during an interview, he would take the interviewee's standard blood pressure readings via an arm cuff and then chart any significant changes in systolic blood pressure.[15]

During World War I, Marston became the assistant secretary of war. He conducted research for the U.S. Army on the feasibility of the galvanometer (GSR) for detecting deception and concluded it was not as accurate as changes in systolic blood pressure. He was also the creator of Wonder Woman who as you may remember forced enemies to tell the truth when she encircled them with her special lasso.

In 1918, Harold E. Burtt, chairman of psychology at Ohio State University, compared the work of Benussi and Marston. His research indicated that both physiological indices were much better than chance; however, the pneumograph (Benussi) was only 73% accurate, while blood pressure (Marston) was 91% accurate.

Sir James Mackenzie, a Scottish physician, developed an ink polygraph instrument. It could continuously record complex physiological changes

Figure 1.13 Photograph of August Vollmer. (From U.S. Library of Congress's Prints and Photographs Division, Washington, DC.)

such as arterial and venous pulses. It was speculated that such a device, if applied to the detection of truthfulness, could measure and record changes as specific questions were being asked, so that a record would be available for later review.

With the encouragement of August Vollmer (Figure 1.13), chief of police in Berkeley, California, Detective John A. Larson (Figure 1.14) combined the Mackenzie ink polygraph[16] to record and monitor changes based on the research of Benussi and Marston. Larson constructed a "two-pen lie detector" that measured breathing and continuous change in cardiovascular activity. He named his instrument the "cardio-pneumo-psychogram," but it quickly was nicknamed the "breadboard polygraph," because in its construction, he used a breadboard for the base. Larson became the first person in law enforcement to administer polygraph tests to criminal suspects to assess their truthfulness (Figure 1.15).

In 1923, Dr. Alexander R. Luria, a Soviet neuropsychologist and developmental psychologist, used word association tests and a device that measured reaction time to detect emotional changes. Luria theorized that during emotional times, there was a breakdown of motor coordination. The subjects were given a word and had to reply and press on the device, which measured reaction time, as they answered.

Figure 1.14 Photograph of Detective John Augustus Larson in 1921.

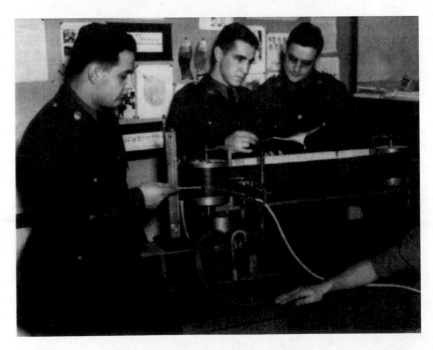

Figure 1.15 John A. Larson employed by the Berkeley Police Department.

Also in 1923, the U.S. Supreme Court made their first ruling on lie detection, in *Frye vs. the United States* (293 F. 1013). A prominent physician in Washington, DC, was murdered. Reward money was offered for information in the case and an informant gave up Alphonso Frye as the perpetrator. The defense hired Marston to conduct a discontinuous blood pressure test on Frye, and Marston, quoting his 10-year accuracy rate as 95%, concluded that Frye was truthful when he denied murdering the doctor.

The prosecutors used the development by Larson to argue that a single parameter test was not sufficient, or state of the art, since Larson had developed a two-parameter instrument that measured breathing and continuous changes in cardiovascular activity. The court ruled against the admissibility of Marston's test states the following:

> Just when a scientific principle or discovery crosses the line between the experimental and demonstrable stages is difficult to define.
>
> Somewhere in the twilight zone, the evidential principle must be recognized, and while courts will go a long way in admitting expert testimony deduced from well recognized principle of discovery, the thing from which deduction is made must be sufficiently established to have "gained general acceptance" in the field which it belongs.
>
> We think the systolic blood pressure deception test has not gained such standing and scientific recognition among physiological and psychological authorities as would justify the courts in admitting expert testimony deduced from the discovery, development, and experiments thus far made.

The jury found Frye guilty of second-degree murder.

In 1926, Leonarde Keeler (Figure 1.16), a high school student, whose father was a personal friend of Chief Vollmer, received a part-time summer job with the Berkeley Police Department. Keeler worked in the photo lab and became a protégé of John Larson. Keeler went on to become known as the "father of modern polygraph." He improved the polygraph instrument of Larson by introducing metal tambours and a synchronized chart drive mechanism that used rolled paper. Keeler was the first person to offer commercial polygraph services and the first to manufacture instrumentation (Figure 1.17).

In 1927, Carl Emil Seashore published a research paper, *Phonophotograph in the Measurement of Emotion in Music and Speech*.[17] Seashore's work involved the possible detection of deception by changes in the tenor of the voice.

In 1929, Harold Randolph Crossland demonstrated that word association tests were a reliable means of detecting deception, but concluded that pulse and blood pressure changes were more accurate.[18]

Figure 1.16 A photograph of Leonarde Keeler, the father of modern polygraph.

Figure 1.17 The Keeler polygraph came on the market in 1926.

In work published in 1935, W.A. Hunt and C. Landis reported that word association tests in conjunction with GSR were an effective means of detecting deception.[19]

That same year, Charles S. Wilson adapted a G.E. photoelectric device to record an additional component for detecting deception.

In 1936, Clarence Lee, a former captain at the Berkeley Police Department, who worked with Larson, improved the polygraph's pneumatic transmissions in both the respiration and cardiovascular components. He began experimenting with electrical systems for monitoring the pulse. He manufactured polygraph instrumentation and in 1953 published the text *The Instrumental Detection of Deception: The Lie Test.*[16]

Reverend Walter G. Summers, head of psychology at Fordham University, developed a galvanometer in 1936. He named the device a "pathometer." He reported 98%–100% accuracy in detecting deception. His single parameter instrument met the same fate as Marston's when he attempted to introduce it into evidence in 1938, *People vs. Forte*, 279 NY 204, 18 N.E. 2d 31. However, he successfully introduced it in *People of New York vs. Raymond Kenny*, 167 misc. 51, 3 NN.Y.S. 2d 348 (1938).

Kenny was convicted of robbery in the first degree. The court threw the decision out and Kenny was retried. Prior to the trial, Kenny was sent to be tested by Reverend Summers with the pathometer or psychogalvanometer. Believing he was measuring emotional changes, Summers testified that research had been performed on 6000 tests. In one study involving 254 people, Summers properly identified 49 of the 50 guilty examinees, 100 out of 102 accomplices, and 100 of the 102 truthful suspects. He testified that due to the intensity of an actual case, accuracy could be expected to be even higher. By laying an excellent foundation, the court ruled to accept his findings. Father Summers died at the early age of 49.

Interestingly, in the 1980s, walking down a major street in Center City, Philadelphia, I noticed a line of tables equipped with people running GSR instruments. Curious, I approached one of the tables where a person who identified himself as a member of the Church of Scientology monitored my GSR responses as he asked me questions about various aspects of my life. He then suggested I come to the Church to receive counseling on the areas in my life that elicited the largest GSR reactions. Still today, these GSR tests are still being conducted with instruments called an E-meter by the Church of Scientology to identify stressful areas in a person's life for which the Church then suggests they undergo counseling sessions (Figure 1.18).

Keeler left Berkley in 1930 to join the new crime laboratory at Northeastern University School of Law, in Chicago. This later became part of the Chicago Police Department. Keeler collaborated with Charles Wilson in 1938 to add the GSR as a third component of the polygraph instrument.

Figure 1.18 The Scientology Mark VIII Ultra E-meter lying in its carrying case. The device's protective cover is shown standing at the back. (Photo by Colliric from Wikipedia, December 14, 2013.)

In 1942, Keeler and Larson are credited with developing the relevant/ irrelevant (R/I) testing technique. The technique consisted of asking relevant questions interspersed with irrelevant ones and was the first technique to require one-word answers from the examinee: "yes" or "no.[16]"

Keeler is also credited with innovating the peak of tension test, the card stimulation test, using the reactions in a card stimulation test when a person denied the number they had picked as a control mechanism for comparison to reactions of relevant questions in the R/I test, and opening the first polygraph school; he is the first to manufacture polygraph instruments and the first polygraphist to offer services commercially to the banks in the Chicago area.

While with the Chicago Crime Lab, Keeler trained Fred Inbau, professor of criminal law at Northwestern University, and Paul Trovillo as examiners. A young college graduate, John E. Reid, later joined the lab and became interested and was trained in polygraph.

In the early 1940s, Frank A. Seckler, a secret service agent, was sent to Chicago to study polygraph. This was the beginning of the use of polygraphy by the federal government. Later, the CIA would send its first agent to be trained, a man who would later have a major impact on the polygraph field, Cleve Backster.

In August, 1945, Keeler was testing German Prisoners of War for the U.S. Army at Fort Getty, Rhode Island. Several examiners interested in starting a polygraph association approached him. This encounter led to the formation of the "International Society for the Detection of Deception."

In 1945, John E. Reid became interested in counter measures. He believed that the cardio tracing could be affected by muscular movement and wanted to identify it. He placed the bladders of blood pressure cuffs into the seat of a chair and connected it to a pen on the polygraph instrument, which enabled him to monitor deliberate muscular movements.

In 1946, various examiners began adding an embarrassing personal question (EPQ) to the R/I test format. This occurred because in some cases, where subjects had been determined truthful, the investigation later verified them as deceptive. Concern was generated that perhaps for some reason these individuals were not capable of emitting psychophysiological reactions, which therefore caused them to be misidentified as truthful. The EPQ was designed to show that a subject had the ability to show psychophysiological reactions and eliminate false negatives (deceptive suspects determined erroneously to be truthful). Unfortunately, regardless of whether a person reacted properly or not in the R/I test, everyone seemed to react to the EPQ, and the problem continued.

In 1947, John E. Reid is credited with innovating the "comparative response question," later termed as the "earlier in life control question," and in recent years renamed as the "comparison question." It is believed by some that the question was actually innovated by William Marston, who called them "hot questions," and decided not to publish information concerning its use to prevent knowledge of it from being shared with the general public.

This question dealt with a matter similar to that under investigation but less severe or dealt with the motivation for the crime. It was very broad in scope, "In your entire life...," and was something everyone would truthfully answer "yes" to; however, the examiner introduced it in a way to elicit a "no" response from the subject. For example, if the examination concerned the theft of a deposit from McDonald's, the relevant questions in the test might have been the following: "Do you know for sure who took that missing deposit?" "Did you take that missing deposit?" "Did you leave McDonald's with that missing deposit?" The examiner might then say,

> What kind of person would do something like this? This is a thief! A leopard doesn't change its spots. A person that's been taught stealing is wrong and is basically honest their whole life doesn't wake up one day and say today I think I'll steal a deposit. Only a thief would do that. Someone who has stolen from their family, stolen from friends, stolen from jobs before. You're not that type of person, are you? I want to be able to show that not only didn't you take that missing deposit, but based on your profile you are not even the type of person that would do something like that. In your entire life, did you ever steal anything? You are not a thief, are you?

To which the truthful examinee, afraid the examiner will misidentify him as the type of person who would steal a deposit, answers, "No."

Reid theorized that this question would cause conflict and concern for the innocent examinee, thus producing greater psychophysiological reactions in the examination than when they truthfully denied committing the crime under investigation. The person who actually stole the deposit could care less about other thefts and would focus on the questions dealing with the current crime, for which if they were detected of committing, would be punished.

This new addition of this question to the polygraph format also answered the earlier problem that the EPQ failed to resolve. Everyone now had to react to questions on a polygraph test for a determination to be made. Truthful suspects had to react to the comparative response questions to be determined truthful, and deceptive suspects had to react to the relevant questions to be determined deceptive.

In 1948, Reid and Inbau faced a new problem. There were some suspects that reacted strongly to both the comparative response questions and relevant questions in their polygraph format. They theorized that some examinees might be "guilt reactors," which was defined by them as a personality type, which would cause them to react to any type of accusatory question. The examiner asks, "Did you do the crime?" and they react. The examiner asks, "In your entire life did you ever...?" and they react. The examiner asks, "Did you shoot Abe Lincoln?" and they react as they wonder where they were on that date in 1865.

Thus, the "guilt complex question" was a question about a make-believe crime. A crime that was never committed. The make-believe crime was described in a manner so that even if this was the perpetrator of a series of serious crimes, he would know this was a crime he didn't commit. For example, on a possible rapist, they may describe a rape of a nurse that never occurred where the rapist also stole the nurse's RN pin. They would then run a test with questions about the make-believe crime along with questions about the real crime under investigation. If the suspect still reacted to the relevant questions but did not react to the guilt complex questions, they were determined to be guilty. If they still reacted to all of the questions, both guilt complex and relevant questions, they were determined to be unsuitable to take a polygraph examination. Later, when we discuss techniques, we will see that this did not prove fruitful, and Reid innovated other options for this problem.

On July 16, 1951, the military opened its own polygraph school in Fort Gordon, Georgia. One of the early school directors who had a great influence on the government's polygraph program was Ron Decker, fondly known as "the wizard."

The International Society for the Detection of Deception changed its name to the Academy for Scientific Interrogation, in 1953. Reid and Inbau, dissatisfied with the association's failure to increase training time and educational requirements for applicants, formed their own organization, the American Academy for Polygraph Examiners. In 1954, the organization met and adopted a minimum training program of 6 months. Potential applicants for their school had to possess a minimum of a baccalaureate degree. Reid maintained that requirement the entire time he offered polygraph training.

In 1958, Chris Gugas formed the National Board of Polygraph Examiners. The organization was revised in 1961 to meet the needs of private examiners interested in uniting to fight antipolygraph legislation.

In 1959, Cleve Backster—who, as previously mentioned, studied under Keeler as the first polygraph examiner to be trained by the Central Intelligence Agency and Richard O. Arther, a Reid-trained examiner—opened their own school in New York, the National Training Center.

In 1960, Backster innovated the Zone Comparison Technique (ZCT). In 1962, the two separated, with Arther maintaining the New York school and Backster opening his own school in San Diego, California. Backster went on to introduce many of the psychological concepts in polygraph, including psychological set, anticlimatic dampening, super dampening, and the seven-point scoring system for chart interpretation.[16]

Arther developed his own technique, the Arther Known Lie Test, and became the first examiner to record thoracic and abdominal breathing, and a leading proponent of utilizing an automatic GSR. In 1970, he introduced the false key peak of tension test.[16]

In 1962, the military school sent examiners to be trained by Reid and Backster. The military then established the Military ZCT (MZCT), also referred to as the federal zone comparison test, based on Backster's technique and the army Modified General Question Technique (MGQT) based on the Reid General Question Technique. For many years, the school was directed by the aforementioned Ronald Decker.

In January 1964, the National Board of Polygraph Examiners, Academy for Scientific Interrogation, American Academy of Polygraph Examiners, and the International Association of Polygraph Examiners formed the "Council of Polygraph Examiners." The Council was made up of members of all four associations in an attempt to show a united front for the polygraph profession.

In August 1966, the Council was dissolved, and the four associations merged to form the APA. The first president of the APA was J. Kirk Barefoot (Figure 1.19).

In 1980, Philip M. Cochetti and I opened the Academy for Scientific Investigative Training in Philadelphia, Pennsylvania (Figure 1.20). We used the early work of Reid and Dr. Frank Horvath to develop the Forensic Assessment Interview Technique. In 1987, we introduced the Horizontal Scoring System, a more objective scoring system, and the first innovation in

Figure 1.19 J. Kirk Barefoot and the author in 2015.

Figure 1.20 Insignia for the Academy for Scientific Investigative Training, cofounded in 1980 by Philip M. Cochetti and the author.

Figure 1.21 Photograph of James Allan Matte.

scoring since Backster's introduced the "7-point scale" in the 1960s. In 1987, we collaborated with William Waid, PhD, and innovated the Integrated ZCT (IZCT). Our goal was to establish a format that allowed the examiner the flexibility to administer single or multi-issue examinations while maintaining the same question format. In 1999, I introduced the Academy's Algorithm for Manual Chart Interpretation. Combined with the earlier Horizontal Scoring System, all areas of subjectivity were eliminated from chart interpretation.

In 1989, James Matte (Figure 1.21) completed his research and introduced the Quadri-Track Zone Comparison Technique. The technique offered a new concept, the "inside issue," which dealt with the innocent examinee's fear of error.[16] Matte replaced the third Comparison–Relevant (C48 and R37) set in the Backster You Phase with his inside issue (C23 and R24), comparing fear of error with hope of error. Matte also authored several texts on polygraph, including the over 700-page book, *Forensic Psychophysiology: Using the Polygraph*, in 1996.

In 2013, the International Society of Polygraph Examiners (Figure 1.22) was formed with the goal of uniting examiners around the world to conduct examinations in a professional and ethical way. The board and membership was truly representative of the global polygraph community.

Figure 1.22 Logo for the International Society of Polygraph Examiners.

Conclusion

The search for truth has been with humans from the beginning of our existence and will continue with us on our journeys into the future. To date, there have been many improvements made in that search. Instrumentation has become computerized and new physiological phenomena are continually being researched. The questioning techniques used with them have also been refined.

Bernard of Chartres used to say, "we [the Moderns] are like dwarves perched on the shoulders of giants [the Ancients], and thus we are able to see more and farther than the latter. And this is not at all because of the acuteness of our sight or the stature of our body, but because we are carried aloft and elevated by the magnitude of the giants."

The polygraph gods, Keeler, Reid, Backster, and Arther, are no longer with us; however, they have left us with a wealth of knowledge. As our art moves forward and our advances continue, it is because we stand on the shoulders of those polygraph giants that came before us! Indeed, the pioneers of modern lie detection did their work well in creating this highly reliable art based on the sound principles found in the sciences of psychology and physiology.

Figure 1.23 Screen still from an interview with Cleve Baxter, Jr.

Grover Cleveland "Cleve" Backster, Jr. (Figure 1.23) was an interrogation specialist and the first examiner trained by the CIA. He was perhaps the greatest innovator in the polygraph profession. He introduced scientific concepts on how polygraph worked, including psychological set, anticlimatic dampening, and super dampening, as well as the first numerical system for analyzing polygraph data. His restructure of polygraph technique to what he named the Zone Comparison Technique gave birth to the most accurate polygraph techniques in existence.

Notes

1. Meta-Analytic Survey of Criterion Accuracy of Validated Polygraph Techniques. Report prepared for the American Polygraph Association Board of Directors: Nate Gordon, President (2010–2011), by The Ad-Hoc Committee on Validated Techniques: Mike Gougler, Committee Chair; Raymond Nelson, Principal Investigator; Mark Handler, Donald Krapohl, Pam Shaw, and Leonard Bierman.

2. American Polygraph Association By-Laws. Effective January 1, 2012.
3. It should be noted that the accuracy for screening/applicant testing was later reduced by the APA to "above chance."
4. Gordon, N. and Fleisher, W. (2011) *Effective Interview and Interrogation Techniques*. Academic Press.
5. Keeler, L. (1938) *Outline of Scientific Criminal Investigation*. Edward Brothers, Ann Arbor, MI.
6. Keeler, L. (1933) Scientific methods of crime detection. *Kansas Bar Association Journal*.
7. Szasz, T. S. (1970) *The Manufacture of Madness*. Harper & Row, New York.
8. Wikipedia. https://en.wikipedia.org/wiki/Erasistratus.
9. Trovillo, P. Y. (1939) A history of lie detection. *Journal of Criminal Law, Criminology and Police Science*, 29, 848–881, March–April; 30, 104–119, May–June 1939.
10. Some writings describe him as a colleague, others as a teacher of Mosso.
11. Lombrosso, C. (1895) *L'Homme Criminel*, 2nd French edition.
12. Lombrosso is also known for his less than scientific theory of physiognomy, which was a system he developed to identify persons prone to criminal behavior based on their physiology and bone structure.
13. Trovillo, P. (1939) A history of lie detection. *Journal of Criminal Law*, 29(6), 848–881.
14. Herbeld-Wooten, H. (1982) Tatbestandsdiagnostik: A historical review of the beginnings of lie detection in Germany. *Polygraph*, 11(3), 246–257.
15. Marston reported 96% correlation between significant differences in systolic blood pressure and attempts at deception using this method. *The Journal of Experimental Psychology*, 11(2), 1017, April.
16. Matte, J. A. (1996) *Forensic Psychophysiology Using the Polygraph*. JAM Publications, Williamsville, NY.
17. Seashore, C. E. (1927) Phonophotograph in the measurement of emotion in music and speech. *Proceedings of the National Academy of Sciences of the USA*, 9, 323–325.
18. Crossland, H. R. (1929) *The Psychological Methods of Word-Association and Reaction-Time as Tests of Deception*. Psychology Series, vol. 1, No. 1, University of Oregon Publication, Eugene, OR.
19. Landis, C. and Hunt, W. A. (1935) The conscious correlates of the galvanic skin response. *Journal of Experimental Psychology*, 18(5), 505–529.

Instrumentation

2

Truth exists; only lies are invented.

—Georges Braque

While the first ink polygraph instrument was developed by Sir James Mackenzie (Figure 2.1) for European physicians, which had the ability to continuously record complex physiological changes,[1] the first polygraph instrument specifically developed to verify truth was in 1921, by John Augustus Larson, at the Berkley, CA, Police Department. It was able to continuously monitor both respiration and cardiovascular activity. It is classified as an analog pneumatic or mechanical instrument because the only electricity needed was for the chart drive mechanism. The two components measuring physiological activity (pneumo and cardio) did not require any electrical input.

Leonarde Keeler is credited with making the instrument portable and developing a much more efficient chart drive mechanism to move the chart paper. In the 1930s a third physiological parameter was added that allowed the monitoring of galvanic skin responses (GSRs), which are changes in sweating monitored from the fingertips.

Today, instrumentation falls into three categories: nonelectronic (also referred to as pneumatic or mechanical) analog instruments, electronic analog instruments, and computerized polygraph instruments.

The analog instrument can still be ordered today with pneumatic or electronic components and is still being used by some examiners in the field. The first manufacturer of polygraph instruments was Leonarde Keeler. The two major manufacturers in the United States of analog instruments still in business today are the Stoelting Company (www.stoeltingco.com) of Illinois and the Lafayette Instrument Company (www.lafayetteinstrument.com) from Indiana.

The mechanical analog instrument was a three-pen device that monitored and recorded the pneumo (respiration), GSR, and the cardio (mean blood pressure, blood volume, and heart rate).

The mechanical pneumo consisted of two pieces of equipment: the pneumo chest assembly that was attached to the examinee and the pneumo instrumentation component (Figure 2.2).

Figure 2.1 Photograph of Sir James Mackenzie.

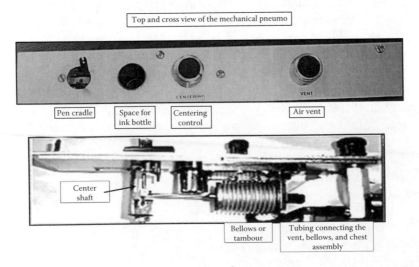

Figure 2.2 The mechanical pneumo.

Figure 2.3 The chest assembly component. (Courtesy of Lafayette Instrument Company, Lafayette, IN, www.lafayettepolygraph.com.)

The pneumo component is a low-pressure system, which operates on atmospheric air pressure (usually around 14.7 lb of pressure per square inch in the United States). When the vent is placed in the down and open position in the Stoelting instrument, or the vent is in the open position of the Lafayette instrument, air is present in the pneumo component; however, it is not operable.

The examiner attaches the chest assembly component (Figure 2.3) to the examinee. Prior to the profession's requirement to monitor breathing from both the examinee's chest and stomach (as inspired by Richard Arther), the attachment was often placed at the solar plexus of the examinee, since it was believed it would monitor both areas of breathing.

When the examiner places the vent in the up or closed position in the Stoelting instrument, or in the closed position in the Lafayette instrument, the air in the atmosphere is trapped in the instrument and the pneumo component becomes operable.

The examiner then centers the tracing with the centering knob. The size of the tracing can only be adjusted by tightening the chest assembly tube in an attempt to increase the tracing size or loosening it in an attempt to decrease the tracing size.

When the person inhales, the chest assembly expands, causing the bellows to contract. This pulls on the connecting link, which in turn moves the center shaft causing the pen cradle to rotate upward. Although the air in the system is constant, the expansion of the chest assembly creates greater space in the component than the contraction of the bellows; thus, there is an overall decrease in system pressure.

When the person exhales, the chest assembly contracts, causing the bellows to expand, which causes the connecting link to move the center shaft, rotating the pen cradle downward, which now results in an increase in system pressure and the recording of a single breath (Figure 2.4).

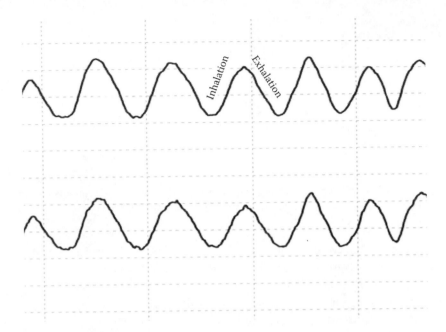

Figure 2.4 Inhalation and exhalation.

The mechanical cardio component (Figure 2.5) is very similar to the pneumo component. The cardio tubing connects the vent, with a standard blood pressure cuff, an encased bellows to prevent excessive stretching during the pumping of air into the system, a pump bulb, and a sphygmomanometer (pressure dial). Since air is actively pumped into the system, unlike the low-pressure pneumo, the cardio component is a high-pressure system.

Usual placement of the blood pressure cuff is on the upper arm with the bladder over the brachial artery. With the mechanical cardio, the vent is in a closed position with the lock bar on. Air is introduced by pumping the cuff up to about 120 mmHg (millimeters of mercury). The cuff is massaged to even the air out in the system, and the pressure is lowered to 80–90 mmHg. If the cuff is repositioned to the forearm, pressure is increased to 90–100 mmHg, and to 100–120 mmHg if placed on the wrist. The lock bar is then released and the pen is centered. Ideal pressure is when the dicrotic notch is centered on the diastolic stroke. A high notch indicates low pressure, and more air is added to the cuff. A low notch indicates the pressure is too high, and air is let out of the cuff.

When the cardio pen rises, it is the systolic stroke caused by the heart contracting and pumping blood. The dicrotic notch is caused by blood pumped into the aortic artery rebounding off of the closing of the aortic semilunar valve preventing it from going back into the heart. When the pen comes back down, it is the diastolic stroke as the heart relaxes and receives blood from the body to be processed (Figure 2.6).

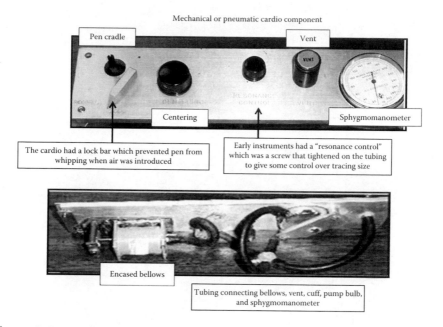

Figure 2.5 Mechanical cardio component.

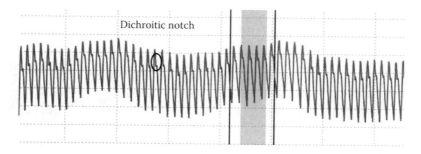

Figure 2.6 Illustration of cardio tracing.

The GSR component is electric and has no air component involved in its operation. Basically, all human beings give off an unknown amount of an electrical current. Through the instrumentation, a very low current of 5 µA is introduced. This current is below the threshold of feeling and establishes a Wheatstone bridge. The unknown current from the body basically meets and resists the known current from the instrument. As the resistance from the body decreases, the GSR reaction on the chart goes up. There are actually two types of resistance from the human body. A quick changing resistance, which is the galvanic resistance (Figure 2.7), and a much slower resistance known as basil or nominal resistance (seen in the baseline changes in Figure 2.8).

The GSR component (Figure 2.9) can be operated in the manual mode, which allows both types of resistance to be observed, or the automatic mode,

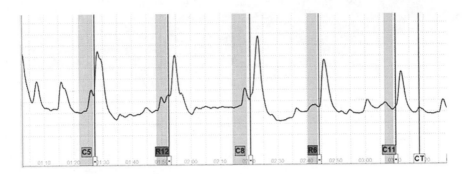

Figure 2.7 Graphic of galvanic resistance (the quick upward movement of the tracing).

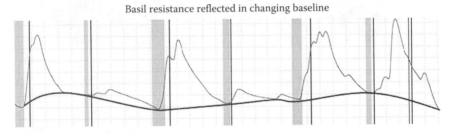

Figure 2.8 Graphic of basil or nominal resistance.

Figure 2.9 The galvanic skin response component.

which cancels the signal of the basil resistance, giving a stable baseline and showing only the quick changing galvanic skin resistance reactions.

Since the GSR component no longer uses air and bellows to move the pen, an electrical signal is delivered to the Galvo Box or pen motor drive, which in turn causes movements in the pen. There is still a pen cradle, a centering knob, and now a switch to allow the component to be operated in either the manual or automatic mode. There is also a "pip" switch for testing the electrical circuit.

While problems in the pneumo and cardio are generally associated with leaks in the tubing or attachments, only two problems can occur with the GSR: an open circuit or a short circuit. An open circuit is created if a wire comes loose breaking the connection. If this happens, the pen will travel to the bottom of the chart and cannot be recentered. A short circuit occurs if the attachment plates or wires touch each other. In this event, the pen goes up to the top of the chart and cannot be recentered down.

In the 1970s, electronically enhanced instrumentation was introduced. This allowed examiners the ability to use lower cuff pressure in the cardio component, and a "sensitivity control," which enabled the examiner to amplify the pneumo and cardio signal making it much more ideal for accurate analysis. This new concept combined air and electricity. Changes in the movement of air in the chest assembly as a person breathed or the cardio cuff as blood was pumped through the artery was changed to an electrical signal via a transducer, which in turn sent a signal to a pen motor box that moved the pen. The bellows was now a thing of the past. Later they introduced a "multichannel" component (Figure 2.10) that allowed for a single component to be used to monitor pneumo, cardio, or an electric auxiliary component, such as a plethysmograph (Figure 2.11) or cardio activity monitor (CAM) introduced by Stoelting.

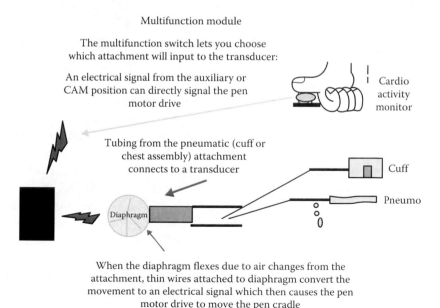

Multifunction module

The multifunction switch lets you choose which attachment will input to the transducer:

An electrical signal from the auxiliary or CAM position can directly signal the pen motor drive

Cardio activity monitor

Tubing from the pneumatic (cuff or chest assembly) attachment connects to a transducer

Cuff

Pneumo

Diaphragm

When the diaphragm flexes due to air changes from the attachment, thin wires attached to diaphragm convert the movement to an electrical signal which then causes the pen motor drive to move the pen cradle

Figure 2.10 Multichannel component.

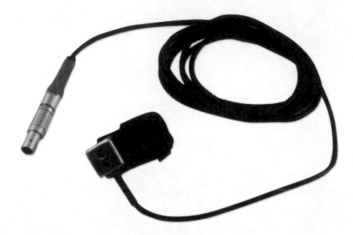

Figure 2.11 An electrical component to measure cardio activity. (Courtesy of Stoelting Company, Wood Dale, IL, www.stoeltingco.com.)

Figure 2.12 A Lafayette instrument multifunction component.

The plethysmograph uses a light to monitor changes in the cardio as blood moves in and out of the finger, while the CAM detects changes in the thumb's pulsation and sends electrical signals to the pen motor drive.

New analog instruments can now be ordered with five components in any combination of mechanical or multifunction components (Figure 2.12). Many instruments were now ordered with four multifunction components and one GSR.

Stoelting introduced the electronic Polyscribe analog instrument in 1974, and in 1979, introduced the Ultrascribe (Figure 2.13) with the newly designed unichannel feature where all of the controls and pen for each component were on the same module. Lafayette introduced its version of a fully electronic instrument called the Ambassador (Figure 2.14).

The analog instrument has two types of inking system. Originally, there was "community inking" where all of the pens shared ink from a common reservoir (Figure 2.15). A part of the pen actually dips into the reservoir and the ink is sucked through the pen with a duck-billed syringe.

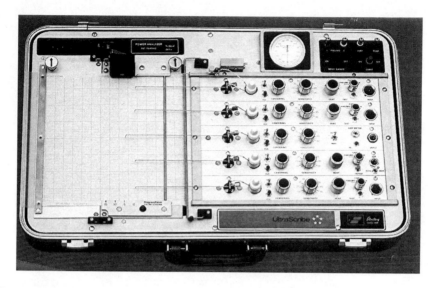

Figure 2.13 An older 1970s' model of Stoelting Ultrascribe.

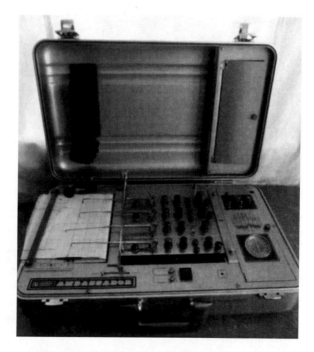

Figure 2.14 Lafayette Ambassador.

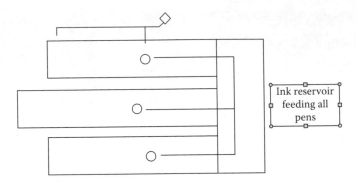

Figure 2.15 Community inking system.

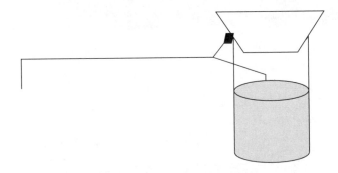

Figure 2.16 Individual or captive inking system.

An individual or captive inking system (Figure 2.16) was then introduced where each pen had its own bottle and individual ink supply. This was
much more convenient for portable use of the instrument. In either inking
system only water soluble ink is used. Both systems rely on a capillary feeding system where each drop of ink pulls the next drop through by molecular
cohesion.

Chart paper in modern times was usually 8 in. wide with markings on
the paper showing 5 second time intervals. Charts are moved by a synchronous chart motor drive mechanism called a kymograph (Figure 2.17), which
moves the chart paper at a speed of 6 in./min.

There are currently four manufactures of computerized polygraph systems in North America: Stoelting, Lafayette, Axciton, and Limestone.

The Lafayette LX-5000 (Figure 2.18) appears to lead the group in sales
and user friendliness (www.lafayetteinstrument.com).

Limestone Technologies offers the Paragon Computerized System
(Figure 2.19), which is manufactured out of Canada (www.limestonetech.com).

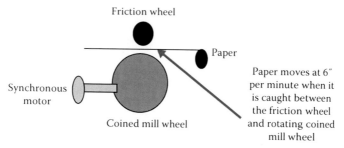

• All modern kymographs (chart drives) have a synchronous motor that consistently moves a metal "coined mill" wheel.

Friction wheel

Paper

Synchronous motor

Coined mill wheel

Paper moves at 6″ per minute when it is caught between the friction wheel and rotating coined mill wheel

Figure 2.17 A kymograph.

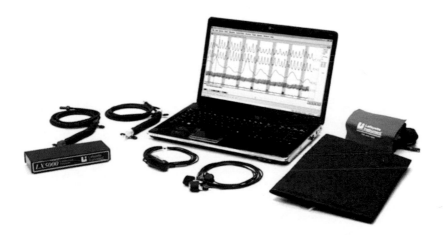

Figure 2.18 The Lafayette LX-5000. (Courtesy of Lafayette Instrument Company, Lafayette, IN, www.lafayettepolygraph.com.)

They are the newest company on the market and have introduced some out of the box concepts that have actually pushed the other manufacturers into making changes that have enhanced their instruments.

Some examiners maintain that the Axciton Computerized System (Figure 2.20) out of Houston, TX, actually produces the best polygraph charts (www.axciton.com).

Stoelting Company, one of the oldest manufacturers of polygraph instrumentation and one of the first manufacturers of computerized polygraph systems, has made some major refinements in their CPS Pro (Figure 2.21) software that should put its system on par with any of the others (www.stoeltingco.com).

Figure 2.19 The Paragon Computerized System from Limestone Technologies. (Courtesy of Limestone Technologies, Inc., Odessa, ON, www.limestonetech.com.)

Figure 2.20 Axciton Computerized System. (Courtesy of Axciton Systems, Inc., Houston, TX, http://www.axciton.com.)

The major advantage of the computerized systems is that they all have scoring algorithms that allow the examiner to utilize as quality control for the decisions made by the examiner in their manual scoring of the polygraph data. These systems also eliminate the need for ink and allow the examiner to have the greatest control over the appearance of the data being collected, both during and after the test, resulting in the finest graphics for analysis of physiological data possible.

Figure 2.21 Stoelting CPS Pro Computerized System. (Courtesy of Stoelting Company, Wood Dale, IL, www.stoeltingco.com.)

Conclusion

While the physiological phenomenon recorded by the polygraph instrumentation has changed very little since its innovation, the search for additional indices continues. The major change in instrumentation has been the development of the equipment, from mechanical instruments to electronically enhanced instruments to computerized system with built-in algorithms to assist in the quality control of the interpretation of the data.

Like the search for truth, the search for better instrumentation that can collect more data goes on. Perhaps the future of instrumentation will someday be a chair that a person sits in with no obvious attachments that will allow the examiner to monitor 6–10 different physiological indices.

Note

1. www.sciencemuseum.org.uk.

Question Formulation

3

By doubting we are led to question, by questioning we arrive at the truth.

—Peter Abelard

All polygraph techniques utilize questions from the four categories of irrelevant, relevant, comparison, and symptomatic questions. Each type of question has its place, and each plays an important role in the polygraph examination.

Irrelevant questions by definition have no connection to the matter under investigation and therefore should pose no threat to the suspect. In short, they are questions to which neither innocent nor guilty suspects have reason to lie to. They traditionally are background-type questions dealing with information the examiner knows to be true. They traditionally were answered "Yes"; however, several techniques, including Marcy, Arther, and the Integrated Zone Comparison Technique (IZCT), now have irrelevant questions requiring both "Yes" and "No" answers.

Obviously every suspect in a criminal investigation, whether innocent or guilty, will be in a heightened psychophysiological state when being administered a polygraph examination. These "neutral" questions are therefore generally used at the beginning of a polygraph technique to establish a physiological "norm" for the examinee or throughout the examination as needed to reestablish a normal physiological pattern. These questions were color-coded "yellow" by Cleve Backster in his attempt to standardize the overall polygraph profession. Here are some examples of irrelevant questions:

- Is your first name Nathan?   Yes.
- Were you born in the United States?   Yes.
- Were you born in March?   Yes.
- Do you live in Pennsylvania?   Yes.
- Is today Tuesday?   Yes.
- Is your last name Gordon?   Yes.
- Are you in Switzerland right now?   No.
- Is today Sunday?   No.

Relevant questions deal with the matter under investigation. They are questions that are designed to solve a piece of the puzzle. Each question deals with

43

a single issue and should be short and direct. Relevant questions dealing with direct involvement in the crime are color-coded solid red.

These questions must be formulated so that the innocent examinee can answer them truthfully, while the guilty examinee is forced to lie to them. As such, these questions are formulated to threaten the guilty person and cause subsequent physiological arousals to occur. Relevant questions cannot imply guilt or infer that the examiner has already reached the conclusion that the examinee is guilty. Examples of direct involvement relevant questions are as follows:

- Did you *commit that crime*?
- Did you start that fire?
- Did you take that missing money from the safe?
- Did you force that woman to have sex?
- Did you shoot that man?

Relevant questions concerning secondary involvement are labeled medium relevant questions and are color-coded red over yellow. Examples of these are as follows:

- Did you conspire with anyone to *commit that crime*?
- Were you present when that crime took place?
- Did you help anyone commit that crime?
- Did you plan with anyone to commit that crime?
- Do you know for sure who committed that crime?
- Did you see who committed that crime?
- Did anyone tell you they committed that crime?

Relevant questions should not contain words that are legalistic or that are so emotional that the language itself may cue responses, regardless of whether the person is lying or telling the truth. Therefore, emotionally charged words, such as "kill," "rape," and "steal," are avoided since they themselves could make examinees uncomfortable and may upon their usage alone elicit a physiological response. For the same reason, intimidating legal words like burglarize, extort, bribe, and rob are avoided. The latter legal language also can be ambiguous and allow the guilty examinee to hide behind a rationalization (e.g., "I didn't take a bribe; I accepted pay for a special job").

Relevant questions should be kept as short and focused as possible. To ensure that the examinee understands the language and question, they should be asked, "What does that question mean?" not "Do you understand that question?" Most examinees would answer "Yes" to the latter question even though they do not understand the meaning to avoid the embarrassment of admitting they do not. Asking the examinee to explain the question also ensures that the examinee's understanding of the question is the same as that of the examiner, which helps prevent examinee rationalization or personal coding.

Rationalization is where an examinee justifies their act. An employee who has stolen company money can rationalize that it was not stealing since they were promised a raise they never received. They took the missing money, but they have rationalized that it was not stealing, but the money was owed to them. Personal coding is where an examinee redefines a crime so it is no longer the crime under investigation. When a young boy was asked about the polygraph examination concerning digital penetration of a 3-year-old, he stated that it was about "bad touching." When I asked what "bad touching" was, he replied, "Ripping a person's clothes, or smacking them." When I asked him, "If you inserted your finger into a little girl's vagina, but did not rip her clothes or smack her, would that be bad touching?" "No," he answered. If I had accepted that the test was about "bad touching," based on his definition, he was innocent of the crime.

In homicides, avoid the question, "Did you cause the death of (victim)?" especially if the suspect had some type of relationship with the deceased. In reinterviewing an innocent man, who failed a polygraph test when asked, "Did you cause the death of your daughter?" we asked him what he had thought about and why he had registered a positive for lying. He said he thought he had caused her death since he felt he was responsible for it by not being there when he was needed. She was 4 years old and taken from his house during the night. She was found sexually molested and beaten to death the next morning. He explained that as her father, it was his responsibility to have been able to protect her. He felt it was his failure and his fault that his daughter had been killed. When asked on a reexamination, "Did you beat _____ to death?" he answered "No" and the polygraph confirmed his innocence.

As you can see, this notion of cause of guilt and responsibility is open to a wide range of interpretations. The examinee can internalize guilt without being the perpetrator or directly involved. An examinee can feel responsible and yet not have performed the act that is the target of the examination.

Consider these hypothetical circumstances: A boyfriend and girlfriend had a fight. She got out of the car and walked away. The boyfriend left in anger but came back for her, didn't find her, and went home. Later he found out that on her way home, she was raped and murdered. How did the boyfriend feel? Did he see himself as responsible? Did he feel guilt for his anger? If he had not given in to his anger, she would not have gotten out of the car, and she would still be alive.

The examiner must make sure he or she deals with only one issue and aspect of a crime at a time. Imagine if the victim mentioned earlier had been raped by one perpetrator but killed by his accomplice. The complex relevant question "Did you rape and kill...?" could be successfully denied by both, thus raising a second instance of ambiguity. In a multiple issue crime, questioning should focus on the most serious act first.

Cleve Backster introduced the theory of psychological set: *A person will focus their mind on those questions in a polygraph test that hold the greatest threat to his or her immediate general well-being.* Considering this theory of psychological set (later redefined as salience), the guilty party could fail to show deceptive reactions to what is perceived as the lesser crime questions because he is waiting to be asked about the more threatening one. Backster identified this possible problem as anticlimactic dampening,[1] which also explains why the deceptive suspect reacts more strongly to the relevant questions than to the comparison questions, even though he is lying to both.

In all cases, extensive preparation for the examination may mean the difference between success and failure. Since relevant questions are meant to force the guilty party to lie, the examiner needs to know as much about the crime and the examinee as possible. That will enable the questions to be well framed and clearly focused. Such questions generate the tensions that most threaten the guilty suspect and cause the psychophysiological changes that occur. Thus, the more known about the crime, the better prepared the examiner will be, and the more productive the examination.

Weak relevant questions are color-coded yellow over red. They are also known as pseudo-relevant, sacrifice relevant, icebreaker, catchall, semirelevant, and throwaway relevant questions because they sound like important questions; however, they are actually used to introduce an examinee into the test or take them out of the test, rather than for determinations of truth or deception. Examples of these questions are as follows:

- Do you intend to deliberately lie to any test question?
- Do you intend to answer every test question truthfully?
- Regarding whether you *did the crime*, do you intend to answer each question truthfully about that?
- Did you deliberately do anything to try and beat this test?

Comparison questions create the environment for properly identifying truthful suspects.[2,3] They are color-coded green. These questions are broad in scope and deal with issues similar but less threatening than the relevant issue to be resolved. They are questions one would expect everyone to truthfully answer, "Yes." In reality, they create a threat to innocent examinees, making them feel as if they must lie. To get an understanding of how comparison questions work, answer each of these sample comparison questions truthfully in your own mind as you read them.

Examples of comparison questions are as follows:

General comparisons

- In your entire life, did you ever tell a lie to get out of trouble?
- In your entire life, did you ever do anything for which you could be arrested?

Theft comparisons

- Prior to working for your current employer, did you ever steal anything from a job?
- In your entire life, did you ever steal anything?
- In your entire life, did you ever steal from someone who trusted you?
- In your entire life, did you ever cheat?
- In your entire life, have you ever taken something that did not belong to you?

Arson comparisons

- In your entire life, did you ever deliberately damage anything?
- During the first 19 years of your life, did you ever play with matches?
- Have you ever done anything you could be arrested for?

Homicide comparisons

- During the first 22 years of your life, did you ever go out of your way to get even with anyone?
- Between the ages of 19 and 23, did you ever lose your temper?
- Have you ever wished harm on anyone?
- Have you ever acted out of anger?
- In your entire life, did you ever deliberately hurt anyone?

Sex comparisons

- In your entire life, did you ever have an unusual sexual fantasy?
- Have you ever done anything sexual to anyone without their permission?
- In your entire life, did you ever masturbate?

- During the first 20 years of your life, did you ever lie about a sexual matter?
- Have you ever done anything sexual you were ashamed of?
- During the first 20 years of your life, did you ever have an unusual sexual fantasy?

You probably answered all or most of these questions "Yes" in your mind. However, almost every truthful suspect will hedge or answer them "No." To understand this, let's look at the dynamics involved with the area of "comparison" questioning.

Assume you are a suspect in the theft of $10,000 from the safe in the office where you work. The relevant question might be, "Yesterday, did you remove that missing safe money?" You did not take the money, so you answer "No." Obviously, since you are a suspect, although you answered truthfully, this question still may hold some threat for you—no one likes to be accused. Now, the examiner states, "A leopard doesn't change its spots." The type of person who would steal $10,000 from his employer is a thief. A basically honest person does not wake up one day and decide to steal a large amount of money. The person who did this will have a history of stealing. This is a person that has stolen from other jobs and from people who trusted him throughout his life. That is the kind of person that would do this. This is the type of person that, even if they did not take the missing safe money, should not be in a sensitive position like yours. That is why I would like to know, "In your entire life, did you ever steal anything? Are you a thief?"

If you took the $10,000, you would not be concerned about this line of inquiry. You are there about the $10,000 you stole. You feel guilty about the $10,000 you stole. You may go to jail for the $10,000 you stole. That you are being asked about ever stealing anything else seems psychologically unimportant to you under the immediate circumstances.

However, we have already said that you are innocent. Think about what is going through your mind as you are asked the comparison question. You do not know what to do: lie or tell the truth. If you lie, will you be caught? If you are caught, will they think you took the $10,000? What if you tell the truth? Will they think you are the type of person that would steal the $10,000 now that you have told them about the 50 cents you took from your mother's purse or the candy bar you ate without paying for on your last job? Even if they do not, the examiner has already said, "That is the type of person, who although he did not take the $10,000, should not be in a sensitive position like yours."

It is important to understand that at some time in their lives, almost all individuals have stolen something, lied about something important to someone who trusted them, cheated someone, deliberately hurt someone, or did some other act of which they are thoroughly ashamed. Committing these minor transgressions are the experiments with the rules by which many of us learn to become responsible members of the community and is an integral part of our socialization. We are testing our social parameters, learning a sense of remorse or guilt, and usually growing into better human beings. However, this experimental antisocial behavior is something we are very reluctant to discuss with other people, let alone a stranger investigating a crime.[4]

Now, if you were an innocent suspect, which question would bother you more? The relevant or comparison question? Obviously, the comparison question holds a greater threat for you because you are being asked to admit to something you actually did. You didn't do the thing under investigation, so the relevant questions represent no threat.

In asking comparison questions, the question framing is less agreed upon. Notice that some of the sample comparison questions begin with globally inclusive phrases like "In your entire life, did you ever...," while other questions involve ages or begin with phrases that seem to exclude a great deal of time, such as "During the first 20 years of your life..." or "Between the ages of 19 and 23, did you ever...?" There is professional disagreement in the field concerning the importance of using inclusive (questions that include the time of crime, such as "In your entire life...") or exclusive comparison questions (questions that exclude the time of crime, such as "During the first 20 years of your life, did you ever...?"). John Reid and Fred Inbau, credited with innovating the comparison question, recommended the use of inclusive questions—those that included the relevant time period under investigation. Thus, they recommended questions worded with the preface, "In your entire life..." or "Have you ever...?" They believed that the examiner should make the comparison question as broad and general as possible. This would ensure that a suspect experienced the maximum threat, forcing him to lie to a question, which he felt might lead the investigator to believe he was guilty of the relevant act.

Cleve Backster recommended that the comparison question be separated in time from the relevant issue. For example, if you are 24 years old at the time of the crime, he would ask, "During the first 21 years of your life..." or "Between the ages of 14 and 18...." Backster argued that this prevented the guilty suspect from perceiving the comparison question as a relevant question. When asked, "In your entire life, did you ever steal anything?" the guilty suspect answers, "No," as he thinks, "I stole the safe money yesterday."

I believe that both Reid and Backster were correct and can be explained by the major difference between the Reid and Backster test question format. In the Reid format, the strong relevant questions come before the comparison questions. In the Backster technique, the comparison questions come first.

Therefore, Backster was right in using exclusive comparisons in his format. If the first question the deceptive examinee heard in the test was

"In your entire life, did you ever steal?" then, he may in fact perceive that it included the deposit he stole yesterday and react to it as if it was a relevant question, resulting in a possible diminished response to the next question in the format, which is the relevant question.

In the Reid technique, the examinee first hears "Did you leave the store with any of that missing deposit money?" and "Did you take that missing deposit money?" and then is asked, "In your entire life, did you ever steal anything?" The chances that the deceptive examinee would come through the two strongest relevant questions and perceive that the comparison question included the deposit theft and therefore react strongest there are almost non-existent. However, for the truthful suspect, who first has to answer the two strongest relevant questions in the test, perceiving that the comparison question includes the time period of the actual theft and therefore lying there may lead the examiner to believe he actually committed the deposit theft, which would add strength to the comparison question and aid in a truthful outcome.

The fact that the inclusive comparison question is more productive in the Reid format is clearly supported by research into the accuracy of the Reid general question test and the army modified general question test. The Reid technique has accuracy rates in the low to mid 80%, while the army modified general question test has accuracy rates in the low 70%. The only difference between the two techniques is that the Reid technique uses inclusive comparison questions and the army modified general question technique uses exclusive comparisons. Therefore, innocent suspects perceive the inclusive comparison question used in the Reid technique as more threatening, and subsequently, the high false-positive rate experienced in the army-modified general question technique is greatly reduced.

Specialized comparison questions are also color-coded green. They are technique specific. They include the "known truth" in the Arther technique, the "known lie" in the Marcy technique, "suspicion" in the Backster and IZCT S-K-Y techniques, "fear or error" in the Matte technique, and the directed lie question.

The "known truths" used in the Arther known lie test are questions dealing with a fictitious character mixed in with actual case facts. For example, in the deposit theft case previously discussed, the examinee may be asked, "Do you know someone named Ralph Bald?" "No," he replies. "Well, you may not know him by name. He is about 6'6", has dark black hair with a silver streak, and was scalded on his face when he was a little boy.[5] Do you know anyone that looks like that?" "No," he replies. "We have information that someone here may have conspired with him to commit this theft. So I am going to ask you, '(3T) Did you plan with Ralph Bald to take that missing deposit money?' and '(8T) Do you know Ralph Bald?'"

Arther theorized that for the truthful examinee, there was no difference between "Did you plan with Ralph Bald to take that missing deposit?"

and "Did you take that missing deposit?" They are both questions about a crime that the examinee knows nothing about and has nothing to do with. In fact, Arther maintained that the "known truth" question may become more threatening to the examinee since the examiner implies that he may have involvement with this person. For the deceptive person, the "known truth" is a question that he is answering truthfully, and "Did you take that missing deposit?" is a question he must lie to. Therefore, the latter holds greater threat.

In the Marcy technique question 2T, the "known lie" question is, "Did you tell the truth about everything we talked about since you have been here today?" Marcy maintains that everyone is lying to this question when they answer, "Yes." Truthful examinees have lied about the comparison questions. Deceptive examinees have lied about the crime and comparison questions. Therefore, everyone is lying to the question and Marcy uses their reaction to this question for comparison purposes with the relevant question, "Are you withholding any information *about that crime?*"

Matte theorizes that all truthful examinees have a fear of error and that the examiner is incompetent or the procedure does not work and the examiner will accuse them of a crime they did not commit. He therefore asks, "Are you afraid that I will make an error in this test concerning whether you *did the crime?*" The examiner introduces the question in a way to elicit a "No" response. Matte uses the reaction to this question as a comparison with "Are you hoping that I will make an error in this test concerning whether you *did the crime?*" that he considers to be a relevant test question. He calls this pair of questions the "inside issue."

The directed lie comparison (DLC) question is being used in the field increasingly as some researchers[6] have continuously suggested its use in a pedantic manner with statistical smoke and mirrors to replace the traditional probable lie comparison (PLC) question.

The DLC is employed by basically informing the examinee that all people have done these things in their lifetime (lied, broke a traffic law, etc.); however, so that the examiner can see exactly what happens physiologically when they lie, they are to answer these questions "No" during the examination.

The concept seems to have gained some support in governmental examinations because it is "politically correct," or because it alleviates the examiner from having to possess the skill and ability to properly structure and introduce the PLC question. The "politically correct" argument is that if an examiner is testing a superior, he or she does not have to go into their actual life background to create a comparison question, which may not be well received by the person of higher rank.

While the DLC may be politically correct and require less skill for the examiner to utilize, I fear it also creates false-negative outcomes for several reasons, some of which were shared by Dr. Stanley Abrams (2001),[7] and is demonstrated in research by Matte and Reuss (1999).[8]

> *Problem 1*: Introducing the DLC does not allow for the natural flow of "psychological set"; instead, it creates a false focus to the DLC. If I tell you that what happens physiologically in your body to this question allows me to identify your body's reaction to deception, which I can then use to compare to the reactions in the relevant questions and determine their veracity, then the DLC becomes the "key" to the revealing of the guilty examinee's involvement. Psychologically, the DLC, the "key," can become more important than the relevant test questions, resulting in false-negative outcomes.
>
> *Problem 2*: You do not have to be a "rocket scientist" to realize that if the reactions to the DLC are greater than those to the relevant test questions, you will pass the test, resulting in an increase in counter-measures and distortions to the DLC. Interestingly, the researchers deny this, and yet they instruct examiners not to score respiration because it can be controlled by the examinee. Distortions of the pneumo will also cause distortions in the other polygraph components. Breathing is the effector and the EDA and cardio are the affected. If we cannot trust the pneumo component, how can we trust what it affects?

Once again we are looking at an increase in false negatives.

Here are three actual field charts (Figures 3.1 through 3.3) with relevant question 5 enveloped by a PLC and a DLC. It resulted in a confession to the relevant issue. Notice the deliberate distortions to the DLCs. Thus, the DLC invites countermeasures. The question now becomes "Who is better, the examinee at employing them or the examiner at spotting them?"

Perhaps the argument for the DLC should be that in a test that has a higher false-positive rate than false-negative rate, a procedure that reduces the former by creating more of the latter is a good solution. I may be behind the times; however, my goal as an examiner has always been to come to a proper conclusion, not create one type of error to try to compensate for another.

The last category of questions is called symptomatic questions. They are color-coded black. Backster calls these questions the "outside issue." Backster's techniques are known as "Tri-Zone Comparison Techniques." Backster believed that a polygraph examination was a procedure that identified the flow of an examinee's psychological set. The red zone (relevant questions) is designed to threaten the deceptive examinee. The green zone (comparison questions) is designed to threaten the truthful examinees. The black zone (symptomatic or outside issue questions) is designed to ensure

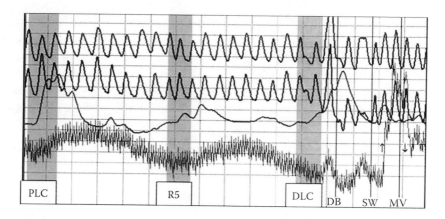

Figure 3.1 Countermeasures to directed lie comparison chart 1.

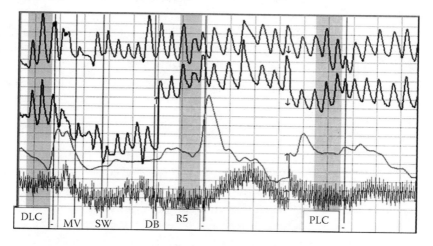

Figure 3.2 Countermeasures to directed lie comparison chart 2.

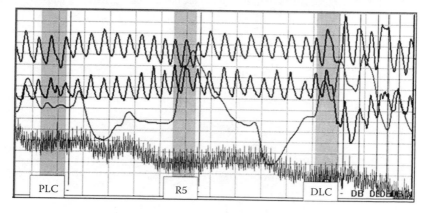

Figure 3.3 Countermeasures to directed lie comparison chart 3.

that the examinee is not afraid the examiner will ask a question that was not reviewed concerning some personal outside issue, which may dampen his ability (called "super dampening") to properly focus on his greatest threat in the test, be it the relevant or comparison questions. The symptomatic question can also serve as a question asked at the beginning of an examination to further allow the examinee to establish a normal or homeostatic physiological testing norm.

Examples are as follows:

- Do you believe me when I promise not to ask a question in this test that I have not gone over word for word?
- Even though I promised that I would not, are you afraid I will ask a question in this test that I have not gone over word for word?
- Do you understand that I will only ask the questions I reviewed?

As you will see, all polygraph techniques derive their format from these four categories of questions. You will learn in the chapter on *Technique Development* that what makes one technique different from another is how the innovator of the technique selected questions from these categories and combined them in their technique format.

Basic Rules for Irrelevant Questions

- The primary purpose of the irrelevant question is to establish or reestablish the examinee's normal physiological/homeostatic pattern to include the examinee's excitement or emotional level with the introduction of a verbal stimulus.
- In some techniques these questions aid in the interpretations of specific reactions (relevant/irrelevant technique) or possible countermeasures.
- There should be no known connection between the irrelevant questions and the relevant issue. For example, using a name in a crime involving conning or scams would be improper. Using a person's place of employment, where the crime involves employment, would be improper.
- When using identifying information, you must make sure that it is correct.
- Be careful not to use irrelevant questions that the examinee may be sensitive to, such as "Do you smoke?" "Did you eat?" and "Are you 44 years old?"

Basic Rules for Relevant Questions

- They must be simple and direct.
- They must not involve legal terminology.
- They must be dichotomous—answerable by "Yes" or "No."
- They should be as short as possible.
- Each question should be clear and unmistakable.
- They must be phrased in a language the examinee can understand.
- They should not be accusatory or infer that the examiner has concluded that the examinee is already guilty.
- They must refer to only one aspect of the offense and only one offense.
- They should force the guilty to lie and allow the innocent to answer truthfully.
- They should solve some aspect of the crime.
- Use the word "that," rather than "the." "That" implies specificity.
- Descriptive phrases, such as "yesterday" and "other than what you said," should be in the beginning of the question.
- There should be no insulting, profane, or obscene words or terms.
- Case facts when included must be correct.
- Do not use words or terms you cannot pronounce.
- Get feedback from the examinee to be certain that he understands the meaning of the question and is not rationalizing or personally coding by asking the examinee, "What does that question mean?"

Basic Rules for Comparison Questions

- The primary purpose of the comparison question is to threaten the innocent examinee.
- The question should be similar in nature to the crime, or motivation of the crime, but less severe.
- The comparison question is used for comparison with the relevant test questions.
- Each comparison questions should be formulated in a manner that the examiner can be reasonably certain that the examinee is lying or unsure of his answer to the question.
- Comparison questions should be answerable by "No."
- Comparison questions should be broad in scope to ensure deception or create doubt in the mind of the examinee as to their truthfulness.

Conclusion

Question formulation is one of the many key aspects of conducting an accurate polygraph examination. For a valid examination, it is imperative that the relevant questions asked resolve the issue under investigation and that the examinee and examiner have the same understanding of what the question means. In the chapter on *Techniques*, you will see that a polygraph format is nothing more than how a creator selected and combined questions from these various categories.

Notes

1. Backster, C. (1974) Anticlimax dampening concept. *Polygraph*, 3(1), 48–50.
2. Reid, J. and Inbau, F. (1947) A revised questioning technique in lie detection. *Journal of Criminal Law and Criminology*, 37(6), 542–547.
3. Although Reid and Inbau were the first to publish information on the comparison question, both Marston and Father Summers were already using similar questions in their techniques.
4. Gordon, N. and Fleisher, W. (2011) *Effective Interview and Interrogation Techniques*. Academic Press, San Diego, CA.
5. The fictitious character is described in a way to ensure even if the suspect knows someone of a similar name it is clear to him or her they do not know this person.
6. Honts, C. R. and Raskin, D. C. (1988) A field study of the validity of the directed lie control question. *Journal of Police Science and Administration*, 16(1), 56–61.
7. Abrams, S. (1991) The directed lie control question. *Polygraph*, 20(1), 26–31.
8. Matte, J. A. and Reuss, R. M. (1999) Validation of potential response elements in the directed lie question. *Polygraph*, 28(2), 124–142.

Psychophysiology

4

If you tell the truth, you don't have to remember anything.

—Mark Twain

To understand the physiological data collected with the polygraph, the examiner should have a basic understanding of physiology, especially the central nervous system, cardiovascular system, integumentary system, and respiratory system. It would take volumes to properly cover the human physiology. This chapter on physiology is written to give a simplified understanding of a very complex topic.

The easiest way to remember how the body is organized is with the acronym CTOS:

Cells: Cells are the smallest units of life and are the building blocks involved in metabolism, growth, reproduction, etc.
Tissues: When similar cells form or work together, they form tissues.
Organs: When tissues work together, they form organs.
Systems: When organs work together, they form systems.

To remember the organs of the body, we can use the acronym I jokingly refer to as Mc Donald's cousin, MC RENDERSS:

Musculatory
Circulatory
Respiration
Endocrine
Nervous
Digestive
Exocrine
Reproductive
Skeletal
Skin

The *central nervous system* is comprised of the brain and spinal cord. As humans evolved, the brain developed from the lowest part, the hindbrain, up to the forebrain. The basic essentials for living are contained in the hindbrain.

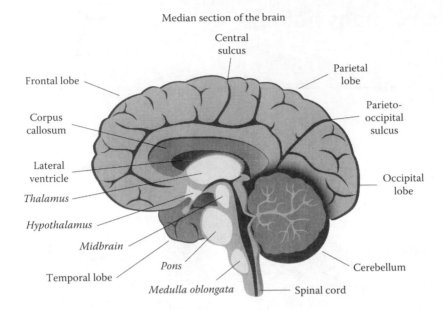

Figure 4.1 Diagram of the brain.

Located in the hindbrain is the medulla oblongata, which is involved in many of our autonomic functions. These include breathing, heart rate, and blood pressure, which obviously are of interest to the polygraph examiner and process (Figure 4.1).

The *limbic system* (Figure 4.2) is a complex set of brain structures that are involved in emotion, epinephrine flow, long-term memory, motivation, and behavior. It includes the olfactory bulbs, hippocampus, amygdala, anterior thalamic nuclei, fornix, columns of fornix, mammillary body, septum pellucidum, habenular commissure, cingulate gyrus, parahippocampal gyrus, limbic cortex, and limbic midbrain areas.

The *hypothalamus* is in the forebrain and contains a number of small nuclei with a variety of functions. One of the most important functions of the hypothalamus is to link the nervous system to the endocrine system via the pituitary gland. The hypothalamus is responsible for certain metabolic processes and other activities of the autonomic nervous system. It synthesizes and secretes certain neurohormones, often called releasing hormones or hypothalamic hormones, and these in turn stimulate or inhibit the secretion of pituitary hormones. The hypothalamus is the highest brain area controlling the autonomic nervous system functions including body temperature, hunger, thirst, fatigue, sleep, and cardiac rhythms.

The *peripheral nervous system* includes all nerves outside the central nervous system and connects the central nervous system to all parts of the body. It divides into two systems: the *somatic nervous system*, which deals

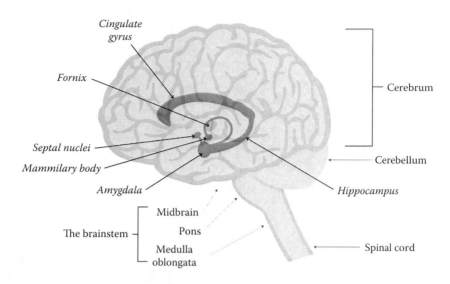

Figure 4.2 Limbic system.

with voluntary actions, and the *autonomic nervous system*, which deals with involuntary actions. For example, your heart is beating right now without you looking at your chest and saying, "Beat! Beat! Beat!"

The autonomic nervous system divides into the parasympathetic nervous system and the sympathetic nervous system. The brain can control every autonomic function in the body through these two systems. If it wants your heartbeat to slow down, it sends a parasympathetic message. If it wants it to speed up, it sends a sympathetic message. The parasympathetic system is considered the "housekeeper" and the sympathetic system the emergency system, often referred to as the "fight or flight" system. As a general rule, the parasympathetic system slows down thoracic activity such as heart rate and breathing, lowers blood pressure, and speeds up abdominal activity so we can digest food and eliminate wastes. The sympathetic system does the opposite, increasing thoracic activity to ensure the body is properly oxygenated for the emergency, and slowing down abdominal activity since digestion and waste elimination are not important if you are about to die (Figure 4.3a and b).

Communication from the nervous system to various parts of the body is done through chains of nerve cells, called *neurons*. There are three types of neurons in the body: afferent or sensory neurons, interneurons, and efferent or motor neurons. Afferent nerves pick up information from our senses and communicate them to our brain. Interneurons are relay areas. Motor neurons are communications from the brain to the body. The autonomic nervous system is made up of motor nerves: the brain telling the body how to change due to information it has received from the environment and sensory nerves.

There are many types of cells in the body: blood cells, skin cells, etc.; however, neurons are the only cells that can communicate. They can send, store, and receive information. The neuron consists of a cell body or soma, receiving ends called dendrites, and a sending end called an axon. The skin of the neuron is made up of a semipermeable membrane. Like a window screen, the membrane lets certain things in and keeps certain things out. The inside of the neuron consists mostly of negatively charged chloride ions, while the exterior is mostly positively charges with sodium ions. Sodium chloride is the chemical that salt derives from. Like a battery, with all positive charges at one end and all negative charges at the other end, you have the potential for an electrical current to happen. When neurons are in this state, it is referred to as resting potential.

The areas between neurons are called synapses. A neural message is a combination of an electrical and chemical process. If the dendrites receive

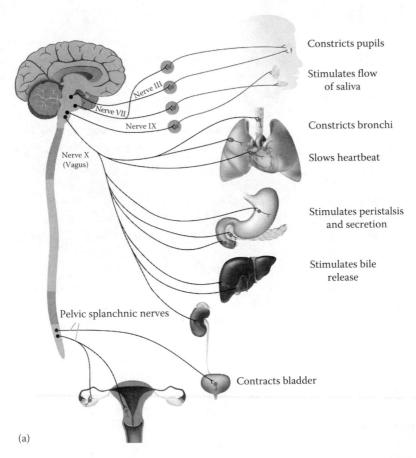

(a)

Figure 4.3 (a) Parasympathetic.   (*Continued*)

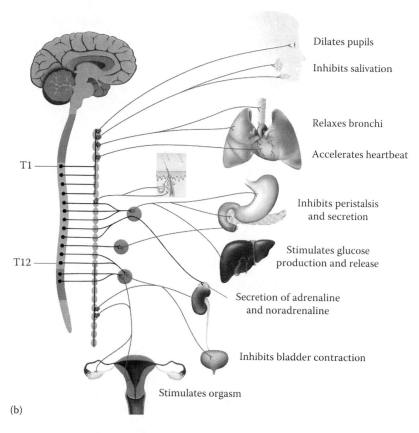

Dilates pupils

Inhibits salivation

Relaxes bronchi

Accelerates heartbeat

T1

Inhibits peristalsis
and secretion

Stimulates glucose
production and release

T12

Secretion of adrenaline
and noradrenaline

Inhibits bladder contraction

Stimulates orgasm

(b)

Figure 4.3 (*Continued*) (b) Sympathetic nervous system.

enough stimulation from neurotransmitter chemicals released from the pre-synaptic neuron into the synapse, the semipermeable membrane suddenly allows the positively charged sodium ions to enter, and an electrical charge occurs, referred to as action potential. The stimulation required either meets the minimum amount needed or it does not—all or nothing.

At the tip of the axon, there are synaptic vessels called telodendria that release the neurotransmitter chemicals into the synapse, and if enough chemicals are released, the postsynaptic neuron will also go through the same process and so on down a chain of neurons until the chemicals are released into a synapse that will stimulate a muscle and organ (Figure 4.4).

Once the neuron fires, it must go through a refractory period where all of the positive sodium ions are pumped out of the cell and it can return to a resting state. The entire process from resting potential to action potential,

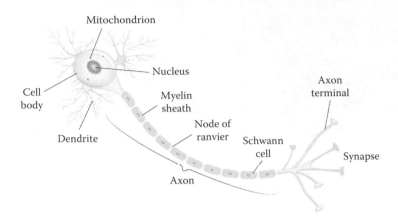

Figure 4.4 Illustration of a neuron.

to a refractory period, and back to resting potential in some neurons only takes a millisecond. Since some neural impulses need to be sent quickly, their axons are myelinated with spaces on the axon produced by Schwann cells or glial cells named "nodes of Ranvier." Through a process known as saltatory conduction, the electrical current skips from space to space rather than traveling straight down the length of an unmyelinated axon. Imagine dropping a rock into a body of water and its speed as it slowly drops to the bottom versus throwing the rock across the water's surface and the speed it travels as it skips across. A current traveling down the length of an axon without myelination moves at about 3 ft/s. Skipping across the myelinated nodes of Ranvier, it travels about 300 ft/s.

The *muscular system* consists of skeletal, smooth, and cardiac muscles. It is this system that allows for body movement, posture, and blood circulation throughout the body. The muscular system in humans is mostly controlled through the nervous system. There are three types of muscles in the human body. Striated or skeletal muscles are involved in voluntary movements. Smooth muscles are controlled by the autonomic nervous system and are involved in involuntary movements. The cardiac muscles are combinations of striated and smooth muscles, which are involuntary and controlled by the sinus node that in turn is controlled by the autonomic nervous system.

The *circulatory system* circulates blood and transports nutrients (such as amino acids and electrolytes), oxygen, carbon dioxide, hormones, and blood cells to and from the cells in the body to provide nourishment and help in fighting diseases, stabilize temperature and pH, and maintain homeostasis.

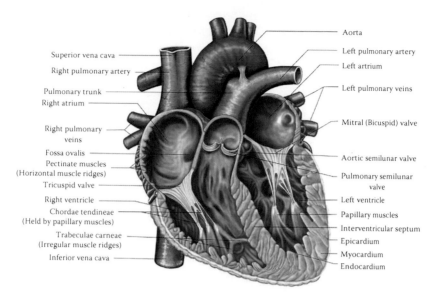

Aorta

Left pulmonary artery

Left artrium

Superior vena cava

Right pulmonary artery

Left pulmonary veins

Pulmonary trunk

Right atrium

Mitral (Bicuspid) valve

Right pulmonary
veins

Fossa ovalis

Aortic semilunar valve

Pectinate muscles
(Horizontal muscle ridges)

Pulmonary semilunar
valve

Tricuspid valve

Right ventricle

Left ventricle

Chordae tendineae
(Held by papillary muscles)

Papillary muscles

Interventricular septum

Trabeculae carneae
(Irregular muscle ridges)

Epicardium

Myocardium

Inferior vena cava

Endocardium

Figure 4.5 Diagram of the human heart.

It consists of the heart, blood, and blood vessels and actually involves two circulatory systems: the greater or systemic circulatory system and the lesser or pulmonary circulatory system. The greater system involves getting the oxygenated blood and nutrients to all of the cells in the body, while removing carbon dioxide and waste. The lesser system transports the carbon dioxide and waste to the lungs where the blood is then oxygenated and returned to the heart to be pumped throughout the body. The cardiovascular systems of humans are closed, meaning that the blood never leaves the network of arteries, veins, and capillaries they travel in.

When we look at the heart, it is as if it is in another person. The right side of the heart is to the viewer's left (Figure 4.5). The heart is divided into four chambers. The top two chambers are called atria and they receive blood. The bottom two chambers are called ventricles and they pump or send blood. The right side of the heart is involved in processing deoxygenated (bad) blood and the left side with oxygenated (good) blood. So you now know the right atrium receives bad blood and the right ventricle pumps it, while the left atrium receives good blood and the left ventricle pumps it. All arteries take blood away from the heart and all veins transport blood to the heart. In the lesser circulatory system, arteries are transporting bad blood and veins good blood, while in the greater system, the arteries transport good blood and the veins bad blood.

In the greater circulatory system, arteries are bringing bad blood from the body back to the right atrium of the heart through the superior and inferior venae cavae. The blood then travels through the tricuspid valve into the right ventricle where it is then pumped through the pulmonary semilunar valve and pulmonary arteries to be transported to the lungs to exchange the deoxygenated blood and wastes for oxygenated blood and nutrients. The good blood now is returned to the left atrium by four pulmonary veins. It then passes through the bicuspid or mitral valve into the left ventricle, where it is pumped through the aortic semilunar valve into the aorta, the largest artery in the body, and transported to all of the body cells.

The exchange from bad blood to good blood at the lungs is called "external respiration" (remember that air entering the lungs comes from the external environment), while the exchange of good blood for bad blood in the body is called "internal respiration."

The left ventricle is the strongest chamber of the heart responsible for pumping blood throughout the entire body and therefore meets the most resistance. Both atria receive blood at the same time and both ventricles pump at the same time. The dicrotic notch that appears on the cardio tracing is created due to blood that has just been pumped rebounding off the closing aortic semilunar valve, which prevents it from returning back into the heart.

The normal rhythmical heartbeat is called sinus rhythm. It is established by the sinoatrial (SA) node, which is the heart's pacemaker. The SA node is found in the upper part of the right atrium. It is influenced by sympathetic and parasympathetic signals from the medulla oblongata, located in the hindbrain causing the SA node to generate an electrical signal to the left atrium via the Bachmann's bundle, causing both the left and right atria to contract together. Through the parasympathetic system's vagus nerve, the signal is slowed, and through sympathetic stimulation, it is increased. From there the signal travels to the atrioventricular node, which is at the bottom of the right atrium. The signal then travels along the bundle of His to both of the ventricles of the heart. In the ventricles the signal is carried by specialized tissue called the Purkinje fibers, which then transmit the electric charge to the cardiac muscle causing ventricular contraction and blood to be pumped to the lungs from the right ventricle and the body from the left ventricle. A normal resting heart rate for adults is between 60 and 100 beats/min.

Cardiac output is the volume of blood pumped by the heart per minute (mL blood/min). Cardiac output is a function of heart rate and stroke volume. The heart rate is simply the number of heartbeats per minute. The stroke volume is the volume of blood, in milliliters (mL), pumped out of the heart with each beat. From a polygraph standpoint, heartbeat can easily be assessed by counting the number of beats on the graph for 10 seconds and multiplying by 6. Most of the computerized systems will automatically be able to show these data. On the other hand, stroke volume is difficult to identify since the size of the tracing that is expected to show changes in stroke volume is also influenced by the relationship between changes in the examinee's mean blood pressure and the pressure being exerted by the instrument's blood pressure cuff.

The *respiratory system* is responsible for supplying life-sustaining oxygen to your body and removing waste and carbon dioxide from it through the act of breathing. Breathing ideally starts at the nose, but can be done through the mouth.

When you inhale air into your nose, nasal hairs act like a screen to eliminate any debris and the mucus membranes warm the air to body temperature. It then travels down the back of the throat and into the windpipe, or trachea. The trachea then divides into air passages called bronchial tubes. As the bronchial tubes pass through the lungs, they divide into smaller airways called bronchioles. The bronchioles end in tiny balloon-like air sacs called alveoli located in the lungs. There are over 300 million alveoli in the body. The alveoli are surrounded by a mesh of tiny blood vessels called capillaries. This is where external respiration takes place, in which carbon dioxide passes from the blood into the lungs to be exhaled and oxygen from the inhaled air passes through to the capillaries and travels to larger vessels and finally into the four pulmonary veins and brought back to the heart for disbursement to the cells in the body (Figure 4.6).

The lungs are protected by the rib cage and sit on top of the diaphragm, the major muscle involved in breathing. The medulla oblongata in the

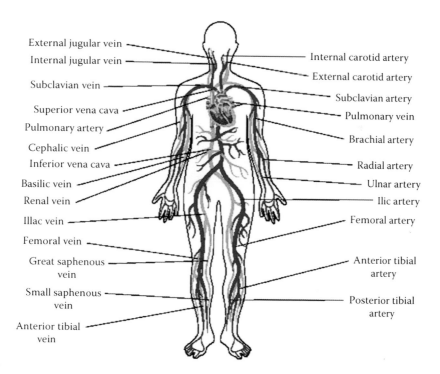

External jugular vein
Internal jugular vein
Subclavian vein
Superior vena cava
Pulmonary artery
Cephalic vein
Inferior vena cava
Basilic vein
Renal vein
Illac vein
Femoral vein
Great saphenous vein
Small saphenous vein
Anterior tibial vein

Internal carotid artery
External carotid artery
Subclavian artery
Pulmonary vein
Brachial artery
Radial artery
Ulnar artery
Ilic artery
Femoral artery
Anterior tibial artery
Posterior tibial artery

Figure 4.6 Diagram of the circulatory system.

hindbrain sends a signal to the diaphragm to contract and for the intercostal muscles to contract. Think about the space around the lungs as an airtight box, like an accordion. When the intercostal muscles contract pulling up on the rib cage and the diaphragm contracts, the box expands and the inhaled air is sucked into the lungs. When they relax, air is removed from the lungs via exhalation.

There are two types of glands in the body which are referred to as duct glands and ductless glands. All glands secrete chemicals or hormones into the body. Duct glands secrete their hormones into specific body cavities, for example, sweat glands. Ductless glands secrete their hormones into the blood stream, thereby affecting the entire body. Ductless glands make up the *endocrine system* and include the pituitary gland, or "master gland," which not only regulates other glands but also produces some hormones. The pineal gland regulates the body clock and is influenced by daylight. The thyroid gland regulates energy and bone growth. The parathyroid gland, located behind the thyroid gland, removes calcium from bones. The thymus gland activates the body's immune cells. The adrenal glands regulate blood flow and involuntary muscle activity in the "fight or flight" response and control mineral content of blood, as well as produce stress response hormones. The pancreas gland regulates the glucose content of blood using insulin and glucagon.

The integumentary system includes the skin and its appendages, such as hair and nails. The skin is the largest organ in the body. This system separates our internal body from the external environment and has multiple roles in homeostasis. The skin acts as the body's first line of defense against infection, temperature change, and other challenges to homeostasis. Changes in the electrodermal activity monitored by the polygraph are caused by changes occurring in this system affecting sweat gland activity (Figure 4.7).

The integumentary system's functions include the following:

- Protecting the body's internal living tissues and organs
- Protecting against invasion by infectious organisms
- Protecting the body from dehydration
- Protecting the body against abrupt changes in temperature to maintain homeostasis
- Helping excrete waste materials through perspiration
- Acting as a receptor for touch, pressure, pain, heat, and cold
- Protecting the body against sunburns by secreting melanin
- Generating vitamin D through exposure to ultraviolet (UV) light
- Storing water, fat, glucose, and vitamin D
- Maintaining the body form
- Forming new cells from stratum germanium to repair minor injuries
- Protecting from UV rays

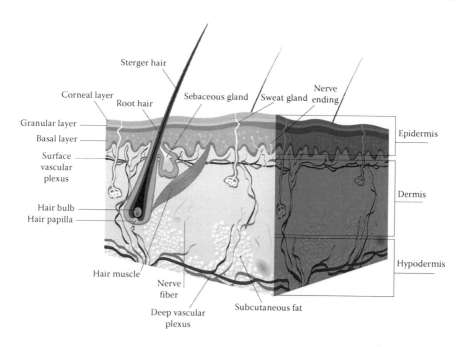

Figure 4.7 Diagram of the structure of skin.

Having a basic understanding of physiology is necessary for the polygraph examiner in understanding the polygraph language and making accurate determinations of the data they collect. The question now becomes, "Why should physiological changes occur when a mental act such as lying occurs?"[1]

The study of psychology involves our thoughts, feelings, and behaviors and how these three areas are connected and influence the individual. Theory can be defined as an organized and studied hypothesis to explain why things occur. There are many theories that evolved over time in both psychology and polygraph. Quite often we see that one individual's original ideas get built upon by another theorist and the concepts get taken a step further. There is no clear right or wrong within a theory—we look at what is functional in a given situation or context.

One of the more interesting psychological theorists was Sigmund Freud. Freud perceived the mind as constantly in a state of conflict with itself and understood this conflict as the primary cause of all human anxiety and unhappiness. This led him to an eventual division of the mind into three parts, of conflicting internal tendencies, the well-known id, ego, and superego. Perhaps it is easier to think of these as the child, the self, and the parent.

The child in us is the id. It just wants! The reality of life is we want only to eat, drink, urinate, defecate, be warm, and gain sexual pleasure. These urges are the demands of the id, the most primitive motivational force. In pursuit of these ends, the id demands immediate gratification: it is ruled by the pleasure principle, demanding satisfaction now, regardless of circumstances and possible undesirable effects. Some urges, such as urination, are easily satisfied. However, if the urge is not immediately discharged, the id will form a memory of the end of the motivation: the thirsty infant will form an image of the mother's breast. This act of wish-fulfillment satisfies the id's desire for the moment, though obviously it does not reduce the tension of the unfulfilled urge.

The superego is "the parent," demanding that we do what is morale and correct in life. The superego is subdividable into two parts: the conscience and ego ideal. The ego ideal aims the individual's path of life toward the ideal, perfect goals instilled by society. The conscience tells us what is right and wrong. If a person does something that is acceptable to the superego, he experiences pride and self-satisfaction. However, since the id's demands often go against what the superego believes is right behavior, the superego uses guilt and self-reproach as its primary means of enforcement of its rules.

The ego represents "the self" and is ruled by the reality principle. The ego is the negotiator between the demands of the id and the principles set forth by the superego. While the ego may temporarily repress certain urges of the id in fear of punishment, eventually these external sources of punishment are internalized, and ideally, the child who later develops into an adult will not, for example, "steal," even when unwatched, because he has taken the ideas of punishment, right, and wrong into himself.

The ego as the negotiator often just suppresses the id's urges until an appropriate situation arises. This repression of inappropriate desires and urges represents the greatest strain on the mind, and the ego often utilizes defense mechanisms to achieve and aid this repression. These mechanisms help to maintain the stability and sanity of the individual, though they take up a considerable amount of our psychic energy in the process. As a polygraph examiner, it is important to be familiar with these ego defense mechanisms to ensure an examination does not result in a false negative due to the examinee's ability to deploy them.

> *Reaction formation*: To ward off an anxiety-causing and unacceptable impulse, one may replace it with its overemphasized diametrical opposite. For example, the young boy who hates his older brother for his accomplishments and the rewards and praise that his older brother receives may transform this hatred into aggressive love and praise. This replacement of his hatred with its opposite, love, represses the hatred and satisfies his superego's rules for what is acceptable, but does not eliminate the original impulse.

Projection: In projection, forbidden, unacceptable urges build up and break into consciousness, but are then attributed to others. A jealous husband may call his wife unfaithful, while it is he who wants to have an affair but cannot face this. His projection means that he has first repressed his own urge and then projects it upon his wife.

Rationalization: This relieves a person of anxiety or guilt by formulating perfectly reasonable reasons for their unacceptable behavior. An employee steals a deposit from his or her employer; however he justifies it by rationalizing that it was not stealing. The employer promised the employee a raise after 6 months of employment that has never occurred. The employee rationalizes that the money they took is only a partial payment for the raise they never received; it was not stealing and in fact they are still owed more compensation.

Displacement: When a natural urge related to anger is not immediately able to be vented and therefore repressed, it is often displaced to another, less threatening, disguised outlet. A man's anger at his boss, which is unacceptable because of his position within this hierarchy, may be displaced by reprimanding and taking it out on his secretary. The secretary may take her anger home and punish her son. Here the unacceptable urge is vented in a manner that feels more acceptable to the ego and superego.

Repression: This is an attempt to repress inappropriate, unfeasible, or guilt-causing urges, memories, and wishes (all usually of the id) to the level of the unconscious, where they will be out of sight, if not out of mind. The ability to repress dangerous or unsettling thoughts turns out to be vital to the individual's ability to negotiate his way through life. If a child had never learned to repress the urge to steal his sister's ice cream cone, for example, he would have spent years in punishment. This is the most common of the defense mechanisms and we will often see repression used by sexual abuse victims and war veterans as a means to attempt functioning in their daily lives by "putting away" these memories that are too difficult to recall.

Identification: It attempts to increase your feelings of self-worth by identifying with a person or institution of higher, more illustrious standing (i.e., joining a fraternity, religious affiliations, and professional organizations).

Somatization: It is the unconscious transformation of unacceptable impulses or feelings into physical symptoms. For example, head or stomach aches that can't be confirmed medically yet are present and specifically related to triggering stimuli.

Regression: It is defined as returning to an earlier level of functioning (childlike behaviors) or a lower-level aspiration during stressful
periods in one's life. An example is an older child returning to bed
wetting or thumb sucking after the birth of a new sibling or midlife
crisis behaviors for adults.

Denial: It is the unconscious discounting of external reality. This is
exemplified by the parent who finds drug paraphernalia in their
child's bag and accepts the child's explanation that they were holding it for a friend versus dealing with the reality of their discovery
that their child may have a problem.

Sublimation: It is acting out an unacceptable impulse in a sociably
acceptable way. Rather than give into the urge of hurting people the
individual takes up boxing.

Splitting: This is selectively focusing on only part of a person to meet
a current state of need, seeing people as either all good or all bad,
which serves to relieve the uncertainty engendered by the fact that
people have both bad and good qualities. This is quite normal in
childhood, since as children develop, they have a "black and white"
absolute way of viewing the world.

Dissociation: It is mentally separating part of consciousness from reality, which can result in forgetting certain events. An example is dis-
sociative amnesia, that is, witnessing a violent act and afterward not
being able to recall the events, even leading up to or directly after the
triggering event.

Compensation: It attempts to cover up a weakness by emphasizing a more
desirable trait or making up for frustration in one area by gratification in another. This is demonstrated by the student poor in academ-
ics and makes up for it with their strength in athletics or vice versa.

Cleve Backster introduced major psychological concepts to assist in understanding the workings of polygraph as well as major refinements in polygraph
formatting and data analysis. He introduced theories such as psychological
set, anticlimactic dampening, super dampening, case intensity factor, basic
emotionality factor (BEF), spot analysis, individual reaction capability, and
numerical scoring.

Since 1980, I have defined Backster's concept of "psychological set" as
the focusing of the mind on those questions in a polygraph format that holds
the greatest interest or greatest immediate threat to the examinee's general
well-being.

In very recent times, this theory has been redefined as "salience"[2]; however, the definition is almost the same, but replaces the concept of reacting
due to fear of detection and then replaces this concept with reactions to the
questions of the greatest importance. Dr. Senter and his associates coined the

term differential salience[3] to identify the varied degrees of importance an examinee places on various questions in an examination based on the degree of intensity emitted to different questions in a polygraph test. While some researchers argue that fear plays no part in the detection of deception ruling out Backster's concept of psychological set for salience, recent research[5] examined different cognitive processes that cause physiological reactions associated with deception during concealed information peak of tension tests (CIT). The research concluded that there are different mechanisms that drive the responding psychophysiological measures used in the CIT, of which the orienting reflex (OR) is but one. Implying that fear or withholding information (inhibition) about a crime plays no role in an examinee's perception of importance/salience and the drive of psychophysiological reaction seems to clearly be an over simplification of the process.

There are several other theories that explain why a mental act, such as lying, causes physiological changes to occur. A spin-off of this concept of psychological set or salience is the orienting response. The orienting response is defined as a behavioral reaction to a changed, new, or abrupt stimulant, for instance, a physiological reaction to a salient question.

Another explanation for why lying might cause physiological arousal is conditioning. There are two types of conditioning: Pavlovian/classical conditioning and operant conditioning.

Anyone who has taken a basic course in psychology will remember Ivan Pavlov and his experiment with dogs. Pavlov was studying digestion by measuring physiological functions, such as salivation, when he presented the dogs with food. Eventually, the dogs began salivating as soon as Pavlov entered the lab and before he had the chance to monitor changes taking place. Pavlov was sidetracked, wondering why he suddenly caused dogs to salivate. This led to his theory of classical conditioning. Pavlov stated that there were certain stimuli that automatically cause a response to occur, without any prior learning. For example, place food (stimuli) in front of a dog and the dog will salivate (response), without any prior learning. Pavlov called these stimuli unconditioned stimuli (UCSs) and the response they caused an unconditioned response (UCR). There were many other things (such as Pavlov) that did not cause this response to occur, and he labeled these as neutral stimuli (NSs). Pavlov theorized that if a NS is continually present at the same time a UCS is presented, eventually, the NS will be able to cause the UCR, which is now classified as a conditioned response (CR) and the NS a conditioned stimulus (CS).

If your father takes off his belt and gives you a hiding (UCS), you will experience physiological arousal (UCR). If every time your father catches you lying (NS), he gives you a hiding (UCS), eventually when you lie, your brain will cause your body to become physiologically aroused (UCR), which has now become a CR (Figure 4.8).

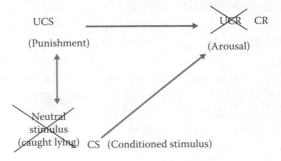

Figure 4.8 Illustration of classical conditioning.

Figure 4.9 Illustration of operant conditioning.

In operant conditioning, first, the organism responds, and depending on whether they receive a reward or punishment for what they did, they will have a future expectation of receiving the same outcome (Figure 4.9). If the person has learned that when they are caught lying they receive punishment, now when they lie, they have an expectation of oncoming punishment, and the brain prepares them for it by enervating their emergency system.

A third possibility is based on the conflict model. There are three types of conflict: approach–approach, avoidance–avoidance, and approach–avoidance.

An "approach–approach conflict" takes place when you must choose between two things you want, and choosing one means you may never obtain the other.

An "avoidance–avoidance conflict" is where you must choose between two things you do not want, but must select one. The greater the conflict between these choices, the greater the individual will experience frustration and emotional changes, and the greater the physiological changes will occur due to them.

The last type of conflict, "approach–avoidance," is the one of interest to us. It is where a single act can result in either reward or punishment, and we are unsure which will occur. The more we desire the reward and the more we do not want to experience the punishment, the greater the conflict. In polygraph we ask a question, "Did you do the crime?" and with a single word, "No," the examinee either goes undetected (reward) or is identified (punishment). Hence, the person experiences physiological changes due to the emotional changes caused by the conflict.

Dr. Avital Ginton published another psychological theory of relevant issue gravity (RIG).[4] His theory is based on attention; due to the gravity of the situation, the deceptive suspect's attention will be drawn to the relevant test questions, while a truthful suspect's attention to relevant questions will be interfered with and drawn to the comparison questions. Like salience, the concept of fear of detection is eliminated from Ginton's RIG concept.

Backster's theory on anticlimactic dampening holds that the more important threat has the ability to dampen out less important threats. A mother with a new born baby is lying on the couch taking a nap. The baby is also sleeping close by in a bassinet. The school across the street from their house has just ended classes and there are children outside playing and yelling. The mother remains fast asleep. Ten minutes later the baby makes a soft sound, "Wah!" and the mother jumps up. Why didn't the noise from all of the school children wake her? Because of the fact that she was so focused on her greatest concern, the baby, all other sounds were dampened out. This is anticlimactic dampening that also explains why a deceptive person who is lying to both comparison and relevant questions reacts stronger to the relevant questions. It also explains why in multifaceted and multi-issue tests it could create problems and confusion for the examiner since there is competition between different degrees of relevant questions.

For example, a person commits a theft and a multifaceted test is administered. The examinee is asked, "Do you know for sure who took that missing deposit?" "Did you take that missing deposit?" "Were you present when that missing deposit was taken?" The examinee knows who took the deposit, he was present when it was taken, and he in fact took it, yet he only reacts to the question, "Did you take that missing deposit?" The examiner is in a quandary! How could he have taken it, and yet not know who did it or have been present when it happened? The answer is anticlimactic dampening; the greatest threat has dampened the examinee's ability to react to lesser threats.

This problem is probably even more prevalent in preemployment screening tests where an applicant is given a multi-issue examination and asked several different relevant questions, having no relationship to each other, all of which are competing for psychological set. Lee Feathers graduated the first Academy for Scientific Investigative Training class in 1980.

He returned to his Ohio Police Department and was conducting screening examinations for the local fire department. He asked a young applicant four relevant questions: "Have you ever been fired from a job?" "Have you had any personal involvement with illegal drugs?" "As an adult have you committed a serious undetected crime?" and "In the past 3 years, are the total of your employee thefts more than $200.00?" The applicant showed significant reactions to the question concerning theft and during the posttest interview made major theft admissions. Feathers did not recommend him for the position. Several days later he was told that the applicant was related to a high ranking official of the fire department, and employee theft was not something they were interested in; "after all, you can't steal a fire engine," he was told. The applicant was sent back for a reexamination, where the theft question was eliminated. The applicant now showed significant reactions to the question concerning illegal drugs and again made admissions after the test. In the initial test, this question showed no significant reactions, because of anticlimactic dampening. The greater threat, employee theft, dampened the applicant's ability to react to the lesser threat of illegal drug use.

Case intensity factor proposed by Backster held that an examinee's ability to respond was directly correlated to the punishment they would anticipate if discovered. He set up a hierarchy based on punishment of life, liberty, security, and reputation. If based on being identified as the perpetrator of the crime under investigation you could be executed, Backster theorized that case intensity would be at its highest, followed by being incarcerated, by losing your job, and least by being thought of as an indecent person.

I personally have never given much credence to case intensity factor, believing that for the deceptive person, arousal would not be based on punishment, but on the individual's own reaction capability. Backster defined the variables of individual reaction capability as

- *Phlegmatic*: Very poor reactor, emitting very little differences in reactions to comparison or relevant questions
- Below average
- Average
- Above average
- *Super reactor*: Extremely large reactions to all test questions

When Backster reviewed the quality of a case, he considered how "case intensity" may affect the data as well as the examinee's "individual reaction capability." If the possible punishment for committing the act under investigation was of low intensity and/or the examinee's reaction capability was in the phlegmatic or super areas, he would consider the examination results to be less reliable.

The concept of "spot analysis" is an extremely important concept that I believe Backster borrowed from the 1936 research of Hans Selye on "general adaptation syndrome," since the theoretical models of both are identical.

Selye's model showed in three phases what the alleged effects of stress have on the body. He developed the theory that stress is a major cause of disease because chronic stress causes long-term chemical changes. He observed that the body would respond to any external biological source of stress with a predictable biological pattern in an attempt to restore the body's internal homeostasis. This initial hormonal reaction is your fight or flight stress response and its purpose is for handling stress very quickly! The process of the body's struggle to maintain balance is what Selye termed the "general adaptation syndrome." Pressures, tensions, and other stressors can greatly influence your normal metabolism. Selye determined that there is a limited supply of adaptive energy to deal with stress. That amount *declines* with continuous exposure. He proposed the following stages a person goes through under stress.

Alarm/fight or flight response: This is the immediate response to a stressor that would result in increasing one's heart rate, blood pressure, and respirations. This stage of the general adaptation syndrome is influenced by the secretion of our adrenaline. This would then serve as a stimulator with accompanying physiological changes and reactions.

Adaptation or resistance: Right after the alarm/fight or flight response, a person can attain his or her relation phase. The pituitary gland stops the secretion of hormones responsible for the alarm response. This would also entirely depend if a person is still exposed to the stressor responsible for starting the first stage. As the first reaction takes place, a person shall then slowly adapt to the stressor. In this stage, a person can take control of the situation right after the first response or take control of the given situation as required of them.

Exhaustion: This is the stage wherein a person has exhausted all his efforts from the reaction he has given to a stressor. Usually, a person will have depleted strength right after a stressor. Worst case scenarios come when great stressors have taken place, which would usually end to death.

Backster postulated his model of "Basic Emotionality Factor" also in similar stages as Selye's.

Basic emotionality factor: It is a person's day-to-day emotional norm. Everyone has little emotional ups and downs.

Heightened emotionality: This is the aroused emotional state a person would enter as they commit a crime. If they did not get caught, they

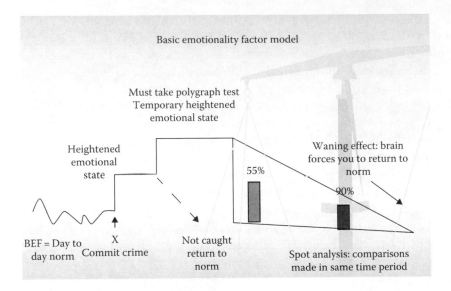

Figure 4.10 Illustration of spot analysis.

would return to their normal emotional state. However, if they were a suspect and told to take a polygraph test, they would enter a new emotional state.

Temporary heightened emotional state: This emotional state causes extreme stress. The brain will force a person to gradually return to its norm. That was called the "waning effect."

Waning effect: The gradual declining of stress anticipated is not something the polygraph examiner can see and affects different examinees in different ways. Therefore, Backster believed that if we are going to compare data, comparison and relevant questions, these questions should be in the same time zone on the test to ensure that the "waning effect" did not cause us to make an erroneous decision. Backster called it "spot analysis," which is an extremely important factor in analyzing data, especially in multifaceted and multi-issue cases (Figure 4.10).

Conclusion

A polygraph examination is a psychophysiological process. While the examiner does not have to be a psychologist or physiologist to be a good examiner, a basic understanding of these sciences is necessary and required to conduct the examination and understand the data being collected.

Notes

1. Gordon-Mazur, Faith Lectures performed at the Academy for Scientific Investigative Training, Philadelphia, PA.
2. Handler, M. and Nelson, R. (2007) Polygraph terms for the 21st century. *Polygraph*, 36(3), 157–164.
3. Senter, S. et al. (2010) Psychological set or differential salience: A proposal for reconciling theory and terminology in polygraph testing. *Polygraph*, 39(2), 109–117.
4. Ginton, A. (2009) Relevant Issue Gravity (RIG) strength—A new concept. *Polygraph*, 38(3), 204–217.
5. Selle, N. K., Verschuere, B., Kindt, M., Meijer, E., and Ben-Shakkar, G. (April 2016) Orienting versus inhibition in the Concealed Information Test: Different cognitive processes drive different physiological measures. *Psychophysiology*, 53(4), 579–590. doi: 10.1111/psyp.12583.

Technique Development 5

I hope martial artists are more interested in the root of martial arts and not the different decorative branches, flowers or leaves.

—**Bruce Lee**

Polygraph techniques can be categorized into recognition tests and truth tests, with the latter group divided into noncomparison question tests and comparison question tests.

Recognition Tests

The first documented technique, used by Cesare Lombroso in 1895, was a recognition test. A child had been molested and murdered. He showed a suspect a series of pictures of children while using an instrument to monitor changes in blood volume in the suspect's hand. He theorized that if the suspect was innocent, none of the pictures would have any meaning to him since they were all pictures of children he did not know. However, if this was the guilty person, when he viewed and recognized the picture of the child he murdered, he would experience a psychophysiological change resulting in detectable blood volume changes in his hand.

Today, this test would be identified as a "known solution peak of tension test." The known solution peak of tension test consists of approximately five to nine choices or questions to which one is the correct item, known as the "key." The other choices are called "buffers." Only the examiner and the guilty person would know and therefore recognize the *key*. The placement of the *key* is usually somewhere in the middle of the sequence and surrounded by the buffer questions. The examinee is told the order of the questions, and if they are guilty, the closer and closer they come to the question they know they will lie to, the more their tension builds resulting in the test's actual name, peak of tension.

For example, let's say a computer flat-screen monitor has been stolen from an office. The suspect denies any knowledge of what was stolen. A sample peak of tension test would be made up of the following type of questions:

Preparatory question:	Regarding that item stolen from the ABC office last week
Prefix question:	Do you know if it was a
Buffer question:	1. Telephone
Buffer question:	2. Typewriter
Buffer question:	3. Calculator
Key question:	**4. Monitor**
Buffer question:	5. Deposit
Buffer question:	6. Attaché
Buffer question:	7. Computer
Buffer question:	8. Safe

The examinee is traditionally aware of the order; however, the sequencing I prefer is to run the first chart in the order reviewed with the examinee, the second chart with the examinee knowing it will be in reverse order, and the third chart in a mixed order, unknown to the examinee.

Richard Arthur introduced a variation of this test known as a "false key peak of tension.[1]" In this test, the examiner mentions something very early in the interview to infer the possible answer to the examinee. For example, asking the suspect in the previous case if he ever took a typing class in school may lead him, if innocent of the theft, to believe the actual item stolen was a typewriter. Question 2 should then be the most salient question in the test, drawing the examinee's psychological set and creating the largest psychophysiological reactions. If the examinee actually stole the monitor in question that should still create the most salience for him resulting in the largest psychophysiological reactions to occur to the "key."

Still another variation of this test is the "guilty knowledge test." Much research was done on this procedure by David Lykken.[2] In this test, the examinee never knows the order of the questions and in each chart the position of the "key" question is moved to any position except the first or last question, and the examiner evaluates whether the examinee consistently follows and reacts to the moving "key."

A final version of this test is the Concealed Information Test (CIT).[3] In this test, single charts about different aspects of a crime are collected with the "key" in each individual chart placed in a different position.

Let's assume that the monitor mentioned earlier was taken during a burglary of an office building at 1704 Locust Street. Entry was made through a rear window of the building.

A CIT would consist of several charts:

Chart 1

Preparatory question:	Regarding that item stolen from the ABC office last week
Prefix question:	Do you know if it was taken from a building on
Buffer question:	1. Pine street
Buffer question:	2. Walnut street
Key question:	**3. Locust street**
Buffer question:	4. Chestnut street
Buffer question:	5. Lombard street
Buffer question:	6. Arch street
Buffer question:	7. Market street
Buffer question:	8. South street

Chart 2

Preparatory question:	Regarding that item stolen from the ABC office last week
Prefix question:	Do you know if entry was made through the
Buffer question:	1. Back door
Buffer question:	2. Basement window
Buffer question:	3. Roof
Key question:	**4. Rear window**
Buffer question:	5. Front door
Buffer question:	6. Side door

Chart 3

Preparatory question:	Regarding that item stolen from the ABC office last week
Prefix question:	Do you know if it was a
Buffer question:	1. Telephone
Buffer question:	2. Typewriter
Buffer question:	3. Calculator
Buffer question:	4. Computer
Buffer question:	5. Deposit
Buffer question:	6. Attaché
Key question:	**7. Monitor**
Buffer question:	8. Safe

What is the likelihood that an innocent person would react strongest to the "key" question in each of these charts? Obviously, it is not very likely at all.

Scoring of this chart according to its users focuses only on electrodermal activity (EDA); the galvanic skin response or galvanic skin conductance.

This scoring process is credited to David Lykken.[3] The largest EDA reaction on each chart receives a 2, and the second largest a 1. If the total scores of the key questions add up to a number equal to or greater than the number of charts collected, the decision is *recognition indicated* (RI). If it fails to meet those criteria, then the decision is *no recognition indicated*. The examiner could also make a decision of *no opinion*.

In the example mentioned earlier, three charts of data were collected. Let's assume in Chart 1 the largest EDA reaction was to the key (Locust Street). It would receive a score of a 2. On Chart 2 the biggest reaction was to question 2 again (basement door). It would receive a 2. The second biggest reaction was to question 3 (roof). It would receive a 1. The key would therefore receive a 0. On Chart 3 the biggest reaction was to question 4 (computer). It would receive a 2. The second largest reaction was to question 7, the key (monitor). It would receive a 1. We ran three charts, so to conclude recognition, the score for the keys must add up to a 3 or higher. In Chart 1 the "key" was a 2; in Chart 2 it was a 0, and in Chart 3 it was a 1. The total score for the "key" is a 3; therefore, our opinion would be RI. Recent research utilizing the CIT found that analyzing changes in respiration and cardiovascular activity in addition to EDA is also important.[25]

The most popular use of peak of tension tests is in demonstration tests, also known as acquaintance or stimulation tests. These tests are administered in examinations to demonstrate to the examinee that the polygraph procedure works and can properly identify when they are telling the truth or lying. The easiest demonstration test is a known numbers test where the examinee is asked to circle a number between 2 and 5. The examiner then collects a chart of data, asking the examinee if they circled the numbers 1 through 6. The examinee is instructed to answer every question "no," even when asked about the number they actually circled and the examiner then ensures the examinee that the data indicated a lie when their number selected was answered "no" and that they were telling the truth to the other numbers they were questioned about. In the following chart, the examinee had circled the number 4. Notice how the cardio tracing increased until the examinee heard their number and then immediately decreased. Also notice the significant EDA activity just before and at the number 4 (Figure 5.1).

The last type of recognition test is searching peak of tension test. This test is administered the same as the known solution peak of tension test; however, in this test, the examiner does not know what the true answer is, only the guilty suspect knows the real answer.

The examiner would put his or her best guess at the answer in the middle of the sequence and then surround it with other possible answers. One of the more interesting searching peak of tension tests was administered years

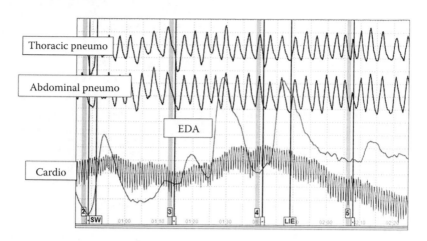

Figure 5.1 Demonstration peak of tension test.

ago in Israel. They had a terrorist that they believed had set a bomb somewhere on a major highway. They did not know where it was located; however, they believed the suspected terrorist did. They attached the suspect to a portable polygraph and slowly drove down the highway monitoring the suspect's physiological reactions. They were able to identify the area of the bomb when the suspect started emitting strong physiological reactions.

Noncomparison Truth Test

The first of the "truth tests" was the relevant/irrelevant (R/I) test that did not utilize comparison questions. They consisted only of relevant questions and irrelevant questions and were credited to John Larson and Leonarde Keeler.

This noncomparison truth test, known as the R/I technique, would look like this:

1. Is your first name Joseph?
2. Is your last name Bailey?
3. Do you know for sure who stole that missing monitor?
4. Is today Monday?
5. Did you steal that missing monitor?
6. Are you sitting down?
7. Is this the month of October?
8. Were those your fingerprints found on that rear window?
9. Did you break into that Locust Street office?
10. Are you withholding any information concerning the theft of that monitor?

Major problems developed with this technique. Sometimes guilty people would not react to any of the questions in the technique and since there was nothing in the test to show reaction capability they were determined to be truthful. This resulted in the development of the "embarrassing personal question," which was usually sexual in nature and asked without review at the end of the test to try and demonstrate the examinee was capable of reacting. However, the problem still continued since the unreviewed sexual question created reactions in everyone, whether they were innocent or guilty, even if they failed to react to any of the test questions.

A second problem with the test was the strength of the relevant questions. Being accused of a crime, especially a heinous crime could create reactions even in an innocent person. For example, I am accused of molesting my child. I am innocent; however, the argument became why wouldn't I show more psychophysiological reaction to questions being asked about whether I did sexual things to my child, such as "Did you stick your penis into your daughter's mouth?" than irrelevant questions, such as "Is today Monday?"

The use of the R/I technique still is used by examiners, though today it is used more often in preemployment screening examinations. The use and accuracy of this application will be discussed in the chapter on preemployment testing.

So, as you can imagine, there was a need for technique refinement that was credited to John E. Reid and his paper on *The Comparative Response Question*.[4] This question would become known as the "Earlier in Life Control Question," which today is called the comparison question. This question not only shows an individual's reaction capability that the R/I technique lacked and needed but also creates a mental environment for properly identifying truthful suspects.

Reid described these questions as broad in scope, dealing with issues similar to, but less threatening than, the relevant issue under investigation. As stated in the previous chapter on Question Formulation, they are questions one would expect every person would truthfully answer "Yes." In reality, comparison questions create a conflict and threat for innocent people, making them feel as if they must lie to be perceived by the examiner as innocent of the issue under investigation.

At a seminar I attended in the late 1970s, John Reid was lecturing. He stated that he never did anything to take away from what his teacher (Keeler) taught him; he only added something to it, which is the "comparative response question."

In the initial Reid General Question Test, the following structure was introduced. (Sometimes there were more than the four relevant questions shown.)

1. Irrelevant   Is your first name Joseph?
2. Irrelevant   Were you born in the United States?

3. Knowledge	Do you know for sure who took that missing deposit?
4. Irrelevant	Were you born in August?
5. Best RQ	Did you take that missing deposit?
6. Comparison	In your entire life, did you ever steal?
7. Irrelevant	Right now are you sitting down?
8. Third best RQ	Were those your fingerprints on that safe?
9. Second best RQ	Did you leave this store with any of that missing deposit money?
10. Comparison	Have you ever broken the trust of a friend?

In the Reid technique, this test was administered as Chart 1. Chart 2 was a demonstration/acquaintance test. Chart 3 would be the original questions in the same order again, and Chart 4, if needed, could be the same questions in a mixed order.

If countermeasures were suspected, Chart 5 could be what Reid called a "yes test." Since most countermeasures during this time period consisted of naive examinees, who often tried to distort their irrelevant questions hoping that if the questions where they were telling the truth were distorted their lies to the relevant questions would not look so bad. In the "yes test" the comparison questions were not asked, and the examinee was instructed to answer all test questions "yes."

1. Irrelevant	Is your first name Joseph? Yes.
2. Irrelevant	Were you born in the United States? Yes.
3. Knowledge	Do you know for sure who took that missing deposit? Yes.
4. Irrelevant	Were you born in August? Yes.
5. Best RQ	Did you take that missing deposit? Yes.
6. Comparison	In your entire life, did you ever steal?
7. Irrelevant	Right now are you sitting down? Yes.
8. Third best RQ	Were those your fingerprints on that safe? Yes.
9. Second best RQ	Did you leave this store with any of that missing deposit money? Yes.
10. Have you ever broken the trust of someone who trusted you?	

Since the deceptive examinee would now be telling the truth to the relevant questions when they answered them "Yes," they now felt forced to distort all of the relevant test questions to make their reactions to the relevant questions appear to be lies.

If there were no attempts at distortions, however, and more data were still needed to make a decision; Chart 5 could be "silent answer test." The examinee was instructed that a person could lie to other people; however, they could not lie to themselves, in this test, they were instructed to answer each question silently in their own mind.

Reid also believed that if the reaction to the medium/relevant "knowledge" question was greater than the other stronger relevant questions, it demonstrated that the examinee may have knowledge about the crime but, however, indicated that he or she did not commit the crime.

After some examinees had been cleared using this approach and were later determined to be guilty, Reid reevaluated his theory. He decided that this error may be due to the fact that the knowledge question in position 3, being the first question asked dealing with the actual crime, might be causing these strong responses in some deceptive examinees. He did not abandon his theory. Instead, he switched the positions of 3 (knowledge) and 9 (the second strongest relevant question). If the examinee now showed less reaction to the strongest relevant question (5), the second strongest question (3), and the third strongest question (8) than to the knowledge question that was now at position 9, regardless of the reaction to the comparison questions, it indicated the examinee did not do the crime.

The Reid family of techniques includes the Arther Known Lie Test, the Army Mixed General Question Technique (AMGQT), and, to some extent, the Marcy Technique. As of this time, research has shown that the AMGQT, a high false positive rate (many truthful suspects fail this test), rendering the technique only about 73% accurate. It is therefore no longer considered a validated technique. The Arther and Marcy techniques have not yet published sufficient research for validation. Even so, it is interesting to see how these techniques developed. The AMGQT was developed from the Reid technique that eventually used Backster exclusive comparisons with some window dressing for questions numbers.

Updated New Version of the Reid General Question Technique

1. Irrelevant	Is your first name Joseph?	
2. Irrelevant	Were you born in the United States?	
3. Second best RQ	Did you leave this store with any of that missing deposit money?	
4. Irrelevant	Were you born in August?	
5. Best RQ	Did you take that missing deposit?	
6. Comparison	In your entire life, did you ever steal?	
7. Irrelevant	Right now are you sitting down?	
8. Third best RQ	Were those your fingerprints on that safe?	
9. Knowledge	Do you know for sure who took that missing deposit?	
10. Comparison	Have you ever broken the trust of a friend?	

AMGQT developed for the above New Version of Reid

1.	Irrelevant	Is your first name Joseph?
2.	Irrelevant	Were you born in the United States?
3.	Second best relevant	Did you leave this store with any of that missing deposit money?
4.	Irrelevant	Were you born in August?
5.	Best relevant	Did you take that missing deposit?
6.	Exclusive comparison	Prior to entering the Army, did you ever steal?
7.	Irrelevant	Right now are you sitting down?
8EC	Evidence connecting	Were those your fingerprints on that safe?
9K	Knowledge	Do you know for sure who took that missing deposit?
10.	Exclusive comparison	While in high school, did you ever break the trust of a friend?

Original Reid

1.	Irrelevant	Is your first name Joseph?
2.	Irrelevant	Were you born in the United States?
3.	Knowledge	Do you know for sure who took that missing deposit?
4.	Irrelevant	Were you born in August?
5.	Best RQ	Did you take that missing deposit?
6.	Comparison	In your entire life, did you ever steal?
7.	Irrelevant	Right now are you sitting down?
8.	Third best RQ	Were those your fingerprints on that safe?
9.	Second best RQ	Did you leave this store with any of that missing deposit money?
10.	Comparison	Have you ever broken the trust of a friend?

The Arther Known Lie Test was developed from this earlier version of the Reid technique. Arther could explain why an examinee reacted to Irrelevant Question 1, since it was the first question a suspect heard in the test. He did not want to have to explain reactions to the other irrelevant questions at positions 2, 4, and 7. Therefore, these questions do not exist in the Arther Known Lie Test. Arther added his two specialized known truth comparison questions.

Arther Known Lie Test

1	Irrelevant (yes)	Right now, are you in the United States?
3T	Known truth	Did you conspire with Ralph Bald (fictitious person) to take that missing deposit (actual crime)?
3K	Knowledge	Do you know for sure who took that missing deposit?
5	Best relevant	Did you take that missing deposit?
6	Comparison	In your entire life, did you ever steal?
8	Third best relevant	Were those your fingerprints on that safe?
8T	Known truth	Do you know Ralph Bald (fictitional character)?
9	Second best relevant	Did you leave this store with any of that missing deposit money?
10	Comparison	Have you ever broken the trust of a friend?
11[5]	Irrelevant (no)	Right now, are you in Canada?

Arther relied heavily on nonpolygraph data information and was famous for some of his pretest presentations. He began his actual testing with a demonstration or acquaintance test he called the polygraph sensitivity test or "PST." This is a very simple yet effective demonstration test that we still use in our office on examinees that are being retested and have already been familiarized with a traditional "numbers" demonstration test. The PST uses three laminated cards: a solid yellow card, a solid red card, and a yellow card with a small red dot in the middle of it. The examinee is instructed,

> I want to make sure the instrument is properly adjusted to your body. I will show you three cards during this test and ask you, "Is this card all yellow in color?" and to all 3 cards, regardless of color, you will answer "Yes." So I will show you this card (solid yellow) and ask, "Is this card all yellow in color?" and you will answer (examinee responds, "Yes"), and I will see exactly what happens in your body when I know you are being truthful. Then I will show you this card (solid red) and ask, "Is this card all yellow in color?" and you will answer (examinee responds, "Yes"), and I will see exactly what happens in your body when I know you are lying. This will also show me how easy it is to distinguish your truths from your lies and whether you are a good candidate to take the examination. Then I will show you a third card (card is not shown at this time) and ask you, "Is this card all yellow in color?" and regardless of what color the card actually is, you will answer (examinee responds, "Yes"). So to all three cards you will answer? (examinee responds, "Yes").[6]

After administering the three-card test, the examinee is assured that there was a significant difference when he said "Yes" to the solid yellow card and told the truth, as compared to when he lied by saying "Yes" to the solid red card. In fact, he is informed that when he said "Yes" to the yellow card with the little red dot, which represents a little lie, the reactions was identical to the big lie told to the solid red card. The examinee was ensured that as long as he tells the truth, he will be fine; however, he is told that even if he tells a little lie, it would appear the same as a major lie.

He then administered his actual crime test question format in order from 1 to 11. Arther then administered a second demonstration test, the double verification test, or DVT, which was a numbered card test, followed by the original crime test format in the same order. If needed, a third crime chart would be collected, asking the same questions in a mixed order.

As stated earlier, Backster lectured that a polygraph examination was a scientific test that monitored the examinee's flow of psychological set. If he or she is guilty, they will focus on the relevant questions, and if innocent on the comparison questions. He introduced his theory of super dampening, which held that if the examinee did not trust the examiner and was afraid of being asked additional unreviewed or surprise questions, it could interfere with their ability to focus on the most salient comparison or relevant test questions. He therefore introduced the symptomatic questions to the test format: "Do you believe me when I promise not to ask a question in this test I have not gone over word for word?" and "Even though I promised I would not, are you afraid I will ask a question I did not go over word for word?"

Some researchers have reported these questions play no role in determining truth or deception. They have missed Backster's point. He never said these questions played a role in determining truth or deception. He stated that these questions assist the examiner in identifying why they may be having problems in their test due to the examinee not being able to properly focus on the relevant or comparison questions because of outside issues. This question also allowed for the examinee to hear an additional question in the test format and establish a normal physiological state before being asked comparison or relevant questions.

Again, it is important to understand that Backster introduced the Tri-Zone Comparison Techniques (ZCT), consisting of the red zone (relevant questions) to draw the psychological set of the guilty, the green zone (comparison questions) to draw the psychological set of the innocent, and the black zone (symptomatic questions) to make sure they had the ability to psychologically set. He also made several important changes to polygraph technique formatting:

1. Comparison questions were placed before relevant questions. Since the problem in polygraph is false positives, he believed we should give the innocent examinees their threat first. By allowing the innocent examinee to react first to the comparison question, the body would want to maintain homeostasis and relieve or compensate to the next question, which was the relevant question. Thus, asking the

comparison question first would be beneficial to the innocent examinee since physiologically there would be less chance of arousal to the following relevant question.

2. Since a person's physiological ability to react waned during the test, he believed that it was very important to compare reactions between comparison and relevant questions when they were next to each other, what he labeled as "spot analysis."

3. He modified Reid's comparison question by making it exclusive. By taking a person's age at the time of the crime, he would establish periods in the examinee's life for the comparison questions that excluded the time of the relevant target issue. For example, if the age of the examinee was 34 at the time of the crime, he may ask the person, "Between the ages of 24 and 31, did you ever steal?" "During the first 24 years of your life did you ever steal?" "During the first 31 years of your life did you ever steal?" He believed this ensured that the guilty examinee would not perceive the comparison question as a relevant question ("In your entire life did you ever steal?" includes the time of the crime that may result in the guilty examinee reacting to it since he stole the deposit).

4. He introduced three ZCT formats: the You Phase, S-K-Y, and exploratory.

   a. The "You Phase" was a single-issue format where all of the relevant questions were about the same act of the same crime. Lying to any one of the relevant questions meant you had to be lying to all of them. This allowed for the greatest focus of psychological set and therefore the greatest accuracy. You will notice he used what appears to be strange question numbering (13, 25, 39, 46, 33, 47, 35, 48, 37, 26). Backster's slogan was "professionalization through standardization." It appears that his initial plan of using these numbers was for examiners to immediately be able to identify the type of question asked based on the number assigned. For example, in American football, if a player is wearing number 7, you can be pretty sure he is a quarterback. If he is wearing the number 55, he is a linebacker, the number 88, a receiver. Backster's original plan was that irrelevant questions would be immediately identified with numbers in the teens (13, 14, 15), symptomatic questions in the 20s, comparison questions in the 40s, and relevant questions in the 30s.

Backster You Phase

13. Is your first name _____?
25. Do you believe me when I promise not to ask a question I have not gone over word for word?
39. Regarding whether you took that missing deposit, do you intend to answer each question truthfully about that?

46. Between the ages of 24 and 31, did you ever steal anything?
33. Did you take that missing deposit?
47. During the first 24 years of your life, did you ever steal anything?
35. Regarding that missing deposit, did you take it?
48. During the first 31 years of your life, did you ever steal anything?
37. (Optional) Were you the person that took that missing deposit?
26. Even though I promised I would not, are you afraid I will ask you a question in this test I have not gone over word for word?

His S-K-Y test is a multifaceted format that ideally was used when there were a group of suspects that knew each other, and where knowledge and/or secondary involvement was important. Fearing that innocent people may react due to personal feelings or intuitions about a general knowledge question, even though they had none, Backster introduced a specialized comparison question (suspect) to draw their attention. As you can see, S-K-Y stood for suspect-know-you.

Backster S-K-Y

13. Is your first name _____?
25. Do you believe me when I promise not to ask a question I have not gone over word for word?
39. Regarding whether you have involvement with that missing deposit, do you intend to answer each question truthfully about that?
31. Regarding that missing deposit, do you *suspect* anyone in particular of taking it? (specialized comparison)
32. Regarding that missing deposit, do you *know* for sure who took it?
47. During the first 24 years of your life, did you ever steal anything?
33. Regarding that missing deposit, did *you* take it?
48. During the first 31 years of your life, did you ever steal anything?
34. Regarding that missing deposit, did you help anyone take it?
26. Even though I promised I would not, are you afraid I will ask you a question in this test I have not gone over word for word?

The third format Backster introduced was the exploratory, which was designed as a multi-issue test. Notice the numbers have significantly changed. Today, this format is mostly used for preemployment screening or postconviction sexual offender testing.

Backster Exploratory

13. Is your first name _____?
25. Do you believe me when I promise not to ask a question I have not gone over word for word?
39. Regarding your background, do you intend to answer each question truthfully about that?

46. Between the ages of 13 and 17, did you ever break a rule?

43. As an adult, have you committed a serious undetected crime?

47. During the first 13 years of your life, can you remember telling a serious lie?

44. As an adult have you had any involvement with illegal drugs?

48. During the first 17 years of your life, did you ever steal anything?

45. As an adult are the total of your employee thefts more than $100.00?

26. Even though I promised I would not, are you afraid I will ask you a question in this test I have not gone over word for word?

I remember attending a seminar where Backster was presented a hypothetical case of four men driving up to a Post Exchange (PX). He was told one man stayed in the car as the driver and three men got out. Two entered the PX with guns and robbed it while one stood outside as a lookout. Several weeks later, a man made a purchase at the PX, and one of the 20 dollar bills he paid with was a marked bill and identified as part of the money that was robbed. The man was taken into custody but denied any knowledge or involvement in the crime. Backster was asked to solve it using his technique.

He stated he would first run a single chart of S-K-Y to determine if the man had any knowledge or direct involvement in the crime. Hypothetically, he reported that the man showed significant reactions to whether he was one of the participants in the robbery.

Backster then stated he ran two charts of a "You Phase," and the man reacted to the relevant target issue of whether he was one of the participants. Backster then said, prior to the interrogation, it would be helpful to know what role the man had played (getaway driver, lookout, or actual gunman), so he asked those three questions in a single chart of an exploratory. Using this information, to the laughter of the audience, he reported the man confessed!

Backster taught his original technique at the U.S. government school the following way:

13. Is your first name _____?

39. Regarding whether you took that missing deposit, do you intend to answer each question truthfully about that?

25. Do you believe me when I promise not to ask a question I have not gone over word for word?

46. Between the ages of 24 and 31, did you ever steal anything?

33. Did you take that missing deposit?

47. During the first 24 years of your life, did you ever steal anything?

35. Regarding that missing deposit, did you take it?

26. Even though I promised I would not, are you afraid I will ask you a question in this test I have not gone over word for word?

The government used it with regular numbers, but added a third comparison and relevant question set at the end.

Federal Zone Comparison Test

1. Is your first name _____?
2. Regarding whether you took that missing deposit, do you intend to answer each question truthfully about that?
3. Do you believe me when I promise not to ask a question I have not gone over word for word?
4. Between the ages of 24 and 31, did you ever steal anything?
5. Did you take that missing deposit?
6. During the first 24 years of your life, did you ever steal anything?
7. Regarding that missing deposit, did you take it?
8. Even though I promised I would not, are you afraid I will ask you a question in this test I have not gone over word for word?
9. During the first 31 years of your life, did you ever steal anything?
10. Were you the person that took that missing deposit?

Originally, they would run two charts of a single-issue test. If the person was deceptive, the examination was over. If the person was truthful, they would run a third chart adding S-K-Y (questions 11, 12, and 13) to the end of the original test questions to ensure the person had no knowledge of the crime. Over time, they shortened their procedure and today question 10 almost always is about knowledge or some other secondary issue, and unfortunately, they rarely use a single-issue format.

Backster was also involved in training several PhDs at the University of Utah, which resulted in the development of the *Utah ZCT*:

1. Do you understand I will only ask the questions I reviewed?
2. Regarding whether you took that missing deposit, do you intend to answer each question truthfully about that?
3. Do you believe me when I promise not to ask a question I have not reviewed?
4. Is today Monday?
5. Between the ages of 24 and 31, did you ever steal anything?
6. Did you take that missing deposit?
7. During the first 24 years of your life, did you ever steal anything?
8. Were you born in the month of December?
9. Regarding that missing deposit, did you take it?
10. During the first 31 years of your life, did you ever steal anything?
11. Were you the person that took that missing deposit?

Backster also trained James Allan Matte, who innovated the Quadri-Track Technique. Through research, Matte came to believe that the reason for a high false-positive rate in polygraph was due to the innocent examinees fear of error, resulting in their inability not to focus on the relevant test questions. To protect against this problem, he introduced what he called the "inside issue," by replacing the last set of comparison/relevant questions in the ZCT with his new concept of fear verses hope of error. He maintains that all truthful people are afraid of error and that all deceptive people are hoping for an error. He uses this dichotomous concept as follows:

13.   Is your first name _____?

25.   Do you believe me when I promise not to ask a question I have not gone over word for word?

39.   Regarding whether you took that missing deposit, do you intend to answer each question truthfully about that?

46C.   Between the ages of 24 and 31, did you ever steal anything?

33R.   Did you take that missing deposit?

47C.   During the first 24 years of your life, did you ever steal anything?

35R.   Regarding that missing deposit, did you take it?

23C.   **Are you afraid I will make an error in this concerning whether you took that missing deposit?**

24R.   **Are you hoping I will make an error in this concerning whether you took that missing deposit?**

26.   Even though I promised I would not, are you afraid I will ask you a question in this test I have not gone over word for word?

Desiring to use four relevant questions in a single format, Dr. Gordon Barland published a paper in *Polygraph* in 1983. He removed the symptomatic questions from the Backster zone and replaced them with an extra set of a comparison and relevant question. He used two of the relevant questions to test on one aspect of a crime and the other two relevant questions on a second aspect of it. A short time later the U.S. Air Force developed the Air Force Modified General Question Technique (AFMGQT).

Like Barland, they removed Backster's two symptomatic questions and replaced them with an extra comparison and relevant question, which has become very popular for multi-issue and multifaceted cases since it allows for four relevant questions.

Interestingly, they took the relevant questions from the AMGQT and inserted them into the better structured Zone format, thus naming it the *Air Force MGQT* rather than the Air Force Zone:

1. Is your first name _____?

2. Regarding whether you took that missing deposit, do you intend to answer each question truthfully about that?

3. Comparison
4. Second best relevant question
5. Comparison
6. Best relevant question
7. Comparison
8. Third best or evidence connecting relevant question
9. Comparison
10. Knowledge or fourth best relevant question

In the 1980s, if you attended the Academy for Scientific Investigative Training, you were required to know every polygraph technique being employed. If you could use a single-issue format, you employed Backster's You Phase. If you had a multifaceted test, you could employ any techniques being used in the field: S-K-Y, Arther, Reid, Marcy, etc.

In the mid-1980s, Dr. William Waid came to work at the Academy. He suggested that we innovate a single format based on what we believed to be best practices that would allow examiners the flexibility to utilize it in any type of examination: single issue, multifaceted, or multi-issue. This resulted in the development of the Integrated Zone Comparison Technique (IZCT).

The IZCT took many of the features introduced by Backster and added some of our own insights into the process. It was a 13-question format[7]:

1. Irrelevant
2. Semirelevant
3. Symptomatic
4. Irrelevant
5. Exclusive comparison
6. Flexible relevant
7. Irrelevant
8. Inclusive comparison
9. Flexible relevant
10. Irrelevant
11. Exclusive comparison
12. Flexible relevant
13. Countermeasure

The IZCT had the following modifications:

1. It only used one simply worded symptomatic question. The traditional symptomatic questions that Backster introduced were very wordy and complicated, which in itself could result in physiological arousal. The IZCT asks, "Do you understand I will only ask the questions we reviewed?" The IZCT only uses this question once in the

beginning of each sequence. Oftentimes when reviewing the questions in a Backster ZCT, we would ask the examinee the traditional symptomatic questions at the end of our question review. "Do you believe me when I promise not to ask a question in this test I have not gone over word for word?" They would answer, "Yes." Then we would review the second one, "Even though I promised I would not, are you afraid I will ask you a question in this test I have not gone over word for word?" Often, they would have a startled look, like "What are you going to ask me???" It seemed like we were creating suspicion for a surprise question resulting in the creation of an outside issue, rather than checking for one. In the IZCT this question is the second question asked, which allows the examinee an extra question to adapt to the testing procedure as well as help the examiner identify possible problems that may affect the examinee's ability to focus on the test questions.

2. We believed Backster was correct in his asking comparison questions before relevant questions, thus allowing the innocent person to react to the comparison question, and subsequently, due to homeostasis diminishing their ability to react to the following relevant question. However, by moving his sacrifice relevant question ("Regarding whether you did the crime, do you intend to answer each question truthfully?") into the third position, he has in fact started his test in the examinee's mind with a relevant question, diminishing their physiological ability to react to the next question in the format, which is the first comparison question.

   In addition, the art of polygraph is getting truthful people to come out truthful. Why do we want to start the test by asking the examinee if they are going to be truthful only to the relevant questions? We wanted to use a semirelevant question that allowed the person to self-direct to their personal zone of threat: comparison or relevant.

   Question 3 in the IZCT is, "Do you intend to answer every test question truthfully?" Everyone is lying to this question when they answer "Yes." Truthful people will be lying to the comparison questions and deceptive people to the comparison and relevant questions. Because this should cause physiological arousal in everyone, when we ask it in position 3 of the first chart, we always follow it with an irrelevant question to allow the examinee to reestablish a normal homeostatic physiological pattern before we begin asking our comparison and relevant questions.

3. In a comparison–relevant format, we believe that the first relevant question must be protected by an exclusive comparison

question to ensure the deceptive examinee does not perceive that it involves the relevant target issue, resulting in physiological arousal that would then diminish their ability to react to the following actual relevant question. Once the comparison–relevant sequence has started, the homeostatic seesaw has begun and the remaining comparison questions can be inclusive or exclusive. Traditionally, the three comparison questions in the IZCT have been exclusive-inclusive-exclusive.

4. We wanted to ensure that an examinee did not experience relief to our last relevant question and what they believed was the last test question, so we decided to end the test with a question that sounded important; however, it was not used for scoring: "Have you deliberately done anything to try and beat this test?" This countermeasure question takes the examinee out of the test and sometimes reinforces an examiner's belief that deliberate distortions have been employed.

5. The relevant questions (6, 9, and 12) are flexible. The examiner decides to use them in a single, multifaceted, or multi-issue manner:
   a. Single issue
      R6 Did you take that missing deposit?
      R9 Regarding that missing deposit, did you take it?
      R12 Were you the person that took that missing deposit?
   b. Multifaceted
      R6 Do you know for sure who took that missing deposit?
      R9 Did you take that missing deposit?
      R12 Did you conspire with anyone to take that missing deposit?
   c. Multi-issue
      R6 As an adult, have you had any personal involvement with illegal drugs?
      R9 As an adult, have you committed a serious undetected crime?
      R12 In any one day as an adult, have you stolen anything valued at more than $50.00?

6. All examiners using IZCT use similar presentations as well as interview formats, which include the Forensic Assessment Interview Technique (FAINT) to evaluate verbal behavior, forensic statement analysis, and nonverbal behavior and may include the Morgan Interview Theme Technique (MITT) projective test in all specific examinations, as well as a standardized interview questionnaire for preemployment, periodic, and other types of testing.

7. All examiners are trained in the Horizontal Scoring System (HSS) and the Academy's Algorithm for objective, rather than subjective, analysis of polygraph data.

After the standardized pretest interview, the following questions are asked:

1. Countermeasure questions
    a. If you were going to take an important test at school, you would have prepared. How did you prepare for this test?
    b. What Internet sites did you go to or research did you do on polygraph?
    c. What do you know about the polygraph and how it works?
2. Agreement of cooperation
    a. Do you understand that to take a polygraph test it requires your total cooperation?
    b. Would you agree that if you are being truthful, you would want to cooperate?
    c. Would you agree the only person that would deliberately not cooperate is someone who is going to lie?
    d. So if you deliberately do not cooperate, do you understand you automatically fail the test?
    e. Please read and sign this "Agreement for Cooperation." (This form is in the Appendix.)
3. Test suitability
    a. Are you aware that not everyone can take a polygraph test?
    b. About 1 in a 100 people cannot be tested because nothing happens in their body when they lie that the polygraph can detect.
    c. So today you will be taking three tests:
        i. The first test is to make sure if you lie, the polygraph can tell you are lying. Just as important, it will make sure when you are telling the truth, the polygraph can tell that you are being truthful.
        ii. The second test is about why you are here (i.e., in a Specific Examination: the incident and whether your profile behaviors indicate you are the type of person that would do something like this, or in a preemployment: or your adult behavior and whether you have the character traits the employer is looking for).
        iii. Before I analyze any of the data, I will give you a third test that will give me an indication if for some reason you do have problems with the test why they may have occurred.
4. Demonstration/acquaintance test (a known number test is employed)
    a. (Write the numbers: 2 3 4 5 on a piece of paper) "I want you to circle any number between 2 and 5." (Add the numbers 1 and 6.) "During the test I will ask you if the number you circled was from 1 to 6, and to every number, even the one you chose, you will answer, 'No'." So the only thing you get to say in this test is the word 'No'."

     i. The subliminal message, according to Dr. Gordon Barland, in the instructions should lead most examinees to choose a number *between* 2 and 5, which is the 3 or 4.[8] If the examinee selects the number 2 or 5, it is a warning sign of possible deception, possible countermeasures, or just an examinee who is mentally challenging you.

  b. *(Engage the examinee with a practice presentation prior to attaching)* "I will ask you if you circled the number 1, and you will answer, 'No'." *(Continue through all the numbers.)* "When I ask you if you picked the number (selected), and you answer 'No,' will that be a truth or a lie?" "You know it is a lie and I know it is a lie, I want to see if the polygraph can identify it as a lie. Just as importantly, I want to make sure when you answer the other numbers truthfully, the polygraph can tell that. If the polygraph can detect you are lying about something as simple as a number I instructed you to say 'No' to, then if you lie about anything of importance, it will be able to detect that. Does that make sense to you?" "And this is the only time today you have my permission to lie!"*

  c. After the test, the examinee will be assured that when they lied and told the truth it was obvious and ensured as long as they tell the truth they will have no problems.

Pretest Phase of the IZCT

1. Attaching the Components
   a. The pad you are sitting on will pick up body movements from your waist down. I am going to put two things around your upper body that will pick up body movements from your waist up. We find truthful people want to cooperate and sit still. Sometimes liars think if they move around during the test the data cannot be analyzed; for example, if you move around in an x-ray machine, the x-rays are no good. In this test if you move around, it shows you are not cooperating, so you automatically fail. So it is important if you want to do well, you sit still. (Attach pneumos.)
   b. These will pick up changes in sweating. (Attach EDA—feeling the fingers/palm to ensure they have not been coated with something to prevent sweating or the skin is calloused that may require you to select different fingers for attaching, or using the top of the fingers for contact.)
   c. This is a blood pressure cuff, just like a doctor uses. During the test there will be air in the cuff, so your arm may become a little

tingly or fall asleep. That is perfectly normal and the only thing you will experience during the test. (Attach the cuff and administer the Demo Test.)

2. Question Formulation

  a. Test questions are now formulated and reviewed with the examinee in the following way for specific tests:

     i. There are three types of questions in this test. The first group of questions is truth or control questions (actually these will be the irrelevant questions). These are questions where I know you are telling the truth and allow the polygraph to establish a baseline of what is happening in your body when I know you are being truthful. I will ask you:

       4. Is today (correct day)? Yes.

       1. Is today (incorrect day)? No.

       7. Right now are in you (correct country)? Yes.

       10. Right now are you in (incorrect country)? No.

     ii. The second group of questions are incident questions. I will ask you:

       R6

       R9

       R12

     iii. The third group of questions are profile questions. (Set the stage: "A leopard doesn't change its spots..." and compound the question, "So I will ask, in your entire life did you ever steal? Are you a thief?")

       C5

       C8

       C11

     iv. Then I will ask you:

       13 Have you deliberately done anything to try and beat this test?

       3 Are you going to answer every test question truthfully?

       2 Do you understand I will only ask the questions I reviewed?

  b. For four relevant questions, preemployment test questions are formulated and reviewed with the examinee in the following ways:

     i. There are three types of questions in this test. The first group of questions are truth or control questions. These are questions where I know you are telling the truth and allow the polygraph to establish a baseline of what is happening in your body when I know you are being truthful. I will ask you:

       4. Is today (correct day)? Yes.

       1. Is today (incorrect day)? No.

       7. Right now are you in (correct country)? Yes.

       10. Right now are you in (incorrect country)? No.

    ii. The second group of questions are adult behavior questions. I will ask you:

R6 (i.e., As an adult, have you ever been fired from a job?)

R9 (i.e., As an adult, have you committed a serious undetected crime?)

R12 (i.e., …, have you had any personal involvement with illegal drugs?)

R14 (i.e., …, in any one day, have you stolen anything valued at more than $50.00?)

As these questions are reviewed, it is important to define each question. For example, in R12, "What do I mean by personal involvement? If coming to the office today you passed someone on the street and smelled that they were smoking marijuana, that is not personal involvement. If you were at a party last weekend and the person next to you used cocaine, that is not personal involvement. Personal involvement means that you personally used, bought, or sold." In R9, "What do I mean by serious crime? I am talking about a felony: rape, murder, arson, car theft, and child molestation. I am not asking you if you ever had a beer and drove a car or ever broke a traffic law."

    iii. The third group of questions are character questions. This employer has had psychologists perform tests on their best employees and have developed certain character traits they believe make for the best employee. So I will ask:

C5 Can you remember ever breaking the trust of a friend?

C8 Are you the type of person that repeats a mistake?

C11 Are you the type of person that would lie to get out of trouble?

C13 Would there be any reason anyone would say you are a person of poor character?

    iv. Then I will ask you:

15 Have you deliberately done anything to try and beat this test?

3 Do you intend to answer every test question truthfully?

2 Do you understand I will only ask the questions we reviewed?

4. Anticountermeasure Chart and the Strengthening of Comparisons

    a. The examiner saves the questions in the computerized system and starts recording an "anticountermeasure chart" without the examinee's awareness, as he or she asks, "Of all the questions we just reviewed, which question or questions do you think are most important?" No matter what the examinee answers,

"That is what most people think, so let me explain something to you" (write):

Here is a school test and here is a polygraph test:

School Polygraph
"If you take a school test and get 100, you pass."
100 = P

"If you answer every question truthfully in a polygraph test, you also pass."
100 = P 100% Truth = P

"If you take a school test and get 10, you fail." "If you only answer 10% of the polygraph questions truthfully, you also fail."
100 = P 100% Truth = P
10 = F 10% Truth = F

"If you take a school test and get 98, you pass. If you answer 98% of the questions truthfully in a polygraph test … you fail!"
100 = P 100% Truth = P
10 = F 10% Truth = F
98 = P 98% Truth = F

"Because a polygraph test is not like a school test. A polygraph test is like a pregnancy test. You are either pregnant or you are not. You can't be a little bit pregnant. In a polygraph test you are either answering the questions truthfully or you are lying"

| Pregnancy | Polygraph test |
| Yes/no | Truth/lie |

"So I want you to understand that every test question is important. Is today (correct day) is as important as anything else. You want to get a 100."

The "anticountermeasure chart" allows for the recording of breathing for several minutes and allows the examiner to establish and document the examinee's normal breathing pattern. If the examinee chooses to distort their breathing during the administration of the actual test, they have already agreed to a final result of failure in their Agreement of Cooperation.

5. The following is one of the explanations I use to inform the examinee of how the polygraph works:

The polygraph is a scientific instrument made up of three different machines originally designed for doctors of medicine to monitor a person's body. That's all it lets me do, monitor your body: your heart rate, blood pressure, sweating of your finger tips, and body movements. The way it works is that all people have an emergency system in them. For example, imagine you were walking down a dark street, in a bad neighborhood, all alone late at night. As you walked down that street you'd be a little apprehensive and nervous. Even though you were nervous, if you walked by an alley and someone came out of the shadows, and said, "Hey you!" your heart would start pounding, and your adrenaline would start flowing. Even though you were already nervous, those sudden changes would take place as your brain turned on your emergency system to get you ready for whatever was going to happen. That is a good analogy to how the polygraph works. Everyone who takes a polygraph test is nervous and apprehensive. If you told the truth to all of the test questions, it is like walking down a dark street in a bad neighborhood late at night, being a little nervous and apprehensive, and nothing happens. You will be nervous during the whole test, but because you are answering all of the questions truthfully, your nervousness will stay the same. If you are going to lie to a question, then for your brain it is a threat, just like someone jumping out of the alley, and it will turn your emergency system on, and you will feel a sudden change take place, and of course I will see it. Is there anything you'd like to ask before the first test?

At least three charts of data are now collected:
    Chart 1 is a silent answer test.

In this first test, I want to give you the opportunity to get used to being attached and having me ask you questions. I do not want you to answer them. Just sit there silently and listen. Make sure you understand the questions, make sure you feel comfortable with the questions, and most importantly, make sure you answered all of them truthfully. Sometimes the first test will jar the memory. If you remember anything you haven't told me about, you can tell me after the test, and we can still change questions if we need to before I start recording your answers.

1, 2, 3, 4, C5, R6, C8, R9, C11, R12, C13, R14, 15

After the test, if it is a utility test (preemployment, sexual history, monitor, etc.), ask, "What did you remember that you didn't tell me about?" This question often results in additional admissions. If it is a specific test (criminal, instant offense), we do not expect the examinee to make admissions about the target issue. If any admissions are going to occur, they will relate to the comparisons issues, which could weaken their affect. Therefore, we want to discourage admissions by asking, "Did you remember anything you did not tell me about? You weren't lying to any of the questions, were you?"
    Chart 2 is administered with the examinee answering out loud and the relevant test questions being rotated. As you begin the test say, "The test is about to begin. Remember it is very important you now answer every test question truthfully, 'Yes' or 'No'. The data will be numerically analyzed, and

lying to any question, no matter what it is about, could cause you to fail the test" (this will help innocent examinees focus on the comparison questions).

10, 2, C5, R14, C8, R6, C11, R9, C13, R12, 15

Chart 3 out loud with the relevant test question again rotated.

1, 2, 3, R12, C5, R14, C8, R6, C11, R9, C13, 15

A fourth chart of data using all test questions can be collected if necessary to allow for additional data required to make a decision, or if deliberate distortions are suspected.

1, 2, 3, 4, C5, R9, 7, C8, R12, 10, C11, R14, C13, R6, 15

Several structures of the IZCT are currently being used. The previously discussed IZCT can be used in single-issue, multifaceted, and multi-issue cases.

In cases where there are several suspects who know each other and the knowledge of the crime is an important factor, we use the IZCT S-K-Y, adapted from the Backster S-K-Y. Again, "S-K-Y" stands for suspicion-knowledge-you. In this type of case many of the innocent suspects may react to a question such as, "Do you know for sure who shot James?" not because of actual knowledge, but due to their suspicions of one of the other suspects they know. To allow these innocent suspects a place to focus this suspicion, Backster used "suspicion" as a specialized comparison question.

5C. Regarding James, do you suspect anyone in particular of shooting him?
6R. Regarding James, do you know for sure who shot him?
8C. In your entire life, did you ever try to get even with anyone?
9R. Did you shoot James?
11C. During the first ___ years of your life, did you ever deliberately hurt anyone?
12R. Did you have any involvement in the shooting of James?

If the relevant issue is extremely sensitive, or the examinee seems extremely upset about the issue, or if the test issue has become sensitized like in a reexamination where the examinee already knows they have failed the question, an IZCT evidence statement test is utilized.

This concept was originally suggested through conversations with Dr. Stanley Abrams, who advocated its use. The sensitive or stigmatic question is placed in an evidence statement as shown in the following box:

EVIDENCE STATEMENT OF JOHN EXAMINEE

August 25, 2015
1. Did you stick your penis into your daughter's mouth?
   NO

John Examinee

The examinee writes his answer on the statement and signs it. He then reads the entire statement from first word to signature out loud. The comparison and relevant questions become the following:

5C. During the first ___ years of your life, did you ever lie to avoid punishment for something you did?

6R. Today, did you answer that question on your evidence statement truthfully?

8C. In your entire life, have you ever lied about a sexual matter?

9R. Regarding your evidence statement today, did you answer that question truthfully?

11C. During the first ___ years of your life, did you ever tell a serious lie?

12R. Was your answer on your evidence statement today true?

An evidence statement *is not* having a person write a detailed statement about the issue under investigation, and then testing them on whether they told the entire truth in their statement. Every statement is edited. Truthful people edit out what they consider to be unimportant information, while deceptive people edit out important information about the crime. No statement made in this manner is "the entire truth."

Another option for this type of scenario would be to utilize the IZCT2, which is our adaptation of Matte's Quadri-Track. In this format, Comparison Question 11 and Relevant Question 12 are changed to the "inside issue" questions Matte developed. This negates the effect of the sensitive or stigmatic wording by placing it in both the comparison and relevant questions, allowing the examiner to analyze which question holds the greater threat or salience: the truthful examinee's "fear of error" or the deceptive examinee's "hope for error."

C11. Are you concerned I will make an error in this test about whether you stuck your penis in your daughter's mouth?

R12. Are you hoping I will make an error in this test about whether you stuck your penis in your daughter's mouth?

In 2003, William Fleisher and I introduced an innovated polygraph technique, the Polygraph Validation Test (PVT) (referred to in research studies by Tuvia Shurany as the Polygraph Verification Test).

The goal of the test was to protect against false positives and to assist examiners in breaking through deceptive examinee's, as later verified, denials. The greatest fear of members in our profession is mistakenly concluding an innocent examinee is guilty; a false positive. In a polygraph examiner's career, there will be times a test is concluded, and before the examiner says anything, the examinee immediately makes statements to explain why they felt they reacted to the relevant questions, even though they were innocent. There may even be occasions where the examinee is actually being truthful.

One of our clients had a major jewelry business and discovered that five parcels of diamonds they had received were missing. We sent out an investigator to conduct FAINT interviews on several employees that had access to the missing parcels. During the interviews, one employee admitted to other thefts from the company, but maintained he had nothing to do with the disappearance of the missing parcels. Based on the interview, this employee was scheduled for a polygraph examination.

The employee had other relatives also working for the company, and the client wanted to know if the employee had committed the theft in question whether any of his relatives were also involved. This turned what would have been a single-issue examination into a multifaceted examination.

Three relevant questions were asked, with the primary question being, "Other than what you said, did you take any of that other merchandise missing from the company?" The examinee showed consistent significant reactions to this question. When I gave the examinee the results and questioned him about them, he strongly denied committing the theft. He stated that one of his relatives overheard the two owners of the company discussing their shrinkage. During the year the company shrinkage was $240,000.00, and according to his relative, the owners said that they had insurance to protect against employee theft and that they intended to turn the examinee into the insurance company and accuse him of stealing the entire $240,000.00 of missing inventory. He stated that every time I asked him about stealing other company merchandise during the test he immediately thought about being accused of stealing the entire inventory and could feel his heart pound.

Is it possible an innocent suspect given these circumstances could focus on the target question, find it most salient, and fail the polygraph test? I thought it could be possible. I remembered a concept my partner, William Fleisher, had shared with me. I told the examinee to go to lunch and then return and I would give him another test to resolve the problem.

When he returned, I reviewed the new list of test questions and instructed him to answer all of the questions, "No."

1. Did you fail your polygraph test because you were tired?
2. Were you afraid I would ask a question I did not review?
3. Did you not understand the test questions?
4. Did you lie to questions in the test unrelated to your company?
5. Did you lie about your thefts from the company?
6. Were you afraid of being accused of company thefts you did not commit?
7. Did you not believe the polygraph works?

Question 4 referred to the actual comparison questions used in the original test. Question 5 referred to the relevant question that showed significant reactions in the original test. Question 6 was the reason the examinee gave for reacting to the relevant question and, since he was instructed to answer the question "No," served as a directed lie question (DLC). I felt that if the examinee was innocent, his greatest reactions should be to questions 4 or 6. If guilty, I expected him to react strongest to question 5, which is exactly what happened. I was now confident the original test was not a false positive, and using the second test, I was able to show the examinee that the reason he gave for failing the first test was not true. He now lowered his head and admitted stealing the five parcels of missing diamonds as well as the majority of missing inventory. The PVT was no longer a Fleisher theory.

Tuvia Shurany read our article about the PVT test and began using it as part of every examination he and his team of examiners performed in Costa Rica, regardless if the examinee's charts indicated truth or deception. During the pretest interview, the examinees were informed they would be taking three tests: the first test is to ensure they were capable of taking an examination, the second one concerns the incident and whether they were the type of person that would have committed such an act, and finally, before any of the data were analyzed, they would be given a third test that would indicate if the examinees did have problems with their test why they may have occurred. His first of three research papers on the PVT was published in 2011.[9]

As a result of Shurany's paper, we started employing the PVT in a similar manner in all polygraph examinations in our office and discovered it was extremely useful in confirming our original test results and helping us make decisions in what otherwise would have been an inconclusive outcome. It has also continued to give us leverage during posttest interviews to ascertain admissions from deceptive examinees.

Shurany's most recent research paper, *Using the Polygraph Validation Test (PVT) in Solving Conflicted Polygraph Results and Confirming Deliberate*

Distortions by Examinees, was published in 2015.[10] Shurany used the PVT as reexaminations for suspects that produced distorted test data in their original examinations. The research involved 51 reexaminations. Shurany found that the PVT was successful in these reexaminations to rectify the original problems and/or confirm attempts by examinees at countermeasures or augmentations.[11]

Currently, we use the following sequence for the PVT that is administered as a single chart:

If you had problems with your polygraph test today, was it because

1. You were tired?
2. You were afraid I would ask a question I did not review?
3. You did not understand the test questions?
4. You lied to profile questions in the test?
5. You lied to questions about the target issue?
6. (The reason the examinee gives as a possibility of why they may have had a problem)
7. You did not believe the polygraph works?
8. You were hungry
   Reask 6 (Figure 5.2).
   Reask 5.
   Reask 4.

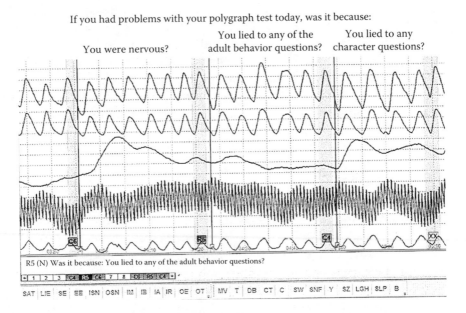

Figure 5.2 Truthful PE polygraph validation test.

This allows for two evaluations of C4 (comparison), R5 (relevant), and C6 (directed lie). In preemployment tests, C4 refers to "character test questions" and R5 to "adult behavior questions."

The last tool in the IZCT box is the "positive control technique.[12]" In 1953, Captain Clarence Lee, who worked with Keeler at the Berkley Police Department, published *The Instrumental Detection of Deception: The Lie Test*. In his book, he writes of a 4-question test theorized by Keeler. The examinee would be instructed to answer the first two questions "Yes" and the second two questions "No."

    1. Are you innocent of that crime?   Yes.
    2. Are you guilty of that crime?   Yes.
    3. Are you innocent of that crime?   No.
    4. Are you guilty of that crime?   No.

These four questions make up two sets of dichotomous questions where the answer to one question in each set has to be true and the other has to be a lie. Keeler's belief was that an innocent examinee answering, "Yes," indicating that they were guilty of the crime and "No" they were not innocent of it would elicit the greatest physiological reactions, and for deceptive examinees denying their crime "Yes" they were innocent and "No" they were not guilty would be the most salient questions. He also believed a third possibility for deceptive examinees would be strong reactions to all four questions, since two involved denials of the crime committed and two involved confessions. There is no evidence the test format was ever employed.

In 1969, at an *American Polygraph Association Annual Seminar* in Houston, Texas, Richard Golden did a presentation on the "Sinks' Yes–No Technique." Golden was in charge of polygraph for a national investigative company and Sinks was a polygraphist located in their Ohio office.

Sinks technique asked each question in the test twice, with the examinee instructed to first answer with what they said was the truth, and then with what they said was a lie when the question was repeated. Like the previously described Keeler theory, each set of questions was dichotomous where one answer had to be the truth and one had to be a lie. Sinks then compared the physiological reactions within each question set to determine where the greatest arousal took place. Like Keeler, he believed that for a truthful examinee having to admit to a crime they did not do should cause the greatest reaction, and for the deceptive examinee denying their crime should elicit the greatest reaction.

Golden on the other hand, while liking the dichotomous pairs of questions Sinks was using, did not like the way he was interpreting the data. Where Sinks was comparing the question with itself to make decisions, Golden compared the greatest reaction in the traditional comparison question set, whether it was when the examinee said they were being truthful or lying to it, with the greatest overall reaction in the relevant question set. Where Sinks was doing an intraset comparison, Golden did the traditional intercomparison. Golden reported that his findings indicated that the technique was just as sensitive in detecting deception; however, he had better specificity in identifying innocent examinees.

In 1968, Sylvestro Reali, a sergeant in the Philadelphia Police Department, was sent to the Backster School of Lie Detection and became a polygraphist. He returned to the school and was promoted as lieutenant and became commander of the department's polygraph unit. In 1969, he attended the APA seminar where Golden presented the "Sinks Yes–No Technique." He left the police department after being injured and opened up his own polygraph school, Polygraph Personnel Research School for Lie Detection, and in 1973, he introduced the positive control technique, which was almost identical to the Sinks Yes–No Technique.

Each question in the test was asked twice. The examinee was instructed to answer first with their "subjective truth," and when the question was repeated to answer with their "subjective lie." Reali used the Sinks method of data analysis, comparing the subjective truth with the subjective lie. If when an examinee reacted stronger to their subjective truth (Did you do the crime? "No."), they were determined to be deceptive. If they reacted stronger to their subjective lie (Did you do the crime? "Yes."), they were determined to be truthful.

Since the data were analyzed in this manner, Reali maintained that there was no need for the traditional comparison question. This eliminated the skill necessary for an examiner to select and introduce comparison questions. Since the wording in the positive control relevant and comparison question were exactly the same, he also maintained that there was perfect balance between the questions, and that any concerns about emotional wording were therefore eliminated. If the relevant part of the question set was, "Did you stick your penis into your baby's mouth?" the wording of the comparison part of the question set was exactly the same. The only difference was what bothered the examinee more, when they denied doing their crime (deceptive) or admitted doing a crime they were innocent of (truthful).

Harry Armitage attended Reali's school and learned the technique that Reali was teaching as a single chart of questions sequenced "tell the truth and then tell a lie."

Returning to the Warminster Police Department, Armitage was concerned that a single chart of data may not be sufficient and started running two charts of data. The first chart was collected as a truth–lie sequence and the second as a lie–truth sequence. He reported back to Reali that he discovered the latter sequence was more productive which resulted in Reali teaching the technique as a single chart sequenced as lie–truth.

Positive Control was more than a technique; it was a concept. Any existing technique could be turned into a positive control sequence by instructing the examinee that in the next chart each question would be asked twice and instruct them to answer first with a lie and then with the truth, or vice versa. Again, the "subjective lie" represented the comparison question and the "subjective truth" the relevant question. For example, here is a Federal Zone bi-spot being administered as a lie–truth positive control:

1L   Is your first name John?   No
1T   Is your first name John?   Yes
2L   Regarding your involvement in that shooting, do you intend to answer each question truthfully about that?   No
2T   Regarding your involvement in that shooting, do you intend to answer each question truthfully about that?   Yes
3L   Do you believe me when I promise not to ask a question I did not review?   No
3T   Do you believe me when I promise not to ask a question I did not review?   Yes
4C   Prior to entering the military, did you ever hurt anyone?   Yes
4R   Prior to entering the military, did you ever hurt anyone?   No
5C   Did you shoot Ed?   Yes
5R   Did you shoot Ed?   No
6C   As a teenager did you act out of anger?   Yes
6R   As a teenager did you act out of anger?   No
7C   Last week, did you shoot Ed?   Yes
7R   Last week, did you shoot Ed?   No
8L   Even though I promised I would not, are you afraid I will ask you a question I did not review?   Yes
8T   Even though I promised I would not, are you afraid I will ask you a question I did not review?   No

While positive control made great theoretical sense, in practice there surfaced major problems that were identified in a paper published by Cochetti and me.[12] Among them was that it appeared for some deceptive individuals admitting their crime evoked greater responses than denying it. Research done at our suggestion by Driscoll and Honts indicated a high false-negative rate of 22% and a 40% inconclusive rate.[13]

In a multi-issue screening type test, some people were what we called "spot reactors." As soon as they heard their most salient question for the first time, they reacted to it. If it was a truth–lie sequence, they reacted to the "truth" and if it was a lie–truth sequence, to the "lie."

Another problem we identified was an increase in countermeasures. It did not take a rocket scientist to figure out if their reaction was greater when they said they did the crime (subjective lie) than when they denied it (subjective truth) they would pass the test.

Based on our findings and the research performed on positive control if a person fails the test, it is highly accurate; however, passing it is meaningless. However, the positive control test can be very effective in identifying deliberate distortions and flushing out "countermeasure signatures."

When the American Polygraph Association published its meta-analysis of validated techniques[14] under my presidency, they classified the IZCT as an outlier. The published research on the IZCT showed it to be more accurate than most other zone techniques. Some people in the profession seemed more concerned with the fact that other examiners may perceive it to be a better technique than theirs.

What is an Outlier? Wikipedia defines an outlier:

A statistical term describing an observation point that is distant from other observations.[15] It points out that an outlier may be due to variability in the measurement or it may indicate experimental error; the latter are sometimes excluded from the data set.[16]

Outliers can occur by chance in any distribution, but they are often indicative either of measurement error or that the population has a heavy-tailed distribution. In the former case one wishes to discard them or use statistics that are robust to outliers, while in the latter case they indicate that the distribution has high kurtosis and that one should be very cautious in using tools or intuitions that assume a normal distribution.

In many larger samplings of data, some data points will be further away from the sample mean than what is deemed reasonable. This can be due to incidental systematic error or flaws in the theory that generated an assumed family of probability distributions, or it may be that some observations are far from the center of the data. Outlier points can therefore indicate faulty data, erroneous procedures, or areas where a certain theory might not be valid. However, in large samples, a small number of outliers is to be expected (and not due to any anomalous condition).

Outliers, being the most extreme observations, may include the sample maximum or sample minimum, or both, depending on whether they are extremely high or low. However, the sample maximum and minimum are not always outliers because they may not be unusually far from other observations.

Naive interpretation of statistics derived from data sets that include outliers may be misleading. For example, if one is calculating the average temperature of 10 objects in a room, and nine of them are between 20°C and 25°C, but an oven is at 175°C, the median of the data will be between 20°C and 25°C but the mean temperature will be between 35.5°C and 40°C. In this case, the median better reflects the temperature of a randomly sampled object than the mean; naively interpreting the mean as "a typical sample," equivalent to the median, is incorrect. As illustrated in this case, outliers may be indicative of data points that belong to a different population than the rest of the sample set.

So simply put, an outlier is a data point so different from the rest of the data that it is unlikely to be accurate or correct and is caused by experimenter error or by an incorrect measurement or affect. When evaluating polygraph techniques, an outlier technique would be a technique that is too accurate, or too good to be true. This would most likely be caused by biased research, faulty research, or something different about the technique that makes it slightly more accurate than other techniques currently being used in the field.

To date, there have been eight research studies performed on the IZCT and the HSS. These studies have been both analog and field studies conducted in five countries, consisting of probably the most diverse population involved in research of any polygraph technique.

The first study conducted was done by the Egyptian government.[17] This field study tested the validity of the IZCT designed for specific issue tests, utilizing 309 confirmed field cases by examiners of the Egyptian government during the period from 1998 to 1999. All examinations were conducted utilizing a HSS for data analysis. The IZCT correctly identified 100% of the innocent examinees and 99.5% of the guilty examinees, excluding inconclusives, or 94.8% of innocent examinees and 90.5% of the deceptive examinees, including inconclusives. This validation study demonstrated the efficacy of the IZCT and concluded the IZCT is an innovative and powerful technique that ethically directs the examinee to his or her proper zone of greatest threat, resulting in accurate determinations of truth or deception. Because this study was conducted within the Egyptian government, raw data were not readily available to independent evaluators.

In 2004, I was contacted by Dr. Scott Faro, then with the Medical School of Drexel University, and now with Temple University's Medical School. Dr. Faro is a radiologist who was interested in testing the fMRI in detecting deception and comparing its accuracy against that of the polygraph. We designed an analog study where 12 medical students were recruited to participate; five were told by Dr. Faro that someone had fired a gun in the hospital and they were a suspect; seven were instructed to fire a gun and deny it.[18] All were told that if they were determined to be truthful by the polygraph and fMRI procedures, they would receive a monetary reward. All 12 were given FAINT interviews. Half were then given fMRI tests followed by IZCT polygraph examinations, and half were tested in the reverse order. One of the deceptive participants confessed during the FAINT interview, leaving a population of five truthful and six deceptive participants. The fMRI testing was done by radiologist Dr. Mohamed Feroze, along with two doctors of neuropsychology and a graduate student. All IZCT tests were performed by me and scored using the Academy for Scientific Investigative Trainings' ASIT PolySuite, which is a manually driven computerized system using the HSS, as well as by the PolyScore and Objective Scoring System algorithms. Only Dr. Faro knew ground zero truth. Everyone else in the study was blind.

A gun was fired whether each participant was truthful or deceptive to ensure that the sound or smell of gun powder did not influence any of the examiners who were blind in the study. Dr. Faro's goal was to show that fMRI testing was more accurate than the polygraph. The fMRI had accuracy rates in the mid 80%. The IZCT with ASIT PolySuite had 90% accuracy when inconclusives were counted as errors, with no incorrect calls, and 100% accuracy when inconclusives were not considered errors.

Those who, for some reason, are intimidated by the accuracy of the IZCT in this study, argue this high degree of accuracy indicates it must be an outlier; that the study was faulty or biased. This study involved totally blind research with two prominent radiologists, two prominent neuropsychologists, and me. I cannot see how anyone could believe these professionals, aimed at proving their fMRI technology was more accurate than the polygraph, would involve themselves in biased or unscrupulous behavior to favor the polygraph or the IZCT technique.

In 2010, a field study was conducted in Costa Rica by Tuvia Shurany and Fabiola Chaves.[19] They investigated 27 cases involving 113 suspects with polygraph and successfully resolved 21 cases by confession. The solved cases involved 84 confirmed suspects, of whom 44 were confirmed deceptive and 40 were confirmed truthful. The charts were analyzed using ASIT PolySuite, which resulted in an overall accuracy of 92.9% with inconclusives, as well as by manual scoring using a 3-point system that resulted in 91.7% accuracy with inconclusives.

In 2011, Tuvia Shurany did a field study in Costa Rica using the IZCT and PVT that consisted of 188 examinees.[9] Of the 188 examinees tested, the IZCT comparison question test (CQT) analysis resulted in two inclusive determinations that were eliminated from the study. Of the 186 remaining IZCT CQT examinations, the PVT results were in total agreement with 184 of the initial determinations.

The results of the PVT for the remaining two were inconclusive due to a lack of reactions to C4, R5, or C6. Interestingly, both of these examinees were truthful to the target issues, and it appears had no psychological commitment to the questions in the PVT. In the two inconclusive examinations eliminated from the study, the PVT indicated both examinees were deceptive. Both of these PVT results were then verified by confession. Shurany concluded that based on this study, it appears that the PVT is a valid way to confirm the results of the CQT, which takes minimal time to complete, and can actually serve to increase the accuracy of the polygraph procedure (Figures 5.3 and 5.4).

Another critique of the IZCT research was that the tests were conducted by experienced examiners, and perhaps the high accuracy rates that resulted for the IZCT would not be the same with less experienced examiners. In 2012, with students in their seventh and eighth week of basic polygraph examiner training in South Africa, 16 tests were conducted on mock thefts

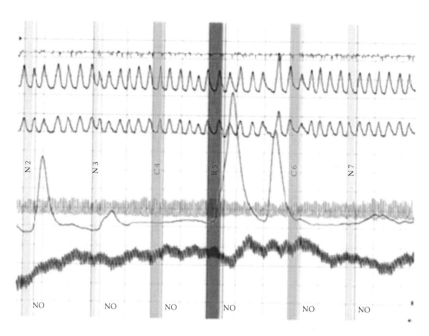

Figure 5.3 Polygraph validation test (PVT) of a deceptive examinee. An example of a case with three examinees showing their PVT. A significant reaction in the PVT to R5, with a deceptive, as later verified, examinee. Note the lack of reaction to C4 and C6, as well as the classic peak of tension "global" evaluation.

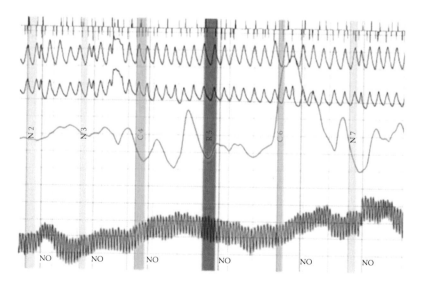

Figure 5.4 Polygraph validation test (PVT) of truthful examinee. The PVT chart of the third examinee, later verified as truthful. The more significant reactions occurred to comparison questions.

using the IZCT and   PVT.[20] The suspects consisted of volunteers from the South African Air Force. Eight were instructed to commit a theft and deny it, and eight were informed a theft had taken place, but had no knowledge or complicity in the thefts. All were told they would receive a monetary reward if they were found to be truthful. All of the students were blind as to who the truthful or deceptive suspects were. The overall accuracy of the IZCT with students using the HSS was 93% without inconclusive and 88% with inconclusives counted as errors. Using a 3-point scoring system, accuracy was 83% without inconclusives and 56% when inconclusives were counted as errors. Using a 7-point scoring system, accuracy was 90% without inconclusives and 69% when inconclusives were counted as errors.

It should be noted again that when the students scored using the HSS reactions were determined by making measurements of all components, verses their ability to make determinations by their eye with traditional 3- and 7-point scoring.

In this study, all participants were also given single charts of a PVT. Decisions made with the PVT resulted in 87% accuracy without inconclusives, and 81% accuracy when inconclusives were counted as errors.

A study conducted by Donald Krapohl, Christopher Lombardi, and me used 100 confirmed Federal Zone Comparison Technique field cases that were blindly scored using the HSS.[21] For the most part, these were multifaceted cases where two relevant questions dealt with the target issue and the third dealt with knowledge. Average accuracy for truthful and deceptive cases, excluding inconclusives, was 86.6%. Cutoffs from this study used an overall score of a +13 or higher for determinations of truthfulness and a −13 or lower for decisions of deception. When the cutoff scores for truth were lowered, overall accuracy increased. Based on this and earlier research, it is apparent that by lowering the requirement for truthful determinations to +2.25 for three relevant questions asked on three charts would increase the decision accuracy to above 90%, with an extremely low inconclusive rate.

In a 2013 laboratory study in South Korea by Cheol Bang et al., of the Supreme Prosecutor's Office, consisting of 46 participants; 23 truthful and 23 deceptive, they found the IZCT to be 84% accurate with a 8.7 inconclusive rate. When they combined the PVT results that agreed with the IZCT results accuracy increased to 97%.

The following is an abstract of the article "Identifying and Cultivating Superforecasters as a Method of Improving Probabilistic Predictions," written by James Matte which was published in the International Society of Polygraph Examiners Research Digest:

"The authors of the study, found support for four mutually reinforcing explanations of superforecaster performance: (a) cognitive abilities and styles, (b) task-specific skills, (c) motivation and commitment, and (d) enriched environments" and that "Accurate probability estimates are critical for good decision making in fields as diverse as medical diagnosis, portfolio management, and intelligence analysis." In tests with area under the curve (AUC), a measure of accuracy or discrimination ability from signal detection theory, the computed values of AUC were 96% for superforecasters, 84% for top-team individuals, and 75% for all others. "Superforecaster superiority held up strongly on this metric as well. Indeed, in one analysis, the receiver operating characteristic (ROC) for superforecasters was as accurate 300-plus days into the future, when the ROC for regular forecasters was only 60 days out." The study showed that fluid intelligence was the strongest dispositional predictor of accuracy. In fact, superforecasters scored higher than top-team individuals and all others on all measures of fluid intelligence, including the Raven's Advanced Progressive Matrices, the Shipley-2 Abstraction Test, the Cognitive Reflection Test, an extended version of the Cognitive Reflection Test, and two Numeracy scales. The authors indicated that "superforecasters have distinctive dispositional profiles, scoring higher on several measures of fluid intelligence and crystalized intelligence, higher on the desire to be the best, the need for cognition, open-minded thinking, and endorsements of a scientific worldview with little tolerance for supernaturalism."

The aforesaid Superforecasters performance would probably be regarded by many leaders in the discipline of forensic psychophysiology using the polygraph, whose results are probabilistic information (Nelson, Handler 2015), as "outliers" due to their unique and exceptional accuracy significantly above regular forecasters, without a thought about the four distinguishing features identified in aforementioned Mellers et al study that sets the Superforecasters apart from the regular forecasters. In an article published in Polygraph (Krapohl 2007), the author discusses "advocacy research" and cites the Arther technique (R. Arther) 99% accuracy, the Guilty Knowledge Test (D. Lykken) 96%–100% accuracy, the Integrated Zone Comparison Technique (N. Gordon) 99.5%–100% accuracy, and the Quadri-Track Zone Comparison Technique (J. A. Matte) 100% accuracy, as examples of advocacy research which "often tends to produce highly favorable results for the interests of the advocate." Krapohl's position indicates a bias potential, which may be justified in those cases that are supported by compelling evidence. However, labeling a study and its involved performance as Advocacy Research and Outliers (Krapohl 2007; see also Gougler, Nelson, Handler, Krapohl, Shaw and Bierman 2011), is like passing sentence before trial, and implies incompetency, negligence or intellectual dishonesty on the part of its authors, which raises the old proverb that suspicion of others is aroused by what we know of ourselves. Without substantial and convincing evidence of research malpractice, the positive alternative that the aforementioned innovators are indeed Superforecasters should be adopted and their work be examined without prejudice, and accepted for the benefit of the entire profession. The above creators of their respective polygraph techniques are individuals who devoted the better part of their adult life in creating and perfecting their polygraph techniques to a high degree of accuracy not expected of their students who graduate with less than 100% recollection and understanding of the psychophysiological aspects of the technique. Nevertheless some of them become involved in research of the technique they learned while other researchers gain information about the technique in study from lectures and/or published articles and textbooks. In a lecture at an American Polygraph Association (APA) seminar a few years ago, the Backster Either-Or Rule was mentioned, and when the lecture ended, an APA member with some 30 years of experience as a government examiner schooled in the Backster You-Phase and its Federal derivative, asked this author, a Backster graduate, to explain how the Either-Or Rule works, to the astonishment of this author, which according to Cleve Backster, forms the nucleus of the Backster Zone Comparison Technique. This is but one example of polygraph examiners who either failed to grasp all of the information provided them during their training, or the fault of the instructor who failed to provide that information through ignorance, negligence or design.

In the authors' four decades of conducting quality control reviews of other examiners' work, it became evident that a significant percentage of them had failed to understand the psychological aspects of the technique they were using, and forgotten important elements of the technique's protocol as evidenced by the numerous procedural violations.

The fact that the creators of the above cited techniques taught their systems on a continuing basis for several decades, reinforced retention of details regarding its structure and application. Hence there was no deviation to the format and procedure in the conduct of polygraph examinations used in their field research studies, thus providing an absolute and pure representation of the polygraph technique in action. The above cited technique creators/administrators, all recognized as court experts, would meet the qualities expressed in above Mellers et al study, to wit: (1) cognitive abilities and styles, (2) task-specific skills, (3) motivation and commitment, and (4) enriched environments, which would undoubtedly merit the title of Superforecasters of truth and deception. As stated by Mellers et al, Superforecasters have a higher desire to be the best, the need for cognition, open-minded thinking, and endorsements of a scientific worldview with little tolerance for supernaturalism. To label their work as "advocacy research" and its results as "outliers" without supporting evidence other than the fact that their research shows a higher degree of accuracy than other techniques, deprives the polygraph profession of its benefits and significantly curtails the advancement of the polygraph profession.

It is clear to me that for a polygraph technique to achieve high degrees of accuracy, it must adhere to the validated principles laid down by Cleve Backster that has led the way for the ZCT to become the most accurate formats in use today. It is only formats in the Backster "family" of techniques that polygraph accuracy rates reach in the high 80% and above.

The question is, "Why does the IZCT perform slightly better than some of the other zone technique family members?" Is it because it is an outlier, due to biased or faulty research studies, or because it clearly outperforms many of the others? I believe it is the latter!

In almost every published study of polygraph that compares the accuracy of the original examiner with that of blind reviewers analyzing the same data, the original examiner is almost always more accurate. Why is that? It is because the original examiner, consciously or unconsciously, is analyzing more than the chart data.

A polygraph technique is much more than an approved or validated question format. A polygraph technique is everything that is said to the examinee from the time he or she arrives, until the data are analyzed. Deviations in this process affect outcome and accuracy, regardless of the research on the format.

In 2014, I was asked to quality control a polygraph examination for a prosecutor performed on a suspect accused of molesting two young children. The polygraph performed for the defense was conducted by a high profile academically recognized examiner. The technique used was the modified Utah ZCT, which resembles the AFMGQT2, a "C R R C R R C" format.

Two different tests were administered. The first test consisted of five charts, utilizing DLCs. The names have been eliminated; however, here are the actual test questions:

1. Do you understand I will ask only the questions we have discussed?
2. Do you intend to answer truthfully all of the questions about allegations that you sexually abused (victim 1) and (victim 2)?
3. Is your name (first name used)?
4. DLQ. (D1) During the first 18 years of your life, did you ever tell even one lie?
5. (R1) Did you ever have oral sex with (victim 1)?
6. (R2) Did you ever put your penis in (victim 1)'s genitals?
7. DLQ. (D2) Prior to age 19, did you ever break even one rule or regulation?
8. (R3) Did you ever have oral sex with (victim 2)?
9. (R4) Did you ever touch (victim 2)'s anus with your penis?
10. DLQ. (D3) Before the age of 19, did you ever make even one mistake?
11. Do you live in (State)?

Two victims and four different alleged crimes in one test format! Where is the research supporting a test with two victims and four crimes in a single test? Five charts were administered, with the examiner selecting the comparison question on either side of the pair of relevant questions that was strongest, leaning the score toward a truthful outcome. The examiner scores are as follows:

R1   +3
R2   0
R3   −3
R4   +3

I scored these charts using the HSS[23] and ASIT PolySuite[24] and had the following results:

R1	R2	R3	R4
−21	−23	−46	−12

These same charts were blindly scored by four school directors and six government examiners. The blind reviewers were only told that the test consisted of four different relevant questions. They had no idea what the questions were, or who the original examiner was. All of the blind evaluators had determinations of deception.

No evaluator was told which scoring system to use, 3- or 7-point system, only to score and report vertical scores and decisions using standard cutoffs. They analyzed 24 spots and determined 22 to be *deceptive* and 2 to be *inconclusive*. The following were the scores of the six blind government examiners:

	R1	R2	R3	R4
Examiner 1	−8	−8	−5	+1
Examiner 2	−3	−9	−10	−8
Examiner 3	+3	−4	−7	−3
Examiner 4	−5	−4	−7	−6
Examiner 5	+3	−9	−12	−4
Examiner 6	−3	−2	−9	−5

The five crime charts administered in Test 1 are shown in Figure 5.5a through e.

These were the comments of the blind evaluators. "Some of the EDA responses are questionable. There seems to be movement at places which were ignored. There was no movement sensor used even though this test was administered after the APA deadline requiring it."

The original examiner had a −3 at R3 indicating a "significant response." The examiner called the test inconclusive. What should have been the next step? I would think you would use the generally accepted hurdle approach and run a more accurate single-issue zone on R3, the relevant question that showed a "significant response." Instead, the examiner changed all of the DLCs to probable lie comparison questions. We have no idea as to how the new "comparison questions" were introduced or stimulated. The relevant

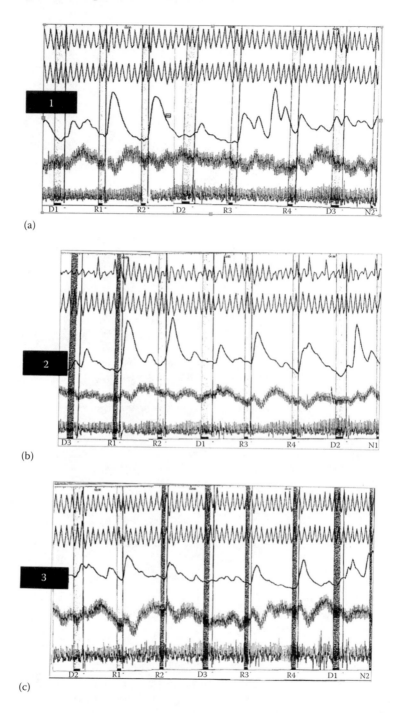

Figure 5.5 Five (crime charts). (a) Chart 1, (b) Chart 2, (c) Chart 3. (*Continued*)

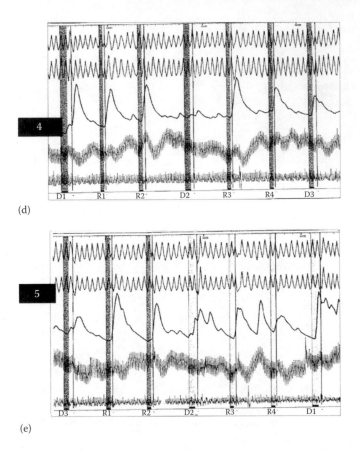

(d)

(e)

Figure 5.5 (*Continued*) Five (crime charts). (d) Chart 4, and (e) Chart 5.

questions were slightly reworded but contained the same material. Three charts were now collected using the following questions:

1. Do you understand I will ask only the questions we have discussed?
2. Do you intend to answer truthfully all of the questions about allegations that you sexually abused (victim 1) and (victim 2)?
3. Is your last name (name)?
4. PLC1. During the first 20 years of your life, did you ever engage in a sexual act of which you were ashamed?
5. R1. Did you ever have mouth to genital contact with (victim 1)?
6. R2. Did you ever touch (victim 1)'s genitals with your penis?
7. PLC2. Between the ages of 18 and 21, did you ever think about having sex with a minor?
8. R3. Did you ever have mouth to genital contact with (victim 2)?

9. R4. Did you ever touch (victim 2)'s anus with your penis?
10. PLC3. Before the age of 21, did you ever take advantage of someone for sexual purposes?
11. Do you live in the United States?

The examiner now made a determination of truthful with the following scores:

R1   +1
R2   +2
R3   +5
R4   +6

I scored these charts using the HSS and ASIT PolySuite and had the following results:

R1	R2	R3	R4
−16	+2.5	+9	−9.75

These same charts were again blindly scored by four school directors and six government examiners. All of the blind evaluators also had determinations of deception. I did not get to testify in the case because polygraph evidence was never introduced. The perpetrator pleaded guilty to all charges.

Researched formats are fine; however, as you can see in the case mentioned earlier, formats do not equate to polygraph techniques. A lot more than a question structure goes into what makes a polygraph technique.

The IZCT differs in many ways from the other "family" members of the ZCTs. The IZCT utilizes standardized presentations in every aspect of the examination; starting with the consent form and continuing through the entire process. The pretest interview itself is the FAINT, which has been researched, and allows the examiner to accurately assess nonverbal behavior, unwitting verbal cues, as well as apply forensic statement analysis, and often involves the MITT. Data are not analyzed based on the examiner's "eye" and experience, but are objectively measured to differentiate the degree of reactions, and the examiner utilizes the HSS to further eliminate any degree of subjectivity.

It is this standardization and elimination of subjectivity that makes the IZCT an outperformer. I think the substantial research on the technique clearly shows that it is not an outlier; instead, it is clearly an out performer! As much as some in our profession wishes it to be, polygraph is not pure science. Polygraph *is an art*, based on principles from the sciences of psychology and physiology.

Conclusion

As a profession we should continue research to validate the techniques we are using and how to improve the art we practice. We must recognize the difference between a "technique" and a "format." Validating a list of questions used in research is validating the format used in that specific research. Three different examiners could take that exact format; questions and sequences, and arrive at three different levels of accuracy based on their technique. Technique encompasses everything said to an examinee from the time they arrive until the data are analyzed. We cannot allow ourselves to be led down a path that misleads us to believe what we do is purely a science. It is the technique and skill of the examiner that is the art, and it is just as important as the format used and the scientific aspects of psychology and physiology involved in polygraph.

Notes

1. Arther, R. O. (1970) Peak of tension: Question formulation. *Journal of Polygraph Studies*, 4(5), 1–4.
2. Lykken, D. (1960) The validity of the guilty knowledge test. *Journal of Applied Psychology*, 44(4), 258–262.
3. Krapohl, D., Mc Cloughan, J., and Senter, S. (2006) How to use the concealed information test. *Polygraph*, 35(3), 123–138.
4. Reid, J. E. (1947) A revised questioning technique in lie detection tests. *Journal of Criminal Law and Criminology*, 37(6), 542–547.
5. Originally Arther used what is called a "Catch All" at question 11: *Are you now withholding any information about that missing deposit?* Much later in time he changed it to an Irrelevant Question designed to be answered "No."
6. When we use the PST, we review the cards in the original order (yellow–red); however, when we actually administer the test, we use the card order: red–yellow–yellow/red dot.
7. For preemployment and PCSOT testing requiring four relevant questions, the countermeasure question becomes Q# 15, and 13C and 14R are inserted.
8. Barland, G. (1978) A fail-proof blind numbers test. *Polygraph*, 7(3), 203–208.
9. Shurany, T. (2011) Polygraph verification test. *European Polygraph*, 5(2), 16, 61–70.
10. Shurany, T. (2015) Using the polygraph validation test (PVT) in solving conflicted polygraph results and confirming deliberate distortions by examinees. *European Polygraph*, 9(3), 33, 123–132.
11. Countermeasures are deliberate distortion created by deceptive examinees in the hopes of beating the test or causing an inconclusive outcome, while augmentations are deliberate distortions created by truthful examinees believing they need to assist the examiner in arriving at the correct determination.
12. Gordon, N. and Cochetti, P. (1982) The positive control concept and technique. *Polygraph*, 11(4), 330–342.

13. Driscoll, L. and Honnts, C. (1987) The validity of the positive control physiological detection of deception technique. *Polygraph*, 16(3), 218–225.
14. APA Ad-hoc Committee. (2011) Meta-analytic survey of criterion accuracy of validated polygraph techniques. *Polygraph*, 44(4), 194–305.
15. Grubbs, F. E. (February 1969) Procedures for detecting outlying observations in samples. *Technometrics*, 11(1), 1–21, "An outlying observation, or 'outlier,' is one that appears to deviate markedly from other members of the sample in which it occurs."
16. Grubbs (1969, p. 1) stating "An outlying observation may be merely an extreme manifestation of the random variability inherent in the data.… On the other hand, an outlying observation may be the result of gross deviation from prescribed experimental procedure or an error in calculating or recording the numerical value."
17. Gordon, N. J., Fleisher, W. L., Morsie, H., Habib, W., and Salah, K. (2000) A field validity study of the integrated zone comparison technique. *Polygraph*, 29(3), 220–225.
18. Gordon, N. J. et al. (2005) Integrated zone comparison polygraph technique accuracy with scoring algorithms. *Physiology and Behavior*.
19. Shurany, T. and Chaves, F. (2010) The integrated zone comparison technique and ASIT polySuite algorithm: A field validity study. *European Journal*, 4(2), 12, 71–80.
20. Gordon, N. and Fleisher, W. (2012) Effectiveness of the integrated zone comparison technique (IZCT) with various scoring techniques in a Mock crime experiment by students. *European Journal*, 6(1), 19, 5–18.
21. Krapohl, D., Gordon, N., and Lombardi, C. (2008) Accuracy demonstration of the horizontal scoring system using field cases conducted with the federal zone comparison technique. *Polygraph*, 37(4), 263–268.
22. Matte, J. (2015) Identifying and cultivating superforecasters as a method of improving probabilistic predictions. *Research Digest*, 2(4), 1–4.
23. Gordon, N. and Cochetti, P. (1987) The horizontal scoring system. *Polygraph*, 16(2), 118–125.
24. ASIT PolySuite is a manually driven computerized algorithm for analysis of polygraph data.
25. Selle, N. K., Verschuere, B., Kindt, M., Meijer, E., and Ben-Shakkar, G. (April 2016) Orienting versus inhibition in the Concealed Information Test: Different cognitive processes drive different physiological measures. *Psychophysiology*, 53(4), 579–590. doi: 10.1111/psyp.12583.

Preemployment Polygraph Examination

6

I am a firm believer in the people. If given the truth, they can be depended upon to meet any national crisis. The great point is to bring them the real facts.

—**Abraham Lincoln**

The purpose of preemployment testing is to get information from the source: residential stability, employment history, gambling, indebtedness, honesty, illegal drug involvement, driving record, military history, and sometimes loyalty. No one knows more about the person seeking employment than the applicant themselves. Today in most modernized countries, there is a host of data services one could use to find out information about criminal convictions, indebtedness, driving records, and even various tests that screen for illegal drug use.

However, when you consider what percentage of the criminals committing serious crimes are caught and what percentage of them are successfully convicted, what we will find by checking criminal records is only the tip of the iceberg. However, the applicant definitely knows whether he or she has committed a serious crime: detected or undetected.

I conducted a preemployment interview on a woman applying for a job as a cashier. During the interview, she admitted to me she had been convicted and incarcerated for a felony. The client also used our services to search for criminal records. To do this, we used one of the largest data-supplying companies in the country. The report came back with no criminal record.

When I called them and enquired how they concluded that she had no criminal record since the applicant had already admitted being convicted of a felony, their response was that not all localities are computerized, so often they send people in to physically go through files. Sometimes, a file is misplaced, and on occasion, it may be missed.

In the United States, we live in a litigious society. Trying to find out an applicant's employment performance and history by calling former places of employment generally gets you, "They worked from this date to that date." Employers do not divulge any other information because they are afraid of being sued. Even if they did, again I ask you, "What percentage of employees committing thefts are caught?" Once again, the applicant knows!

Most drug tests will indicate illegal drug use in the past 30 days. We have no idea what was used prior to that or for that matter whether the applicant has ever been involved in buying or selling illegal drugs. Once again, the applicant knows all!

So how effective is the polygraph as a screening tool? In 1982, my partner at the time, Philip M. Cochetti, did his master's degree thesis on this very topic entitled *The Effectiveness of Polygraph in the Personnel Selection Process.*

A purposeful sampling of 500 preemployment polygraph applicants was surveyed to determine the need for polygraph screening in the business community selection process. An applicant job profile for the metropolitan Philadelphia area was established, and comparisons between applicant pretest admissions and polygraph question determinations were analyzed.

At the time of this study, Scientific Investigation Services was one of eleven commercial companies in Philadelphia, PA, conducting preemployment polygraph screening. The company was established in January 1980. Files pertaining to preemployment screening, periodic honesty tests, specific situation testing, and legal tests had been maintained from that date forward according to the year and in numerical order.

A purposeful sampling technique was used to select all the preemployment files for analysis. The Scientific Investigative Services files were listed consecutively from one to infinity by the year in which the test was given. Since files were listed numerically and not by test classification, 900 files from the year 1982 were examined to select the 502 preemployment tests performed for that year for the purposes of the study.

The population surveyed was composed of job applicants who were selected by small business personnel as candidates for positions that were needed to be filled by their companies. The applicants came from the City of Philadelphia and its surrounding counties and from a diversified employment background. The job spectrum consisted of sales clerks, cashiers, bartenders, waiters, waitresses, assistant managers, managers, and gas station attendants and ranged from minimal to white collar job categories.

Every job applicant file was reviewed individually and all self-reported admissions were recorded. A checklist was developed for the purpose of recording each applicant's admissions in 19 different categories that included suspension of driver's license, gambling, criminal convictions, felony arrests, undetected crimes, number of jobs held, number of times fired from jobs, drug use, and employee theft.

The study utilized a standard preemployment screening data form from Scientific Investigative Services to obtain the self-reported admissions of the 500 applicants surveyed. This data form was completed by every job applicant who agreed to the preemployment polygraph screening examination. The data form was designed to give the job applicant an understanding of what types of questions he or she would be asked during the polygraph testing sequence itself. Of the 502 files selected, two applicants refused to take the examination causing the actual population to be a sample of 500 applicant files.

The applicants' ages ranged from 16 to 60 years with a mean age of 23.9 years. The total population consisted of 285 males (57%) and 215 females (43%). The applicants' marital status consisted of 80 (16%) married, 378 (76%) never married, 33 (7%) divorced or separated, and 1 (0.2%) widowed.

Levels of education ranged from the 4th grade to the postgraduate level. The overall mean education was 13.2 years. There was virtually no difference between the male applicants, 13.09 years of education, and the female applicant's average of 13.35 years.

Of the populations surveyed, 381 (84%) of the applicants had never taken a polygraph examination prior to applying for the particular job. The remaining 74 (16%) applicants had taken at least one polygraph before.

All applicants were informed that under the laws of the Commonwealth of Pennsylvania, no one could be forced to take a polygraph examination. If they desired, they could choose a preemployment background investigation as an alternative to the polygraph test and that they could change their mind at any time during the entire procedure.

The applicants were further advised that all the test questions would be reviewed with them prior to the test, and an explanation of how the polygraph functions would be given. All applicants signed a standard consent form acknowledging their voluntariness and authorizing the results to be released to only themselves and the potential employer.

Informational data were then obtained for identification and to determine the applicant's mental and physical ability to undergo the examination. Each applicant was then interviewed on the relevant areas of interest. The polygraph test questions were then formulated based on the applicant's admissions or lack of admissions to the relevant question areas. Once formulated, the questions were reviewed with each applicant and an explanation of how the polygraph functions was given. This concluded the pretest interview segment of the examination.

The reviewed polygraph questions were then asked to the applicant while attached to the polygraph instrument. At the end of the first test, the applicant was afforded the opportunity to give an explanation for any significant question reactions that occurred or to offer any further information he or she recalled. At least one more test utilizing the same questions was then administered. At the completion of the testing, each applicant was again afforded the opportunity to explain any significant and consistent reactions emitted during the examination. This portion of the procedure is referred to as the posttest interview and concluded the polygraph examination.

Pretest Admissions of Driving Problems

The category of driving problems was discussed in the pretest interview based on what the job applicant admitted to when answering the data form. This category was not formulated into a test question, so no examiner opinions were reported.

Of the 483 applicants responding to the question about driving problems, 36 males (13% of the male population) and 7 females (3.4% of the female population) self-reported that they had experienced some type of driving problem, such as moving violations, driving under the influence of drugs and/or alcohol, and license suspensions or revocations. Parking violations were not considered as part of this category.

Number of Jobs Reported Held by Applicants

A total population of 466 applicants, consisting of 262 (56.2%) males and 204 (43.8%) females, self-reported that they had from no job experience to a maximum of 60 previously held jobs. The average number of jobs previously held was 5.2 jobs per applicant.

The 204 female applicants reported they had held 999 jobs or an average of 4.9 per female applicant. The 262 male applicants reported they had held 1424 jobs or an average of 5.4 jobs per male applicant.

In the opinion of the polygraph examiners after interpreting the responses to the question, "Are you deliberately withholding any important information about the job you had you don't want me to know about?" Of the female applicants, 148 (73%) were truthful, 49 (24%) were deceptive, and 6 (3%) were inconclusive. Of the male applicants, 182 (70%) were interpreted as truthful, 67 (26%) were deceptive, and 12 (4%) were inconclusive. There appeared to be little difference in the average number of jobs between males and females or the truthfulness of their self-reported admissions.

Of the 465 job applicants surveyed, 338 (73%) self-reported never having been fired from a job, 102 (22%) applicants reported to being fired once, and 23 (5%) applicants reported to being fired three times. Of the 204 female applicants, 157 (77%) applicants reported never having been fired, 41 (21%) applicants reported to being fired once, 5 (2.5%) reported to being fired twice, and 1 (0.5%) applicant reported to being fired three times. Of the 261 male applicants, 181 (69%) applicants reported never having been fired, 61 (23%) applicants reported to being fired once, 18 (7%) applicants reported to being fired twice, and 1 (0.4%) applicant reported to being fired three times.

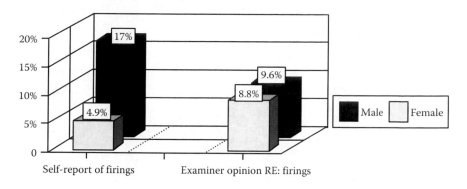

Figure 6.1 Percentage of self-report and polygraph determinations of being fired.

In the opinion of the polygraph examiners after interpreting the responses to the question, "Have you ever been fired from a job?" 37 (14.4%) of the males and 10 (4.9%) of the female applicants were deceptive (Figure 6.1).

Arrests

Of the total population of 462 job applicants surveyed, 417 (90%) reported no prior arrests by any law enforcement or government agency and 45 (10%) reported to being arrested one or more times. Only 3% of the females (6 out 197) reported being arrested, while 15% (39 out of 265) of the males self-reported admissions in this category. Of the applicants self-reporting prior arrests, 87% were males and only 13% females.

Undetected Crimes

Of the total population of 454 job applicants that self-reported to this category, 430 (95%) made no admissions. However, 23 applicants (5%) did admit to committing serious undetected crimes, such as child molestation, robbery, burglary, auto theft, major thefts, and shoplifting.

There were four applicants who had admitted to multiple commissions of crimes, such as one who admitted to committing in excess of 300 auto burglaries, one who admitted to committing 10 strong-arm robberies, one who admitted to committing in excess of 200 thefts of bicycles, and one who admitted shoplifting in excess of 100 times. Only 4 (2%) of the 193 female applicants and 19 (7%) of the 261 male applicants made self-reported admissions. Since this was not a question that was consistently

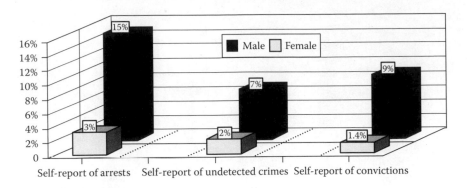

Figure 6.2 Percentage of self-reported admissions by gender.

asked on all of the polygraph examinations, examiner opinion was not reported (Figure 6.2).

Convictions

A total population of 499 job applicants answered the question, "Have you ever been convicted of a serious crime?" Of those, 470 applicants (94%) reported that they had not been convicted of any serious crimes and 29 applicants (6%) reported prior convictions, such as rape, indecent assault, possession of firearms, assault on police officers, theft, bad checks, driving under the influence of alcohol, and disorderly conduct.

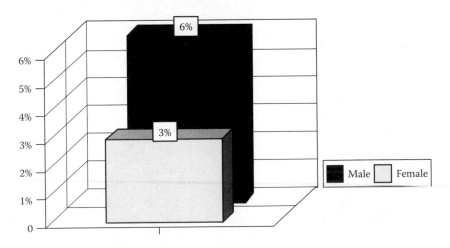

Figure 6.3 Results of the polygraph examiner's determination on the question, "Have you ever been convicted of a serious crime?"

Only 3 (1.4%) of the female applicants reported a prior conviction in relation to 26 (9%) of the male applicants. Those 26 males accounted for 89% of the total population admitting to prior convictions.

When asked the question, "Have you ever been convicted of a serious crime?" the polygraph examiners interpreted that 193 (90%) of the female applicants were truthful, 6 (3%) were deceptive, and 16 (7%) were inconclusive. Of the 249 male applicants, 214 (88%) were interpreted as truthful, 17 (6%) were deceptive, and 18 (6%) were inconclusive (Figure 6.3).

Drug Use and Abuse

Of the 500 applicants tested, 76% admitted some type of illegal drug activity prior to the test. Of the 119 applicants who reported no drug use, 48 (40%) were deceptive in the opinion of the examiners increasing the percentage of applicants with some type of prior illegal drug activity to 85.8%.

Those applicants admitting only marijuana use numbered 169 (33.8%) of the population. There were 96 males (34%) and 73 females (34%) in this category. There was almost no difference between males and females in the truthfulness with this category. Of the male population, 52 (18%) were interpreted as deceptive, while 38 (17.7%) females were also interpreted as deceptive.

Those applicants admitting to the use of two to four illegal drugs were 150 (30% of the total population). The 76 males accounted for 26.7% of this category, while 74 females accounted for 34.4%. In the opinion of the examiner, 49 males (17.2%) and 48 females (22%) were interpreted as deceptive. Females admitted to more use and were interpreted deceptive more than males.

There were only 62 (12.4%) applicants who admitted to the use of five or more illegal drugs and/or selling or addiction. Males clearly dominated this category numbering 47 (16.5% of the male group), while females numbering 15 (7% of their population). Examiners interpreted that 23 of the males (8%) and 9 females (4.7%) were still not completely truthful regarding their drug involvement at this level.

Only five applicants admitted to drug addiction (1% of the total population). All were males (1.8% of male population).

There were 15 applicants who admitted to being drug dealers (3% of the total population). Of those, 13 were males (86.7%) and 2 were females (13.3%).

Of the total population, only two applicants (0.4%) admitted illegal drug use on the job site. Both were males.

It became alarmingly clear that illegal drug use had become the norm rather than the deviant behavior. If employers were to eliminate applicants based on any illegal use of drugs, 86% of the applicants would be unemployable (Figure 6.4).

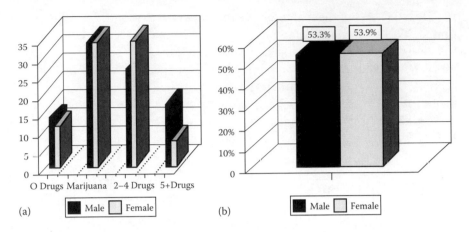

Figure 6.4 (a, b) Responses on drug usage and polygraph examiner's opinion of deception.

Total Employee Thefts

Examining the total population of 500 applicants, 397 (80%) self-reported thefts of property and/or money from previous employers. Of these 197 applicants admitting to employee thefts, 322 (81%) admitted to thefts of property such as saleable merchandise, tools, equipment, supplies, and raw materials and 76 (19%) applicants admitted to thefts of money.

Only 316 of the applicants were able to estimate a dollar value of their thefts during the pretest interview. These applicants reported $31,256.00 in property thefts and $20,101.00 in cash thefts from their employers, totaling $51,357.00.

Each applicant's polygraph examination ended with questions designed to determine the applicant's total thefts from employers. For example, "Have you stolen more than $100.00 in cash or property from all your employers?" Based on the examiner's opinion to these questions, the actual employee thefts committed by the applicants exceeded $150,000.00.

Property Thefts from Employers

Of the 215 females surveyed, 109 (51%) reported no prior employee thefts of property. In the range between $1.00 and $25.00, 73 (34%) reported property thefts that totaled $715.00 or an average of $9.97 per applicant. In the range between $26.00 and $50.00, 14 (7%) reported property thefts that totaled $622.00 or an average of $44.42 per applicant. In the range between $51.00 and $100.00, 8 (4%) reported property thefts that totaled $650.00 or an average of $81.25 per applicant. In the range between $101.00 and $200.00, 3 (1%)

reported property thefts that totaled $535.00 or an average of $178.33 per applicant. In the range between $201.00 and $500.00, 6 (3%) reported property thefts that totaled $2230.00 or an average of $371.66 per applicant. In the range between $901.00 and $10,000.00, 2 (1%) reported property thefts that totaled $7,383.00 or an average of $3,691.50 per applicant.

Of the total female population, 80 (38%) were interpreted as truthful in their polygraph examination to the questions, "Have you ever stolen any property from an employer?" or "Besides what you told me, have you ever stolen any more property from an employer?" There were 127 (59%) interpreted as deceptive and 7 (3%) were inconclusive.

Of the 285 male applicants surveyed, 124 (43%) reported no thefts of property from their employers. In the range between $1.00 and $25.00, 86 (30%) reported property thefts that totaled $882.00 or an average of $10.25 per applicant. In the range between $26.00 and $50.00, 29 (10%) reported property thefts that totaled $1273.00 or an average of $43.89 per applicant. In the range between $51.00 and $100.00, 14 (5%) reported property thefts that totaled $1277.00 or an average of $91.21 per applicant. In the range between $101.00 and $200.00, 16 (6%) reported property thefts that totaled $2602.00 or an average of $162.62 per applicant. In the range between $201.00 and $500.00, 10 (3.5%) reported property thefts that totaled $4312.00 or an average of $431.40 per applicant. In range between $501.00 and $900.00, 2(0.7%) reported property thefts that totaled $1275.00 or an average of $637.50 per applicant. In the range between $901.00 and $10,000.00, 4 (1.5%) reported property theft that totaled $7500.00 or an average of $1875.00 per applicant.

Of the total male population, 92 (32%) were interpreted as truthful in their polygraph examination to the questions, "Have you ever stolen any property from an employer?" or, "Besides what you told me, have you stolen any more property from an employer?" There were 187 (66%) interpreted as deceptive and 6 (2%) interpreted as inconclusive (Figure 6.5).

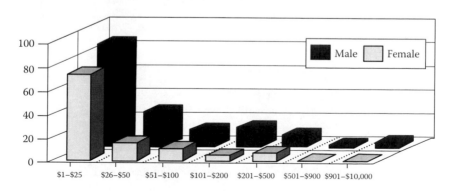

Figure 6.5 Responses to the question, "Have you ever stolen any property from an employer?"

Cash Thefts from Employers

Of the 215 female job applicants surveyed 194 (90%) reported no thefts of money from their employers. In the range between $1.00 and $25.00, 13 (6%) reported cash thefts that totaled $194.00 or an average of $14.92 per applicant. In the range between $51.00 and $100.00, no females reported cash thefts. In the range of $101.00–$200.00, 3 (1.4%) reported cash thefts that totaled $374.00 or an average of $115.00 per applicant. In the range between $901.00 and $10,000.00, (0.5%) reported cash thefts that totaled $1000.00 or an average of $1000.00 per applicant.

Of the total female population, 133 (62%) were interpreted as truthful in their polygraph examination to the question, "Have you ever stolen any cash from an employer?" or "Besides what you told me, have you stolen any more cash from an employer?" There were 57 (27%) interpreted as deceptive and 23 (11%) interpreted as inconclusive.

Of the 285 male job applicants, 245 (86%) reported no thefts of money from their employers. In the range between $1.00 and $25.00, 14 (5%) reported cash thefts that totaled $98.00 or an average of $7.00 per applicant. In the range between $26.00 and $50.00, 9 (3%) reported cash thefts that totaled $397.00 or an average of $44.11 per applicant. In the range between $51.00 and $100.00, 10 (3.5%) reported cash thefts that totaled $820.00 or an average of $82.00 per applicant. In the range between $101.00 and $200.00, 1 (0.25%) reported cash thefts that totaled $200.00. In the range between $201.00 and $500.00, 4 (1.5%) reported cash thefts that totaled an average of $462.00 per applicant. In the range between $901.00 and $10,000.00, 2 (0.7%) reported cash thefts that totaled $15,000.00 or an average of $7,500.00.

Of the total male population, 174 (61%) were interpreted as truthful in their polygraph examination when asked the same questions as females. There were 89 (31%) interpreted as deceptive and 22 (8%) interpreted as inconclusive (Figure 6.6a and b).

Cochetti made the following conclusions of the research:

In considering the use of the polygraph procedure in the hiring process for preemployment analysis, the following four factors must be considered:

1. Does the polygraph procedure produce important and relevant information regarding an applicant's past behavior and therefore assist in predicting future behavior of importance to the potential employer?
2. Is there a genuine need by potential employers for the type of information generated through the polygraph procedure?
3. What infringement, if any, does the polygraph procedure place upon the job applicant?
4. Can the information obtained during the polygraph procedure be gathered in a more practical way?

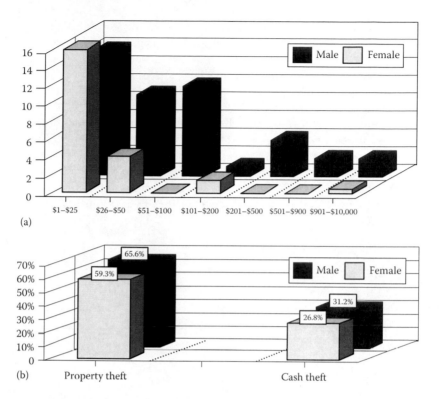

Figure 6.6 (a, b) Responses to the question on cash thefts and examiner opinion of deception.

Deviant employee behavior remains the single most expensive problem to businesses. Employee theft is one of the leading causes of small business bankruptcies in this country. Psychologists believe that an individual's past behavior is highly predictive of future behavior. Though not impossible, it remains highly unlikely that a leopard will change its spots! It is therefore apparent that the hiring process must have the ability to identify applicants that present a high degree of risk to the business for the business to survive.

The information gathered through the polygraph procedure and offered in this survey is obviously vital to the prospective employer in the selection of the most suitable and desired employees. It is just as obvious that most of the crucial information obtained is not available through any other source, since most of the acts disclosed have gone undetected. Even where wrongdoings are discovered by the employer, most employers are unwilling to disclose this type of information due to fear of liability.

In a study conducted by the Department of Sociology, University of Minnesota, in June 1981, only 35% of the individuals surveyed self-reported property theft from their employers. In our study, 80% of the individuals surveyed self-reported employee theft. The one difference between the studies is that the Minnesota sample was not about to be given polygraph examinations.

Several studies have now been conducted indicating that the vast majority of job applicants report a favorable view of their polygraph experience. Barton concluded the reason for these phenomena was each potential employee knew he or she was entering a business where fellow employees could be trusted and where fear of job security due to theft was minimal since everyone had undergone the polygraph procedure.

In view of the important and relevant information that comes out of the polygraph procedure to aid businesses in the selection process versus the small inconvenience, if any, to the job applicant, it would appear that when offered as a real choice (polygraph vs. field investigation) to the job applicant and when properly administrated, the polygraph serves a definite purpose and has a rightful place in the tools available to businesses to aid them in the selection process.

Job Applicant Profile in 1982

The average job applicant profile tested at the offices of Scientific Investigative Services for the year 1982, based on self-reported admissions, was the following:

1. 23.9 years of age.
2. 13.2 years of education.
3. 76% single.
4. 63% will pass the preemployment polygraph examination.
5. 16% had prior polygraph experience.
6. 8.9% driving problems.
7. 10% previously arrested.
8. 5% committed serious undetected crimes.
9. 6% convicted of a serious crime.
10. Five prior jobs.
11. 27% fired from a job.
12. 76% using illegal drugs.
13. 33.8% using marijuana only.
14. 30% using 2–4 different illegal drugs.
15. 12% using five or more different illegal drugs and/or selling or dealing in drugs.
16. 80% have stolen from previous employers.

This 1982 study was accepted by Norman Ansley, editor of the APA Journal; however, it was never published. This is very sad, since in 1988, the Employee Polygraph Protection Act was passed into legislation, which basically eliminated this type of testing to businesses. Paradoxically, the legislation states that preemployment polygraph does not work and is totally inaccurate because it lacks scientific research. It is inaccurate, unless you are a governmental agency, a law enforcement agency, or have a private business that the legislature perceives is important to protect. If you own a convenience store, according to the 1988 Act, preemployment polygraph does not work; if you are the CIA, it does! If you own a shoe store, it does not work; if you have armored car personnel, it does! If you own a department store, it does not work; if you are a law enforcement agency, it does!

With or without the polygraph, the examiner/interviewer must be able to do the following things if they want the applicant to offer truthful information about their past behavior:

1. Plant the seeds for truth.
2. Gain rapport.
3. Use assumptive questions.
4. Use exaggeration.
5. Share.
6. Use projective questions.

Planting the Seeds for Truth

Planting the seeds for truth involves what the examiner says to the applicant prior to starting the interview:

> This process is designed to screen out 1 in 10 applicants. About 9 out of 10 applicants can do well. However, only seven do. Two more should but do not, because they do not tell the truth. Then we do a background investigation or polygraph test and we uncover things they deliberately did not tell us. Usually, its minor things that had they told us wouldn't even of mattered. However, it shows that they lack integrity and maturity and that they probably have not learned from their mistakes. Therefore, they are automatically eliminated. I am not a saint, and I do not expect you to be a saint. I do expect you to tell me the truth.

Gaining Rapport

Obviously, gathering truthful information is much easier if rapport is established. The quickest and easiest way to gain rapport is to find things you have in common with the applicant early in the interview process. People who are alike—*like*!

Assumptive Questions

Always ask questions that assume the applicant has engaged in the behavior and require the applicant to tell you they have not. For example, do not ask, "Have you ever been fired from a job?" Instead, ask, "When we check with your past employers, whether they are right or wrong, and now is your chance to tell your side of it, how many will say you were fired?" Do not ask, "Have you ever been convicted of a crime?" Instead, ask, "When we check for criminal records, what is the most serious crime we will find you were convicted of?" Every question must assume something happened and it is up to the applicant to state it has not.

Use Exaggeration

If an applicant has a problem with tardiness and was late 20 times in the past year, and you ask, "How many times have you been late for work in your past year of employment?" what are the chances you will be given the correct number? Being late 20 times sounds like a lot! If the same applicant is asked, "How many times have you been late in the past year of employment: 100, 50, 20, 10, 5?" By exaggerating the problem and asking the question starting at 100, the 20 latenesses no longer sounds so bad and getting an answer closer to the truth is more likely.

Share

Sharing information with the applicant accomplishes two things to increase your collection of accurate information. You have gained rapport. Many people are afraid to tell you what they have done in their past because they are afraid you will think they are a bad person and will not like them. Everyone wants to be liked. Sharing something with them overcomes this fear! Second, there is an unwritten law in communication, the "law of reciprocity," which states if you tell someone a secret, they must tell you one in return. Imagine these two attempts to ascertain information:

Have you ever used illegal drugs?
          versus
Research shows that 90% of the population has experimented with illegal drugs. What I need for you to do is name every illegal drug you have used or experimented with, even if it was only once, and I'll let you know when you beat me—go!

Because we said, "I'll let you know when you beat me," the applicant can perceive we just admitted using illegal drugs. Therefore, we will not dislike him or her if he or she does. Because the applicant thinks we have shared a secret about ourself, he or she is now obligated to tell one back.

Projective Questions

Projective questions allow us to view the applicant's past by exploring his or her current attitude. There is a psychological concept called "cognitive dissonance" that basically holds that a person cannot have opposing ideas without change taking place. I cannot believe I hate apples—while thinking how much I enjoy eating one, without a change in my attitude. I cannot believe my employer is fair and stealing is wrong, without a change in my attitude taking place if I steal. Most people believe they are part of the majority—not part of the minority. If I am honest, I believe most people are honest, too. We can ask an applicant questions like, "Out of 100 employees, how many do you think steal from their job?" If an employee has been basically honest and has not witnessed a great deal of employee theft from coworkers, we would expect a low number.

"If an employee is caught stealing, what do you think should happen to them?" "Do you think they should be given a second chance?" If an employee has been basically honest, we would expect strong punishment and denial of allowing for a second chance.

"If you owned a company and caught an employee stealing cash, at what point would you fire them: $1.00, $5.00, $10.00, $20.00, $50.00, $100.00, $500.00, or $1000.00?" "At what point would you prosecute them?" "How about if it was property, such as supplies, merchandise, or equipment? At what point would you fire them? At what point would you prosecute them?" Again from a basically honest employee, we expect low numbers and consistency between punishment for cash and property theft.

We often hear examiners, who have conducted a preemployment examination where only irrelevant and relevant questions were asked, describe it as an R/I technique format. I believe this classification is often incorrect.

I define an R/I technique as a mixed issue examination where questions fall into two categories: relevant questions and irrelevant questions. The relevant questions will usually consist of questions of different issues and varied emotional weight/threat.

What I mean by varied emotional weight is that if the suspect is deceptive to the matter under inquiry, his or her perception of the threat of lying to the relevant questions and consequently his or her psychophysiological reactions on the examination to them could and probably will be different, even though the answers to all of the questions are lies.

For example, an applicant has recently stolen $5000.00 from his or her employer. They also occasionally use marijuana. The test questions in the R/I format would consist of irrelevant questions, such as the following:

Is your first name James?
Were you born in the United States?
Is your last name Smith?
Do you live in Philadelphia?
Is today Friday?

They also consist of relevant questions, such as the following:

Have you ever been fired from a job?
As an adult, have you ever committed a serious undetected crime?
In the past 3 years, have you had any involvement with illegal drugs?
In any one day, have you stolen anything valued at more than $50.00?

The determination of this suspect's truth or deception to the relevant questions will be an evaluation by the degree of psychophysiological reactions that occurred to the irrelevant questions, with those emitted to the relevant questions. If the reactions to the relevant questions are significantly greater than those emitted to the irrelevant questions, the suspect will be determined to be nontruthful and vice versa.

Further, as an examiner, I would suspect that there may be differences in the intensity of reactions to the relevant questions based on the suspect's involvement in the crime, even though he has lied to all of them. For example, if this was a specific examination, where the examinee was a former employee who helped plan the holdup of his employer, his reactions to "knowledge" of the holdup or "receiving" stolen money may be significantly greater than those concerning the actual commission of the crime. If this was the perpetrator, perhaps he will react strongly to "Did you stick up...?" and "Did you shoot...?" yet show little reaction to the secondary relevant questions concerning "presence," "knowledge," or "receiving," since they are less threatening areas of inquiry.

How does this differ from a preemployment examination that is commonly referred to as being performed utilizing the R/I technique? There is still a mixture of irrelevant and relevant questions in the format; however, all of the relevant questions have equal emotional weight, in the sense that lying to any of them will result in them not being hired.

Second, the primary determination of this applicant's truth or deception to any relevant question will *not* be an evaluation of the degree of reactions to the irrelevant questions, with the reactions emitted to the relevant questions, but the consistent strong reaction to a relevant question as compared to significantly lesser reactions to other relevant questions of the same emotional weight and threat.

In essence, this preemployment examination is not an R/I test, it is an R/R test. We are saying that all of the relevant questions have the ability to deny employment and therefore are of equal threat and emotional weight. If an applicant is asked relevant questions on the test concerning illegal drugs, undetected crimes, employment honesty, and employment terminations, for example, what other explanation can there be for significant reactions to one relevant question but not to the others, except for the fact that the applicant's past behavior related to this question and his denial of it have made this a threatening and salient issue?

The Israeli "ART Technique" utilizes a format consisting of *all* relevant questions. They compare the relevant questions with each other and then use a "hurdle" technique and administer zone comparison tests (ZCT) on the two strongest reactions in the R/R technique.

The scientific argument we hear concerning the comparison question test is how can we be sure of the threat and significance of the examinee's perception of the comparison question with that of the relevant question? In an R/R test, this argument is eliminated! In theory, the R/R test is easier to explain than the more commonly used and scientifically researched comparison question test.

Lying to any of the relevant questions equals denial of employment, thus all of the relevant questions have equal threat. When there are significant reactions to one of these relevant issues and lack of reaction to the others, we can safely conclude there is past behavior related to this relevant issue that the applicant has chosen not to disclose that has resulted in this outcome.

I recently found a research paper by Gordon Barland on the Internet involving a study he performed on the accuracy of preemployment testing while he was with the Department of Defense Polygraph Institute. Interestingly, he found that strong yet inconsistent psychophysiological reactions to relevant questions in a screening examination were a more accurate determiner of deception than an examiner looking for strong and consistent reactions throughout the testing to the same relevant questions. In other words, those inconsistent reactions to different relevant questions during the examination were more accurate in determining reactions than consistent reactions to the same question throughout the examination. I believe, this finding may be due to the way an examiner asks questions in a preemployment examination versus how questions are asked in a specific examination.

In a specific examination, using a "comparison" question technique, the innocent examinee has identified his or her threat as the comparison questions and has psychologically set to them, while the deceptive examinee has recognized his or her greatest threat as lying to the issue under investigation and has psychologically set to those questions. In this examination, the examinee can recognize if the question being asked is the one that poses them the greatest threat as soon as the examiner asks the first word in the question, since comparison and relevant questions will begin with clearly different wording (such as prior, during, between vs. did, were, regarding). Even in a specific multifaceted examination, the relevant question wording will differ from that of the comparisons.

In a preemployment examination, most, if not all, of the relevant questions, although containing totally different issues, will begin with the same wording (i.e., "As an adult, have you used any illegal drugs?" "As an adult, have you been fired from a job?" "As an adult, have you committed a serious undetected crime?"). Therefore, an applicant lying about one relevant issue but not all may react significantly yet inconsistently to the relevant questions. The examiner begins the question, "As an adult," and before the applicant even knows the substance of the question, he or she is already reacting in anticipation of having to lie to it. The applicant hears, "As an adult," and he already anticipates it is the "drug" question and reacts, as the examiner finishes the question, "committed a serious undetected crime?" Once the physiological reaction begins, it cannot be stopped or taken back.

We have found this problem can be avoided if the examiner announces ahead of time, with a single word, what the substance of the question will be, thus allowing for single word discrimination. We also find that by telling the applicant that their company or agency has identified certain character traits that make for the best employee/officer, introducing comparison questions is relatively easy. For four relevant question preemployment tests, we tell the applicant the following:

> There are three types of questions in this test. The first group of questions is truth or control questions. These are questions where I know you are telling the truth and allow the polygraph to establish a baseline of what is happening in your body when I know you are being truthful. I will ask you:
>
> 4. Monday—Is today (correct day)? Yes.
> 1. Sunday—Is today (incorrect day)? No.
> 7. United States—Right now are you in the (correct country)? Yes.
> 10. United Kingdom—Right now are you in the (incorrect country)? No.
>
> The second group of questions is adult behavior questions. I will ask you:
>
> R6 (i.e., fired—As an adult, have you ever been fired from a job?)
> R9 (i.e., crime—As an adult, have you committed a serious undetected crime?)
> R12 (i.e., drugs—In the past __ years, have you had any personal involvement with illegal drugs?)
> R14 (i.e., theft—In the past ___ years, in any one day, have you stolen anything valued at more than $50.00?)
>
> As these questions are reviewed, it is important to define each question. For example, in R12, "What do I mean by personal involvement? If coming to the office today, you passed someone on the street and smelled that they were smoking marijuana, that is not personal involvement. If you were at a party

last weekend and the person next to you used cocaine, that is not personal involvement. Personal involvement means that you personally used, bought, or sold." In R9, "What do I mean by serious crime? I am talking about a felony: rape, murder, arson, car theft, and child molestation. I am not asking you if you ever had a beer and drove a car or ever broke a traffic law."

The third group of questions is character questions. This employer has had psychologists perform tests on their best employees and have developed certain character traits they believe make for the best employee. So I will ask:

C5. Trust—Can you remember ever breaking the trust of a friend?
C8. Mistake—Are you the type of person that repeats a mistake?
C11. Integrity—Are you the type of person that would lie to get out of trouble?
C13. Character—Would there be any reason anyone would say you are a person of poor character?

Then I will ask you:

15. Beat—Have you deliberately done anything to try and beat this test?
3. Intend—Do you intend to answer every test question truthfully?
2. Understand—Do you understand I will only ask the questions we reviewed?

These questions are reviewed with the examinee and asked during the examination with these single word beginnings. We have found this process greatly assists in allowing examinees to properly and consistently react to those questions that are most salient and use this process in all screening examinations as well as any test, such as a postconviction sexual offender maintenance or monitor examinations, where confusion may take place due to questions beginning with similar phrases yet addressing different issues.

A popular screening technique being used by examiners is the directed lie screening test (DLST[1]). The DLST is modeled after the U.S. government's test for espionage and sabotage. The DLST requires using a hurdle approach since it is not considered a diagnostic test.

The DLST is made up of two neutral questions (N1, N2), a sacrifice relevant question, two separate relevant questions (R1, R2), and two directed lie comparisons (DLC) comparison questions (C1, C2). It is administered as a single chart where the two relevant questions are repeated at least three times. Generally, two relevant questions are asked in a test and two tests are administered, allowing for four relevant issues to be covered.

The examiner explains that the DLCs are "known lie" questions, which will be used for comparison purposes to ensure the truth questions (relevant questions) are truthful. Obviously, the examinee must admit that he or she has done the act covered in the DLC. Some examples of a DLC are as follows:

In your entire life, did you ever lie to avoid responsibility for something you did?
In your entire life, did you ever act out of anger?

In your entire life, did you ever make a mistake?
In your entire life, did you ever make a negative comment about someone?

The sequence is as follows:

N1—Neutral or irrelevant question
N2—Neutral or irrelevant question
SR—Sacrifice relevant question
1C1—First presentation of DLC#1
1R1—First presentation of R1
1R2—First presentation of R2
1C2—First presentation of DLC#2
2R1—Second presentation of R1
2R2—Second presentation of R2
2C1—Second presentation of DLC#1
3R1—Third presentation of R1
3R2—Third presentation of R2
2C2—Second presentation of DLC#2

Additional presentations are allowed when three artifact-free presentations of each have not been obtained. In the latter case, examiners are permitted to present the question sequence a fourth time. This can take place as a fourth presentation of the test stimuli within the single examination chart or through the completion of a second shorter chart, consisting of the following sequence (N1, N2, SR, 3C1, 4R1, 4R2, 3C2).

For analysis, the stronger comparison question to either side of the relevant question is used. Advocates of this procedure warn that the data collected from pneumographs in DLC examinations do not appear to have diagnostic value. A spot total of −3 or lower at either spot or a grand total of −4 or less results in an opinion of significant response (SR). No significant response opinions are made when the grand total is +4 across the two relevant targets, as long as there is a positive numerical score for both issues.

Those researching and using the DLST hail the advantages of the examiner not requiring the skill to introduce a probable lie question and the fact that you do not have to touch on the examinee's personal life, while others in the profession feel strongly that the DLC process invites countermeasures and psychologically will cause an increase in false negatives.

Conclusion

Some examiners still use the R/I technique to conduct preemployment tests. The majority of examiners use ZCT formats that allow for four relevant questions. The importance of polygraph testing in this realm is obvious by its users. That is why almost every government agency (CIA, FBI, Secret Service, ICE, NASA, etc.) and most law enforcement agencies utilize polygraph examinations to verify an applicant's background and ensure they are hiring the best possible candidates. It is a basic fact: no one knows the true past of the applicant better than the applicant him or herself!

Note

1. Handler, M. et al. (2008) A focused polygraph technique for PCSOT and law enforcement screening programs. *Polygraph*, 37(2), 77–86.

Community
Safety Testing

7

People who put themselves on the line and sacrifice their own safety for the greater good and for others, and anyone in any profession whose concern is the welfare for other people instead of the individual, are inspiring and important.

—**Chris Hemsworth**

The use of polygraph examinations within the parole/probation system actually began with what was referred to as polygraph surveillance. It was originally introduced to aid in the management of probationers and to attempt to reduce their high rate of recidivism.

In 1966, Judge Partee of Illinois initially used polygraph testing to question probation applicants about undetected crimes. He then required probationers to take yearly examinations to prevent them from reoffending and identify any who had.

In 1969, Judge Tuttle of Walla Walla, Washington, began using polygraph testing to periodically test probationers to ensure they had not violated their conditions of probation or had reoffended. He found that polygraph testing increased admissions from this population and that polygraph testing also had a deterrent effect on the population. Probationers now knew that even if they could commit a crime and get away with it, it would be discovered when they took their next polygraph examination. Another advantage was that other criminals the probationers were associated with no longer wanted to befriend those in the program fearing that they may divulge information about them during the polygraph testing.

In the 1970s, Judge Cooney of Spokane, Washington, used polygraph testing as a psychological threat. He offered shoplifters the choice of going to jail or admitting all of their thefts, telling them their statements would later be verified by the polygraph. He obtained 1400 additional admissions from 60 defendants; however, he never actually tested anyone.

In 1973, Judge Beatty of Oregon began the first polygraph surveillance program in the state to be used on probationers who would have normally been sent to prison due to their threat to society.

Stanley Abrams, PhD, and his associates performed a study of probationers without polygraph surveillance compared to another group who were required to take polygraph examinations. Their findings were astonishing! Recidivism for the group without polygraph examinations was 74%. Recidivism for the group with polygraph examinations was 31%. Polygraph surveillance resulted in a 43% reduction in recidivism.

Abrams became the father of postconviction sexual offender testing (PCSOT). In the 1970s, he traveled around the United States lecturing about its use at polygraph seminars. He argued that the procedure would

- Reduce prison populations
- Reduce the cost of housing prisoners
- Assist in the management/supervision of this population
- Deter abusers from reoffending
- Identify and help apprehend offenders who reoffended
- Help protect society
- Help in the treatment process

In a large study conducted in 1991, in Jackson County, Oregon, they evaluated the post conviction sexual offender program that was being used and found that of the 173 offenders in the program:

- 95% were free of new sex crimes.
- 96% were free of new felony convictions.
- 89% were free of any new convictions.
- 65% received no revocations of their parole/probation.

It is doubtful that a sexual offender can ever be completely cured; however, for the safety of the community once released back into society, they have to be contained. The concept of the "containment team" was born. The containment team consists of law enforcement (parole/probation), the therapist, and the polygraph examiner (Figure 7.1).

By 1998, 35 states were employing PCSOT examinations in some form. Interestingly, the three types of examinations that were developed were modeled from the pre-EPPA traditional use of polygraph testing: preemployment/screening tests became "sexual history examinations (SHEs)," periodic tests became "Monitor Examinations (MEs)" and specific issue tests became "instant offense (IO) examinations."

Therapists need accurate information about an offender's sexual past, which include types of crimes and number of victims, to effectively assess the offender's risk to the community and/or develop a plan of therapy for the offender. The SHE serves this purpose.

Two types of SHEs are currently being employed. A SHE I deals with an offender's lifetime history of victimization. Information in this examination deals with how they selected their victims, how they gained access to victims, the number of victims they have had, the types of victims they selected,

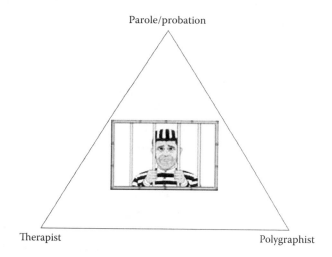

Parole/probation

Therapist   Polygraphist

Figure 7.1 Containment team.

and the various types of sexual offenses they have committed. Since this is a multi-issue examination, consisting of three or four relevant questions administered in a zone format and if the examinee fails a relevant question, a single issue reexamination is administered to accurately determine if the significant reactions on the original examination was correct.

A SHE II deals with an offender's lifetime of sexual deviancy. Rather than focus on just the crime of conviction, this test is used to identify various types of sexual deviancy: voyeurism, sexual molestation, rape, exhibitionism, fetishism, frotteurism, sexual sadism, pedophilia, etc.

Like the SHE I, this is a multi-issue examination utilizing a three or four relevant question zone format, and if the examinee fails a relevant question, a single issue reexamination is administered to accurately determine if the original significant reactions were accurate.

A ME deals with the offender's compliance with terms of parole/probation, or with the terms of treatment. This is a periodic type examination where there are no allegations. It is an exploratory examination into unknown issues. Relevant questions will deal with "Since supervision…" or "Since your last test…" and like the SHEs will usually be formatted into three or four relevant question zone formats. It is suggested that these examinations be performed every 4–6 months, however, at least once a year. A hurdle approach is again used: failing a question or questions result in a reexamination of a more accurate single issue zone test.

A reexamination due to significant reactions to one or more relevant questions in a ME is classified as a sexual offender monitor examination (SOME). A SOME may also be used when a specific request about possible new offenses while under supervision is made or the entire examination concerns reoffending. These tests can again be multifaceted or single issue formats.

An IO examination is given when an offender is released and required to seek therapy for his or her offense. The offender reports to the parole/probation officer (PO) or to the therapist and denies that they committed their crime of conviction and therefore maintains that they do not need treatment. Often they claim that they had a poor defense team or that there were so many charges that they were being prosecuted for that they were advised by their attorney to plead guilty to a minor offense and avoid the possibility of a long jail sentence if they lost their case.

If the offender is in denial of their crime of conviction, this will usually be the first test administered, and many in the profession maintain that an admission of guilt must be obtained before any other type of PCSOT examinations can be administered. An IO test is administered as a specific examination ideally using a single issue zone format specifically about the crime of conviction.

There are times when an IO investigative (IOI) test will be requested. These examinations are where the victim and offender agree on what happened; however, it does not meet the "smell test." That is, it does seem likely that they have told the entire truth. For example, a father is left alone with his 7-year-old daughter for the past year as the mother works at night. One night she becomes sick and comes home early to find the father in bed with the young girl digitally penetrating her. They both claim this is the only instance any form of sexual molestation has taken place. An IOI may be requested to see if there is any additional information or behaviors in context with the crime of conviction that have not been revealed. There are no allegations. This test may deal with the number of times acts were performed, whether there were any other hands-on abuses, whether there was ever any force involved, etc. They are administered as multifaceted or multi-issue examinations, using a hurdle approach, or may be performed as a series of single issue examinations.

The last type of examination dealing with the crime of conviction is the Prior Allegation Examination (PAE). This test is administered where there were original allegations made by the victim(s) left out of the final conviction due to a plea bargain, and now it is of interest to the containment team as to whether these original accusations were true. These examinations can be multifaceted or single issue, again using a hurdle approach.

In a recent case where a grandfather was charged with 26 offenses dealing with attempted rape using the threat of a knife, touching of the young granddaughter's private parts, and masturbating in front of his granddaughter on numerous occasions. He was told that if he pleaded guilty to a single act of masturbation in the presence of his granddaughter, he would receive no incarceration, which he did and now was denied any of the prior allegations.

As part of his risk assessment and treatment plan, it was important to discover if any of these prior allegations were true and a PAE test was requested and performed.

In PCSOT examinations, the time of reference for all relevant test questions in any of the types of IO tests or SHEs will be prior to crime of conviction. For all maintenance and monitor tests they will be since the crime of conviction or since their last test.

Various polygraph associations have established standards of practice for PCSOT examinations, including the American Polygraph Association, which are very similar to those required in any polygraph examination. They include the following:

1. Attended and successfully pass an examination of an accredited PCSOT course.
2. All polygraph tests must be recorded in their entirety (preferred medium is video).
3. At a minimum testing, facilities will
   a. Afford privacy and freedom from interruption
   b. Be free of visual and noise distractions
   c. Have comfortable temperature and proper ventilation
   d. Have an area sufficient for testing (8×8 to 10×10)
   e. Support recording equipment
   f. Have comfortable seating for two and a surface to support polygraph equipment
4. The minimum pretest interview specifications are as follows:
   a. Examinee must be advised of the purpose of the examination.
   b. Examinee must be advised that the exam is voluntary.
   c. Examinee must be advised that the exam can be terminated at any time.
   d. The exam must be conducted in a professional manner and the examinee must be treated with respect and dignity.
   e. The pretest interview must be nonaccusatory.
   f. The exam must comply with governing local, state, and federal regulations and laws, as well as APA standards.
   g. The examiner must properly prepare for the pretest interview; at a minimum, review case facts and information known about examinee and the goal of the examination.
   h. Examinee must agree to the relevant test issues in advance of testing.
   i. Examiner must not show any type of bias, preconceptions, or prejudgments of examinee's guilt or innocence.
   j. Examiner must provide examinee with a complete review of the test procedures.

k. Examiner must provide the examinee with a sufficient explanation of the polygraph, including the physiological activity to be recorded.

l. Examiner must convey to the examinee that the test results will be based solely on the polygraph charts and a thorough analysis will not be conducted until all data have been collected.

m. Examiner must allow sufficient time for a thorough discussion of the test issues and for the examinee to explain his position.

n. All test questions must be reviewed prior to testing.

o. Examiner must verify that the examinee understands each question.

p. Examiner must inform the examinee of the need to cooperate during the examination.

q. Examiner must secure a signed consent and verify the examinee's identity prior to testing and ensure that he or she is mentally and physically capable of taking the examination.

5. The minimum in-test specifications are as follows:

a. Collection of test data must include a permanent recording of the examinee's respiration, electrodermal, and cardiovascular activity.

b. Physiological data will be continuously collected during each chart.

c. These data will be preserved as part of the exam file as long as required by regulation or law, *but for a minimum of 3 years.*

d. Each single issue test shall employ a technique format (zone) that has been validated through research. Utility-based formats may be used to identify issues for single issue testing.

e. Reasonable deviations from the valid format are allowed to the extent that a reviewer would concur that the research and field formats were not significantly dissimilar.

f. Test question pacing shall allow reasonable time for physiological recovery following response distortion (20 second minimum—25–30 seconds is suggested).

g. Examiners will record a sufficient number of charts (minimum three charts), appropriate for the technique. Data collected must be suitable for evaluation, with a minimum of three presentations of each relevant question on three or more charts.

6. If an exam is being conducted as a utility examination and the examinee appears deceptive to a relevant question, prior to rendering a final decision of deception indicated, a single issue examination must be conducted on the specific issue.

7. All polygraph files must be maintained for a minimum period of 3 years and must include the name, date, location of exam, copy of consent form, pretest work sheet, copy of test questions, copies of charts or disk with charts, and examiner score sheet and decision.

8. All exam documentation must list the amount of time it took to conduct the exam.

9. At a minimum, all tests will take at least 90 minutes to conduct.

Sample Comparison Questions for Instant Offense Tests

These can be exclusive (e.g., "Prior to arrest ...") or inclusive (e.g., "In your entire life ...").

- Do you remember ever doing something sexual to someone your own age without their consent?
- Do you recall being involved in any behavior you had to lie about?
- Did you ever do anything sexual with someone your age your parents would be ashamed of?
- Did you ever do anything sexual with someone your age you were ashamed of?
- Did you ever lie about a sexual matter?
- Did you ever lie about someone else?
- Did you ever tell an important lie to get out of trouble?
- Did you ever tell an important lie to avoid responsibility for something you did?
- Did you ever blame someone else for something you did?

Sample Comparison Questions for Sexual History Tests

These can be any of the previous mentioned comparison questions used for IO tests, including the following:

- Have you lied to your PO about anything?
- Prior to your conviction, did you ever excessively masturbate?
- Have you tried to mislead your group about anything?
- Have you lied to anyone who trusted you?
- Prior to your conviction, did you ever do anything to a female your age, after they asked you to stop?
- Have you lied to another group member about anything?

Sample Comparison Questions for Maintenance/Monitor Tests

Since your last test:

- Have you had to lie about anything?
- Have you done anything to intentionally mislead your group?

Since your last test:

- Have you lied to your PO about anything?
- Have you lied to your therapist about anything?
- Have you done anything you wouldn't want probation to know about?

Futuristic comparisons are as follows:

- In the future would you lie to avoid punishment for something you did?
- In the future would you lie to someone who loved you?
- In the future would you commit a crime if you knew you could get away with it?

Sample Relevant Test Questions for Sexual History Tests

- Other than what you said (OTWYS), in the last __ years, have you fondled the sex organs of any child?
- Since the age of 18, have you been involved in an oral sex act with a minor?
- As an adult, have you inserted your penis into a child?
- OTWYS, have you ever exposed your penis in a public place?
- OTWYS, have you ever had sex with a woman against her will?
- OTWYS, have you ever used a weapon to make a person perform a sex act with you?

Sample Relevant Test Questions for Monitor Tests

Since your last test:

- Have you had contact with the sex organs of a minor?
- Have you had sex with anyone under the age of 18?

- Have you secretly been alone with a minor?
- Have you exposed your penis in a public place?
- Have you made any sexual phone calls?
- Have you secretly communicated with a minor?
- Have you observed a minor in the nude?

Sample Relevant Test Questions for Maintenance Tests

Since your last test, or in the past 6 months:

- Have you used any illegal substance?
- Have you consumed any alcohol?
- Have you viewed any pornographic material?
- Have you visited an adult club?
- Have you used a computer?
- Have you had any undisclosed acts of masturbation to thoughts about minors?
- Have you had any undisclosed acts of masturbation to thoughts about victims?
- Have you possessed a weapon?

The use of polygraph for community safety has been expanding. There has been some arguments concerning whether these tests violate an offender's 5th Amendment Rights against self-incrimination. This has led to suggestions by some legal advisors not to ask questions that are not criminal in nature, such as "Since your last test, have you performed a sexual act with a minor?" Instead, they advise to ask noncriminal questions that would indicate behavioral problems for the offender, such as "Since your last test, have you had any secret contact with a minor?"

Many states are now using programs similar to PCSOT testing for offenders on parole and probation in areas such as domestic violence and driving under the influence.

Faith Gordon-Mazur, who spent many years working as a therapist with these populations, points out what she believes works in therapy and what does not.

What Works in Therapy

- Accountability
- Honesty
- A support system
- Homework

- Communication
- Polygraph
- Group versus individual therapy
- Reinforcement of positive self-esteem and positive choices
- Repetition and integration of information
- Team concept

What Does Not Work in Therapy

- Short-term therapy
- Workbook therapy
- Shaming
- Battering
- Self-report only
- Poor/no communication
- Rigidity
- Poor/no boundaries
- Untrained therapy and supervision
- Unclear structure
- No polygraphs

Special Cases

8

I always tell the truth, even if I have to make it up.

—**Alan Trabue**

There are many cases that require special preparation or special consideration. These include the testing of handicapped people, pregnant people, and people with various types of mental or medical problems and tests requiring the use of a translator.

Conducting examinations on deaf people or who are deaf and cannot speak can be performed in two ways. Both cases will probably entail the use of a translator trained in sign language.

During the interview, seating must be done in a way that the examinee can see the translator using signs. During this part of the process, I would recommend the translator to sit next to the examiner, directly across from the examinee (Figure 8.1).

If the examinee is only deaf, I have found that the use of a projector during the test to project the questions onto the wall the examinee is facing is a very effective way to administer the test. Some people will have the translator seated in view of the examinee sending signs or holding up the questions on a piece of paper for the examinee to respond to, or to send signs. I find that this scenario may result in the translator nonverbally doing something, which may cause the examinee to give an incorrect response.

If the examinee is deaf and unable to speak, it presents a much greater problem, especially if this condition existed since birth. First, sign language is not very specific and lends itself to generalizations and possible different interpretations. A second problem is that many people born with this condition actually never learn how to read and often develop their own individual signs they use within their family.

Using a translator to perform a test for someone who does not speak your language can also create problems. The translator and examinee must understand that all communications are between the examiner and examinee.

Many times these examinees actually do speak the language of the examiner; however, they may feel more comfortable with someone else in the room that speaks their primary language or maybe embarrassed to speak in the examiner's language because they feel inadequate using it. Oftentimes the examiner can discover this by attempting to ask some basic

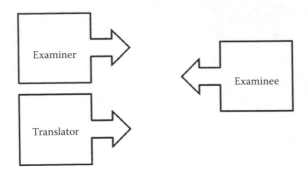

Figure 8.1 Seating arrangement in interviewing a deaf individual so that the examinee can see the translator using signs.

questions of the examinee or observing the examinee when they are speaking to a third person in their own language and monitoring the examinee's behavior and reactions to see if they are listening and comprehending what is being said.

Ideally, I prefer to meet with the translator a day or two before the actual examination and give them a basic overview of the polygraph process if it is the first time I am working with them. I will also give them a list of my intended questions and ask them to rewrite them in the language that will be used in the examination. I will then retain their work product and meet with them again prior to the test. I will give them back the questions they wrote in the foreign language and ask them to tell me what each question says in English. This ensures that the translated questions to be asked convey the content I intended.

I find that the seating in these examinations is best when the translator is seated behind the examiner during the pretest or posttest interview (Figure 8.2).

This seating keeps the line of communication focused directly between the examiner and examinee. Some people will have the translator seated behind the examinee or next to the examiner, which often results in the examinee trying to look over their shoulder to see the translator, or the examinee asks a question, the examinee looks at the translator to understand what was asked, the translator restates the question in the foreign language,

Figure 8.2 When utilizing a translator, it is optimal to have the translator seated behind the examiner during the pretest or posttest interview.

the examinee answers the translator, and the translator then informs the examiner of the answer.

During the actual collection of data, I prefer the translator to sit next to me with his or her list of numbered questions he or she has already written in the foreign language. I can then point to the next question I want to ask and use a hand gesture to alert them when to ask it.

When testing people with medical problems, it is always safer to have their doctor sign a medical release. For example, is it safe to test a pregnant woman? Interestingly, there is no agreement to this question within the profession. Some examiners will always test a pregnant woman, some will never, and some have a policy to only test during certain trimesters of the pregnancy.

Although I believe the polygraph examination is of no danger to a pregnant woman, it is not worth it in my mind to have to defend a law suit if for some reason she loses the baby after the examination. Therefore, I will only test a pregnant woman if she has a medical release signed.

In a post conviction sexual offender instant offense test, I had an examinee inform me during the interview that he had a defibrillator implanted. I decided to complete my forensic assessment interview of the examinee and after informing him I could not administer the polygraph examination. The polygraph introduces a low electrical current of 5 µA to monitor changes in electrodermal responses. This current is below the threshold of feeling; however, I had no idea if it would affect the examinee's defibrillator.

The examinee insisted on taking the test and suggested I contact his physician, which I did. The physician also did not know and suggested I contact the manufacturer of the device. I called the company and explained my situation and was told that the electrical current from the polygraph would not affect the device; however, I was warned that the device may affect the effectiveness of the data I was collecting. Interestingly, the cardio component was the most productive of the polygraph parameters, which led to a deceptive outcome and confession to the examinee's crime of conviction.

In rare occasions, you may have an examinee who is an amputee, or someone with an injury to a usual place for attachment. The cardio cuff can be placed on either calf, which results in much less discomfort and provides an excellent tracing. There is some of the opinion that this may be dangerous if the person is suffering from an aneurism; however, I am not aware of anyone in all the years polygraph has existed having a medical problem due to a blood pressure cuff placed on their calf. In fact, people with these types of problems in their legs are often required to wear some type of restrictive device to assist with the disorder. The cuff can also be placed on the forearm or wrist. The electrodermal activity (EDA) is typically placed on the examinee's fingers or palm; however, the toes and even the forehead offer productive areas for EDA reactions.

There are many psychological disorders or mental problems examinees may have. The profession maintains that a person with a mental age under 12 should not undergo a polygraph examination. When testing people who have mental deficiencies or who can be easily biased the examiner must be very careful not to influence the examinee. I have successfully conducted numerous examinations on mentally deficient examinees and will review one of these cases in Chapter 14.

Many people wonder about the effects of drugs on a polygraph examination. Examinees on medication should be instructed to take their normal dosage as prescribed. In a comparison question test, there is no medication or drug that can cause a false-positive or a false-negative outcome since there is nothing a person could ingest that would allow for him or her to react to only one zone, Comparison or Relevant, but not react in the other. Worst case scenario would be that a mediation or drug would cause an inconclusive outcome by preventing physiological reactions from occurring or resulting in such a hyper state that the distinctions between the degrees of reactions in comparison and relevant questions could not be accurately made.

I received a phone call from a mother many years ago. She explained her son, now in his twenties, was born with multiple sclerosis and mentally deficient. He was in a special school to determine his abilities and was reported to the school's disciplinarian by a female teacher who claimed he had asked her to have sex. When questioned, the young man claimed that the teacher lied, and that she had sexually seduced him and they had engaged in sexual activities over the past couple of weeks. He claimed the teacher told him they had to stop, and when he told her he could not stop because he loved her, she told him she would have him thrown out of the school. I was asked whether or not her son could undergo a polygraph examination. I told her I had no idea; however, she could bring him in and I would determine if I could test him.

Interviewing the young man, it was obvious he was mentally deficient; however, he clearly knew right from wrong, he knew the difference between telling the truth and lying and knew lying was wrong. During the interview, the young man was slow but showed no difficulty with speech. I started the examination with a silent answer test that showed strong reactions to the relevant questions. The second chart was a demonstration/acquaintance test where I asked the young man to circle a number between 2 and 5 and then answer every question "No," including the number 3, which he had circled. Once the test began, the examinee stuttered severely to questions 1, 2, and 3, and the stuttering suddenly stopped once we passed the number he circled. The third chart was the original questions with the examinee instructed to answer each question truthfully out loud. Once again, he stuttered throughout the examination making the data completely useless. The next chart was again administered as a silent answer test, which once again resulted in strong reactions to the relevant questions. Silent answer testing works very well and can be effectively employed in cases of examinee stuttering.

In any case, if it is obvious to the examiner that due to a mental or physical condition the examinee is not suitable for testing, the examination should not be conducted or be terminated immediately.

Conclusion

The need for truth unfortunately does not always take place in pristine locations and with the best of examinees. Challenges will occur; however, in most circumstances with thought and patience, the examination can be conducted and truth will prevail.

Data Analysis

9

The greatest moments are those when you see the result pop up in a graph or in your statistics analysis—that moment you realize you know something no one else does and you get the pleasure of thinking about how to tell them.

—Emily Oster

For accurate scoring and analysis of the chart data, the examiner needs to understand the language of polygraph as well as natural and deliberate distortions. Homeostasis is a complex interactive regulatory system by which the body strives to maintain an internal equilibrium. Being able to recognize an examinee's homeostatic signature for each recording is essential for effective test data analysis. In the polygraph field, homeostasis may also be referred to as "general tracing average," "baseline," "resting state," or "tonic level."

For many years, a great deal of examiners defined reactions as any deviation from a person's homeostatic norm. One of the requirements of any living thing is to maintain this constant internal state. If you were in the desert, by the end of the day, you could probably fry an egg on a stone. However, your body temperature would remain the same through your brain's control of your internal systems via the autonomic nervous system and its dual control through its parasympathetic and sympathetic nervous systems. As a general rule, the parasympathetic system is your body's housekeeper. It slows thoracic activity, while speeding up abdominal activity. Its effects are slowing of heart rate, breathing, and lowering of blood pressure, while it allows for digestion and waste elimination to take place. The sympathetic nervous system, often referred to as the "fight or flight" or emergency system, speeds up the thoracic activity to ensure your body is receiving enough oxygen, while it slows down abdominal activity, since the digestion of food and waste elimination is not of importance if you are about to die.

For over 40 years, Backster had maintained that defining reactions as any change from the homeostatic norm was incorrect and that there were certain changes indicative of reaction and other changes indicative of relief or a lack of reaction. Recent research has supported Backster's beliefs.

There are three possible changes that can occur in an examinee's physiological norm or tonic level:

1. Physiological reaction, also known as a reaction tracing segment, tonic response, or phasic response, indicating an arousal due to threat, interest, or an orienting response. These are generally attributed to sympathetic nervous system enervation.
2. A physiological reaction indicative of relief or compensation to a previous physiological reaction, also known as a relief tracing segment or homeostatic change. These are generally associated with parasympathetic nervous system enervation.
3. A physiological reaction that has no physiological cause because it was created due to a natural or deliberate distortion, the latter due to a countermeasure or augmentation. Countermeasures are deliberate distortions created by a deceptive examinee in an attempt to create an inconclusive or truthful (false negative) outcome, while augmentations are deliberate distortions created by a truthful person trying to ensure the examiner reaches the correct truthful outcome. Unfortunately, while examiners may be able to identify deliberate distortions, they cannot determine the motivation for them: countermeasure or augmentation.

Backster also identified another mechanism our body uses when we are experiencing fear or threat, what he referred to as "holding and hoping," which is more commonly identified as "freezing." When we consider the options of survival for humans faced with a threat we almost always refer to sympathetic arousal, or the "fight or flight" response. However, think about primitive humans. What animal that could eat us were we capable of outrunning? What animal that could eat us could we defeat in a fight without sophisticated weaponry? So, if primitive human's only defense against predators was to run or fight, we would probably be extinct!

The third option for survival was to freeze. Stay perfectly still and hope the faster more ferocious predator didn't see us, or paid no attention to us. Much of what we see and identify as reactions in polygraph can be attributed more to "holding and hoping," or freezing, than to sympathetic arousal.

As previously stated, during sympathetic arousal, we expect an increase in thoracic activity, an increase in respiration, and an increase in heart rate. What we actually find is a decrease in both.

In analyzing physiological data, we should be aware of some useful terminology common to the polygraph profession.

Diagnostic features or criteria refer to the physiological phenomena used in the numerical evaluation of polygraph test data. Latency refers to the period of time between the stimulus onset (the beginning of the examiner's question) and the response onset (the beginning of the examinee's reaction).

When we look at periods of latency, there should be consistency throughout the examination for the examinee's periods of latency between the two primary zones (comparison and relevant questions).

The "response onset window" (ROW) refers to the typical time period, from the stimulus (beginning of question) to the onset of reaction. In other words, where we would predict a physiological response would occur in order for that response to be deemed timely. The ROW differs for each component:

- *Pneumo*: The reaction should begin somewhere between the start of the question and one respiratory cycle past the answer.
- *Electrodermal activity* (EDA): The reaction should begin between the start of the question and the examinee's response.
- *Cardio*: The reaction should begin between the start of the question and the examinee's response.

Respiratory System

Data are collected from the thoracic area of the examinee's body or chest and the abdominal area or stomach by placing attachments around the examinee's body. We refer these components as the pneumo(s). A single breath is made up of two parts: inhalation, which results in an upward stroke, and exhalation, which results in a downward stroke (Figure 9.1).

If we think about the upper body as an airtight box, much like an accordion, we can get a better idea of how breathing takes place. The medulla oblongata, located in the hind brain, has two areas of innervation. Through the phrenic nerve, it causes the intercostal muscles to constrict, which in turn cause the rib cage to pull up, and at the same time it sends a signal to the diaphragm causing it to constrict and pull down. Air is then sucked into the lungs to allow for external respiration to occur (Figure 9.2).

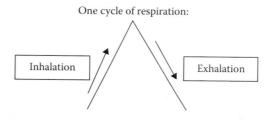

Figure 9.1 A single breath is made up of two parts: inhalation, which results in an upward stroke, and exhalation, which results in a downward stroke.

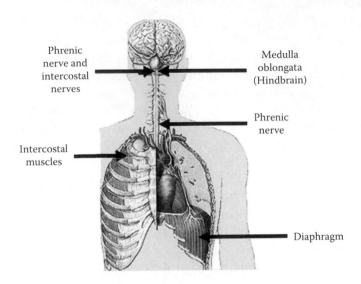

Figure 9.2 Two areas of innervation.

The average adult breathes 12–20 times per minute. Normal breathing is referred to as "eupnoea." Breathing nine times or less a minute should be considered as a sign of possible controlled breathing, and six or less breaths a minute is considered by the American Red Cross to be "distressed respiration" and should definitely be classified as deliberately distorted breathing. Stoppage of breathing is referred to as "apnea."

In analyzing the pneumo, the primary question to ask is where does the examinee get less air? There are basically three ways for this to occur: apnea or stoppage of breathing, suppression or breathing less air than normal, and a slowdown in breathing where a person is actually breathing fewer cycles a minute. Pneumo reactions are also created by changes in the I/E ratio (time of inhalation vs. exhalation as reported by Benussi). These are considered the primary reactions that take place in the pneumo. The only other reaction supported by research is a baseline arousal, which is considered a secondary type reaction.

Apnea can occur in three areas of the breathing cycle. Lower baseline apnea is also referred to as blocking (Figure 9.3). Upper baseline apnea (Figure 9.4) is often referred to as "holding," because it is associated with a deliberate stoppage of breathing rather than a natural stoppage. This would be a great concern to an examiner strongly indicating deliberate distortions if it only appeared in comparison questions.

Median apnea is where there is a stoppage of breathing in the cycle that does not occur at the top or bottom of the breath, but at some point during the inhalation or exhalation period (Figure 9.5).

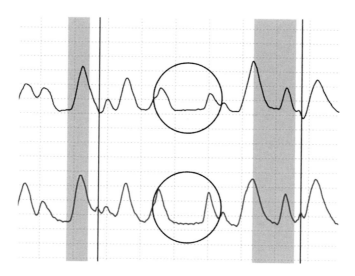

Figure 9.3 Lower baseline apnea.

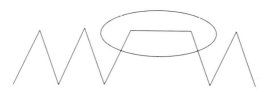

Figure 9.4 Upper baseline apnea.

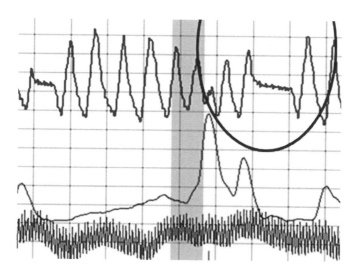

Figure 9.5 Median apnea.

Suppression is where a person breathes in less air in each cycle and can occur in a single cycle, double cycle, or three or more cycles, referred to as sustained suppression (Figure 9.6). Obviously, the greater the suppression, the greater the pneumo reaction.

A slowdown of respiration or an I/E ratio change is also indicative of a reaction (Figure 9.7).

A secondary reaction in the pneumo is a baseline arousal. This is where at least three baseline cycles of the pneumo have been elevated.

With computerized systems, the easiest way to determine where an examinee has breathed less air is by using "respiration line length" (RLL). RLL refers to the linear measurement of a waveform over a specified period of time. Timm and Kircher were early researchers of RLL (1982). Both used consistent preset time windows for all questions being analyzed. RLL identifies all response criteria in the pneumo already described, with the exception of baseline arousal.

The shorter RLL measurement indicates less air and therefore the greater reaction. In the example in Figure 9.8, the line measurements for P2 and P1

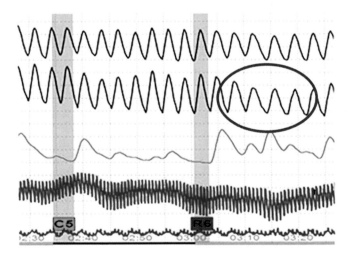

Figure 9.6 Sustained suppression.

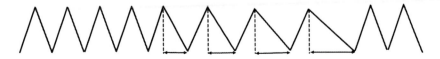

Figure 9.7 Slowdown of respiration. (From Matte, J.A., *Forensic Psychophysiology Using the Polygraph*, J.A.M. Publications, Williamsville, NY, 1996.)

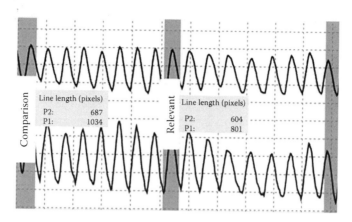

Figure 9.8 Respiration line length.

in the comparison question are larger than those in the relevant question. Therefore, the relevant question represents a shorter line and has less air, constituting a stronger reaction.

Obviously, when using the RLL, you must use a "default time window," or "window of evaluation," which is constant. This window can be determined based on the length of time it takes the examinee to usually respond to a question and for that response to end. Krapohl and Shaw state that another way to look at RLL is to have the computerized software represent it as a continuous line rather than just a number that is displayed on the screen.[1]

They also point out that a more recent concept of analyzing respiration is "respiration excursion[1] (RE)." RE would display respiratory suppression, slowing of respiration, and baseline arousal by measuring the sum of excursions, basically the heights of the pneumos, over a specific period of time. Like the RLL, the RE reflects greater reactions when the numbers generated are less. There is not enough research on RE at this time for it to replace the current methods for respiration analysis; however, it may produce data that can assist examiners in their evaluation of chart analysis.

Electrodermal Response

The electrodermal response (EDR) is also referred to as electrodermal activity (EDA) or can be referred to as the exact mechanism used to monitor it: galvanic skin response (GSR) or galvanic skin resistance (GSR).

All living humans give off an electrical current. The instrument's electrodermal component introduces a very low electrical current (5 μA of electricity) to the examinee, far below the threshold of feeling, and then monitors how the body's current resists the incoming current from the instrument or the speed at which it conducts it.

The monitoring of the resistance of an unknown current by introducing a known current reflecting galvanic skin resistance (GSR) is called a "Wheatstone bridge." GSC, on the other hand, measures the speed the current from the instrument travels from one point on the skin to another point.

EDA appears to have both a mental and physical component to it. The more mental stimulation that occurs for the examinee, the greater the sweat gland activity, and the more sweat gland activity, the greater the reaction.

The EDR is the only component monitored by the polygraph that does not have any parasympathetic control over it. EDR is purely due to sympathetic enervation. The EDR has both a fast changing component to it and a slow changing component. The former, galvanic skin reaction, creates quick upward excursions indicating that the examinee's resistance has decreased, or conductance has increased. The latter is called basil or nominal resistance and slowly changes the baseline of the tracing. Therefore, the component can be operated in a manual mode, which allows for the monitoring of both features (Figure 9.9), and an automatic mode, which cancels the basil or nominal feature and creates a stable baseline for galvanic skin resistance or conductance (Figure 9.10).

In a test such as a peak of tension test, where global evaluations are going to be made, and you are looking for overall changes throughout the entire chart, the slow changing baseline reflecting basil/nominal resistance can be important. For most examinations, however, which are comparison question tests, the automatic mode is more than adequate and much easier to use since it does not require constant centering by the examiner during the test.

The primary reaction in the EDR is the upward movement or height of the tracing. Some scoring systems consider the duration and/or complexity

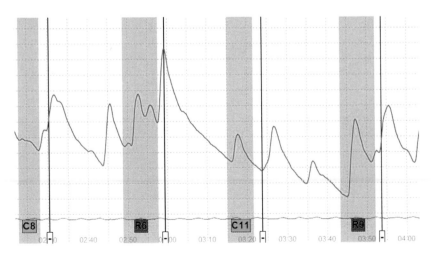

Figure 9.9 Electrodermal activity manual mode.

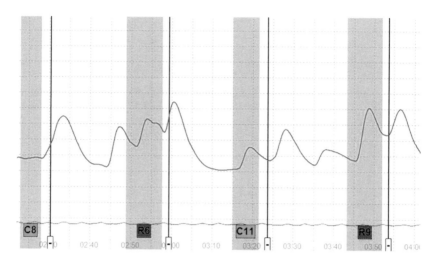

Figure 9.10 Electrodermal activity auto mode.

of the reaction as a secondary reaction. However, height is the primary reaction and cannot be considered to be less of a reaction regardless of the duration or complexity when it clearly is greater (Figures 9.11 and 9.12).

The ROW for the EDR is from the beginning of the question to onset of answer; however, some examiners will accept reactions that begin up to 5 seconds past the answer. Since they are consistently late in both the comparison and relevant questions. Since the EDR has a strong mental component to it, reactions that are delayed could indicate an attempt at mental countermeasures. Therefore, we would only accept delayed reactions in this parameter if they were consistent and existed in both the relevant and comparison zones.

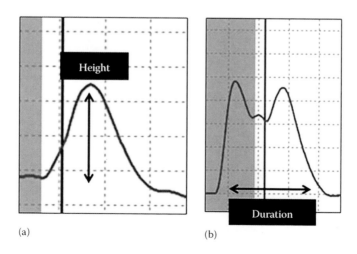

(a)   (b)

Figure 9.11 (a, b) Electrodermal response height versus duration/complexity.

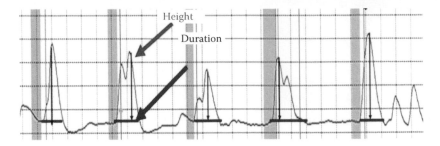

Figure 9.12 Electrodermal activity. EDA—primary reaction is determined from the vertical height, with a secondary consideration given to duration or complexity of the reaction. Complexity never takes precedent over height.

Some examiners also maintain that if the EDR reaction goes up and comes at least one-half ways back down, any secondary reaction after that should not be considered (Figure 9.13).

In either case, consistency in how you are analyzing the EDR is the most important factor. Backster established a ratio for EDR in his scoring system that will be discussed later in this chapter.

All EDRs will be reflected as an upward movement of the tracing from the prestimulus tonic level (baseline). Any sudden downward movement of the electrodermal tracing that is not associated with recovery to the prereaction baseline cannot be considered as part of the criteria since it is not associated with any known physiological response. These downward plunging movements are usually caused by a change of pressure on the finger plates

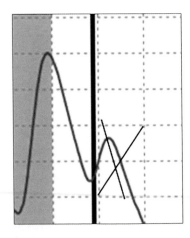

Figure 9.13 If the electrodermal response reaction goes up and comes at least one-half ways back down, any secondary reaction after that should not be considered.

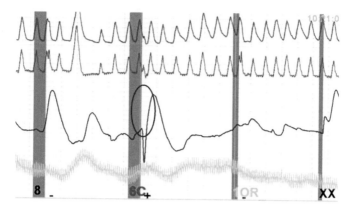

Figure 9.14 Devil's finger.

or loss of contact. For years, it was misconstrued as a reaction and titled the devil's finger (Figure 9.14).

Cardio

Cardiovascular activity is monitored using a standard blood pressure cuff (Figure 9.15) usually placed over the brachial artery on the upper arm. With an electronic or computerized instrument I prefer to use a cuff with a pressure of 70 mmHg. A normal resting heart rate for adults ranges from 60 to 100 beats a minute. Generally, a lower resting heart rate implies a more efficient heart function and better cardiovascular fitness.

For example, a well-trained athlete might have a normal resting heart rate closer to 40 beats a minute. As a general rule, there will be four heartbeats for each breath taken.

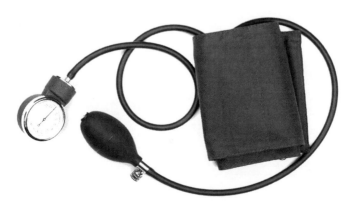

Figure 9.15 A standard blood pressure cuff.

The primary reaction in the cardio is the rise of the bottom of the tracing from the beginning of the question (Figure 9.16). This rise is currently described as an increase in mean blood pressure, although at times it has been described as an increase in blood volume. Perhaps, it is a combination of both. Secondary considerations are the duration of the blood pressure/volume increase and a decrease of the pulse rate (Figure 9.17).

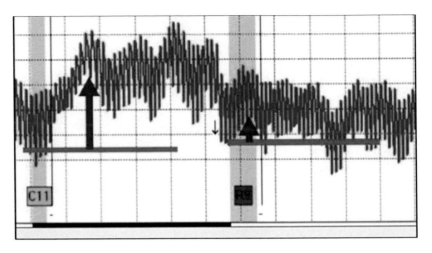

Figure 9.16 The primary reaction in the cardio is the rise of the bottom of the tracing from the beginning of the question. Primary reaction is determined by blood pressure/volume increases.

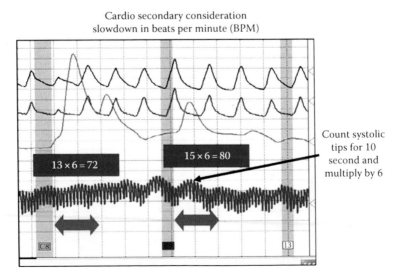

Figure 9.17 Secondary considerations are the duration of the blood pressure/volume increase and a decrease of the pulse rate.

There are several scoring systems used to interpret polygraph data. Backster introduced the traditional 7-point scale in the 1960s, which he described as a subjective system that allowed for the analysis of data in an objective direction by quantifying the chart data. Using the comparison question to compare to the reaction in the relevant question, a number is assigned to each component (pneumo, EDR, and cardio) of the relevant question ranging from a +3 to a −3.

If there is a slight difference between the two, a 1 is assigned. If there was a greater reaction to the comparison question than the relevant question, the relevant question would receive a +1. If the reactions to the relevant question were slightly greater than the reactions to the comparison question, the relevant question would receive a −1. As you can see, the comparison question does not receive a score, we use it to assign a positive or negative number to the relevant question we are analyzing. Clear differences between the two would result in a score a + or −2, and a huge reaction compared to a lack of reaction, with proper spacing and no distortions would result in a score of a + or −3.

In the example in Figure 9.13, there was clearly less air in the comparison pneumo, so the pneumo in the relevant question would receive a +2. The same is true for the EDR, resulting in another +2. There was a slightly greater reaction in the relevant question's cardio, so it received a −1. The score for this relevant question would therefore be a total of a +3 (+2 +2 −1 = +3).

There are three major scoring systems employing Backster's 7-point scale: the original Backster scoring system, the Federal scoring system, and the Utah scoring system. In recent times, what constitute the reaction within each of these systems has become very similar; the selection of comparison questions and the meaning of the scores, however, vary drastically.

Using Backster's original scoring system, the comparison question on either side of the relevant question with the least amount of reaction is used for scoring (unless there was a lack of reaction to the relevant question while there was a presence of reaction to the comparison question, which would then lead to its selection), thus leaning the scores toward a minus or deceptive outcome.

The Federal scoring system selects the comparison question on either side of the relevant question that has the greatest reaction, thus leaning their scores toward a positive or truthful outcome.

The Utah system compares the relevant question to the comparison question that preceded it and rotates the relevant questions in each chart, so that after three charts, the score for any relevant question is how it compared to each of the comparison questions once. Therefore, they do not lean their scores toward truth or deception. Let's look at how these variations in comparison question selection could affect the score outcome.

In the Backster scoring system, the relevant question is compared to the comparison question on either side that is weakest resulting in (Figure 9.18) scores of

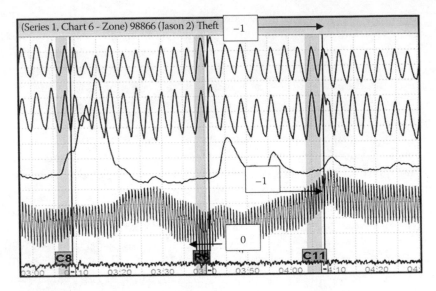

Figure 9.18 Backster scoring system. The direction of the arrow indicates the comparison reaction selected for scoring.

Pneumo compared to C11 = −1
EDR compared to C11 = −1
Cardio compared to C8 = 0
TOTAL SCORE = −2

In the federal scoring system, the relevant question is compared to the comparison question on either side that is strongest (Figure 9.19), resulting in scores of

Pneumo compared to C8 = +2
EDR compared to C8 = +2
Cardio compared to C11 = +1
TOTAL SCORE = +5

In the Utah scoring system, the relevant question is compared to the comparison question that precedes it (Figure 9.20), resulting in scores of

Pneumo compared to C8 = +2
EDR compared to C8 = +2
Cardio compared to C8 = 0
TOTAL SCORE = +4

In addition to differences created by the selection of the comparison question used for generating the score of the relevant question, the meaning of the scores differs between the systems.

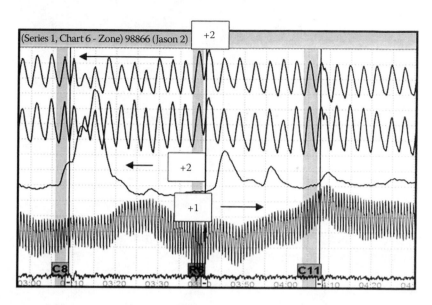

Figure 9.19 Federal scoring system. The direction of the arrow indicates the comparison reaction selected for scoring.

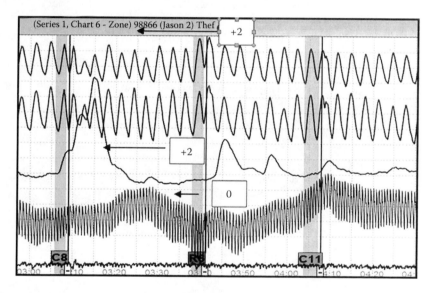

Figure 9.20 Utah scoring system. The direction of the arrow indicates the comparison reaction selected for scoring.

Scores can be looked at as individual question or spot scores in multi-issue or multifaceted tests (also referred to as cut scores), or all the scores can be combined for a total test score if the test is a single issue.

With the Backster scoring system, the score required for a deceptive decision is much more than that needed for a truthful decision. So while

Backster leans his scores toward deception, his interpretation of its meaning leans toward the truth. He seeks balance for what he does in creating his scores toward a negative number with how he interprets the score. The more charts administered, the greater the score required to make a decision (see Tables 9.1 and 9.2).

With the Federal scoring system, which leans their scores toward a truthful or positive outcome, they seek balance after the fact by making it very difficult to have a truthful outcome. Regardless of the number of questions or number of charts in a single or multifaceted test they require a +6 or higher for a truthful determination or a −6 or lower for a deceptive determination. However, every question/spot must have a positive number or the decision is inconclusive. If any question/spot is a −3 or lower, the determination is deceptive for all test questions. Let's see what that means in Table 9.3.

With the Utah scoring system, a total score of a +6 or higher results in a truthful determination, and a score of −6 or lower a deceptive determination, regardless of the number of charts administered, three or five.

In both the Federal and Utah scoring systems, spot scores in multi-issue examinations require a +3 or higher for a determination of "no significant reactions" and scores of a −3 or lower to indicate a "significant reaction."

A 3-point scoring system was developed by the U.S. Army's quality control unit for field examiners by Robert Brisintine, Jr., to allow the field

Table 9.1 Three Relevant Question Scores for a Single Issue Test using Backster Scoring

	Truth	Deception
2 charts	+7 or higher for NDI	−13 or lower for DI
3 charts	+10 or higher for NDI	−19 or lower for DI
4 charts	+13 or higher for NDI	−25 or lower for DI

Table 9.2 Question/SPOT Scores

	Truth	Deception
2 charts	+3	−5
3 charts	+4	−7
4 charts	+5	−9

Table 9.3 Scoring with the Federal Scoring System

	R1	R2	R3	Total Score	Determination
Spot scores	+2	+3	+1	+6	Truthful
Spot scores	+4	+3	0	+7	Inconclusive (All SPOTS are not positive)
Spot scores	+6	+5	−3	+8	Deceptive to all questions (−3 at R3)

examiner to quickly score their charts, which were then submitted for quality control by examiners using the 7-point scoring system.

With the 3-point system, scores are given using only a +1, 0, or −1 for each
component, which resulted in less deviation between examiners scoring the
same charts, however also resulted in a much higher inconclusive rate than
is generated with the 7-point scoring system as was shown in Figure 9.17. The
same decision rules as used in the 7-point system are still used: question/spot
scores of a + or −3 and total scores of a + or −6.

The Federal scoring system also utilizes the Senter two-stage scoring rule
to reduce inconclusive in single-issue tests. This allows for the use of the individual total question scores to achieve a final conclusion when the grand total
score is not significant enough for a determination.

Horizontal Scoring System

The horizontal scoring system[2] (HSS) was introduced by me and Philip M.
Cochetti in 1987 with the aim of reducing the level of subjectivity in the
manual scoring of polygraph examinations conducted using a comparison
question technique. Rather than assigning subjective scores based on an
examiner's eye and experience using a 7- or 3-point scoring scale to identify differences in reaction intensity between question pairings, Cochetti and
I suggested that a ranking strategy across an entire chart for each component
would afford a more objective assessment of the data.

The idea of approaching chart analysis from a ranking perspective as
pointed out by Donald Krapohl in one of the research studies on the HSS
is not new.[3] Lykken proposed an abbreviated ranking system to score his
guilty knowledge test as early as 1959. The Japanese also experimented with
ranking systems for the electrodermal channel (Suzuki, Watanabe, Ohnishi,
Matsuno, and Arasuna, 1973; Suzuki, Ohnishi, Matsuno, Arasuna, 1974) and
Timm (1982) applied a ranking system to RLL. With the HSS, we expanded
ranking to all of the polygraph channels.

In our original (1987) article, we did not identify how features were ranked
from greatest to least reaction. Since that time the HSS has used measurements
of specific features I introduced to further ensure objectivity in the assignment
of numbers used to rank the degree of reactions in each of the tracings as the
Academy's Algorithm for Manual Scoring. The features used in the HSS are

Respiration: Two possible methods: Computerized (1) and Manual (2)
  1. Respiration line length (Timm, 1982) for 20 seconds.
  2. The sum of heights of four respiration cycles squared divided
     into the duration of the four cycles. The formula is $D/H_1 + H_2 + H_3 + H_4$).[1]

Electrodermal: Amplitude squared times the duration. The formula is $(A)^1 \times D$.

Cardiovascular: Amplitude measured by the increase of blood pressure/ volume as shown by the change of the bottom of the tracing from beginning of question to its highest rise within 50 mm (where 1 second = 2.54 mm).

Notes:

A is the amplitude of the response in millimeters.

D is the duration of the response in millimeters (1 second – 2.54 mm).

H is the height of the response in millimeters.

Each question (relevant and comparison) in an individual channel (pneumographs 1 and 2, GSR, cardiograph) is ranked individually greatest to least, with the reaction with the greatest magnitude within each channel receiving the highest rank. To ensure that the pneumo component was not responsible for greater input than the other two components, the rank score for pneumographs 1 and 2 is then averaged and added to the GSR and cardiograph rank score for each question's score.

In a typical zone comparison technique (ZCT), there may be three comparison and three relevant questions, for a total of six questions to be ranked. In this example, the largest reaction in each channel would receive a "6," the second largest a "5" and so forth to a "1" being assigned to the smallest reaction. The sign (+ or –) assigned to the rank depends upon the type of question: the ranks of relevant questions are given a negative sign, while a positive sign is for ranks to comparison questions. The ranks for the channels are then totaled by question, by chart, and for the entire examination.

While doing an American Polygraph Association accreditation certification at the Academy for Scientific Investigative Training, the inspector, Larry Driscoll, asked if there was anything we had developed that he could use for a dissertation in his graduate course. All of our information on horizontal scoring was given to him. After reviewing it he asked permission to a validation study on it, and stated that Dr. Charles Honts wanted to join him in the endeavor. The study was approved and they published their research on horizontal scoring under the name rank order scoring system.[4]

In their research they reported that the new scoring system was just as accurate as traditional 7-point scoring; however, it was much easier to explain. They found that a three relevant question test, analyzing three charts, would have scientific accuracy approaching 90% when decisions of truth or deception were made for total scores of a +13 (or higher) or –13 (or lower), respectively.

Using their research supporting a + or –13 when nine relevant questions (three relevant questions per chart and three charts of data) were totaled we traditionally used decision cutoffs for spot analysis at ±4.5 for three charts, and ±6 for four charts. For single-issue examinations using three relevant questions we maintained their findings of a total score requirement of a +13 or higher for truth and a −13 or lower for deception.

Based on recent research[5,6] we have found that by lowering scores for truthful determinations while maintaining the traditional scores for deceptive decisions we were able to further increase the accuracy to 90% or above.

In 2013, I received an abstract from Raymond Nelson on an unpublished study by him and Mark Handler, entitled *Bootstrap Study of Criterion Validity Using Rank Order Scoring with Field Examinations: An Extension with Normative Data and Statistical Confidence Interval.* The data they used were from the 2008 Krapohl, Gordon, and Lombardi study on horizontal scoring, but they elected to use what Nelson terms a more scientific name of rank order scoring in their title. Their unpublished paper concluded that the HSS was above 90% accurate, with less than a 20% inconclusive rate on the sample used of 100 field Federal ZCT tests of a multifaceted nature (Tables 9.4 and 9.5).

The HSS ranking of a four-question test (two comparison and two relevant questions) is shown in Figure 9.21.

In a traditional test consisting of three comparison and three relevant questions, each component is ranked from 6, representing the greatest reaction to 1, representing the least reaction. In cases where reactions are equal to each other, they will receive the average score of the ranks they are competing for. As shown in Figure 9.22, R12 was the greatest reaction and received the rank of 6, C5 received the rank of 5, C8 and R12 were about the same degree of reaction. They are competing for the ranks of 3 and 4, so they will each receive the average of those positions: 3.5.

Table 9.4   Scores Required for a Three-Relevant-Question Single-Issue Test

	Truth	Deception
3 charts	+2.25 or higher	−13 or lower
4 charts	+3 or higher	−18 or lower

Table 9.5   Question/Spot Scores

	Truth	Deception
3 charts	+0.75	−4.5
4 charts	+1	−6

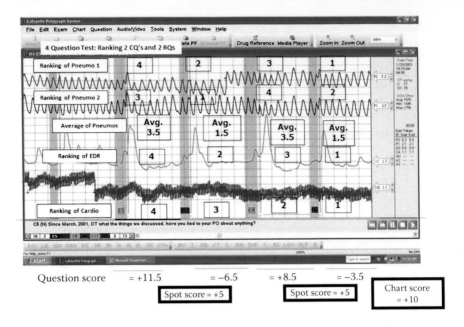

Figure score   = +11.5   = −6.5   = +8.5   = −3.5

Spot score = +5   Spot score = +5

Chart score = +10

Figure 9.21 Horizontal scoring system ranking of a four-question test.

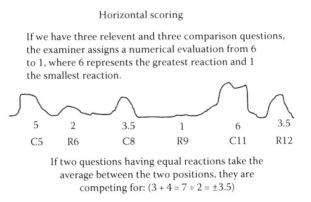

Horizontal scoring

If we have three relevent and three comparison questions, the examiner assigns a numerical evaluation from 6 to 1, where 6 represents the greatest reaction and 1 the smallest reaction.

5   2   3.5   1   6   3.5
C5   R6   C8   R9   C11   R12

If two questions having equal reactions take the average between the two positions, they are competing for: $(3 + 4 = 7 \div 2 = \pm 3.5)$

Figure 9.22 A traditional test consisting of three comparison and three relevant questions.

The IISS allows for every comparison and relevant question to receive a numerical score depicting the degree of each question's reaction. It allows for objective scoring of any type of test: single issue, multi-issue, multifaceted, and peak of tension. It is the only scoring technique that can also be applied to multi-issue screening tests by making comparisons between the comparison and relevant test questions, as well as between each of the relevant test questions, thus giving a CQ–RQ determination, as well as an RQ–RQ determination.

Empirical Scoring System

ESS[7] uses a three-position-weighted scoring system, where the pneumo and cardio are scored +1, 0, −1, and the EDA +2, 0, −2. It also uses a bigger is better philosophy where scores are given regardless of the magnitude of difference in response (i.e., if you can see the difference in the EDA, even though it is slight, it receives a ± 2).

ESS uses the following decision rules[8]:

ZCT (all formats)
- Grand total ≥ +2 = NDI ($a < 0.1$)
- Grand total ≤ −4 = DI ($a < 0.05$)
- Any subtotal ≤ −7 DI (Bonferroni < 0.017)

You-phase (BiZone)
- Grand total ≥ +2 = NDI ($a < 0.1$)
- Grand total ≤ −4 = DI ($a < 0.05$)
- Any subtotal ≤ −6 DI (Bonferroni < 0.025)

Multi-issue screening exams and multifacet investigative/diagnostic exams with 2–4 RQs (MGQT or DLST):
- ANY subtotal ≤ −3 = SR ($a < 0.05$)
- ALL subtotals ≥ +1 = NSR ($a < 0.1$)

(The cut scores remain the same regardless if three, four, or five charts were administered.)

ESS makes the presumption that all examinees are good EDA reactors, that all instruments have good EDA systems, and that the EDA is much more important and more accurate in detecting truth and deception than the other two parameters.

Imagine scoring a spot using a 7-point system where there is a strong presence of reaction in the relevant question's pneumo and cardio resulting in scores of a −2 and −2. The EDA reaction is slightly greater in the comparison question resulting in a score of 0. The spot score total is a −4. It is a single-issue test with similar scores in all three of the relevant questions, resulting in a chart score of −12, and a three chart test score of a −36. This is a very significant score, which is indicative of deception. Using ESS for the same spot would have resulted in a −1 pneumo, a +2 EDA, and a −1 cardio for a total spot score of "0." A three-relevant question, of a three-chart test of similar reactions would result in a "0," as compared to the traditional 7-point scale of a −36. That is very problematic.

Conclusion

There is no part of a polygraph examination that is unimportant. There must be an effective pretest interview, questions that were properly formulated and introduced, and the collection of quality tracings. However, this is all meaningless without an understanding of the polygraph language and the examiner's ability to interpret what they have collected.

While computerized systems offer algorithms to analyze data, it is important that the examiner use these systems as "quality control" for their own manual scoring decisions. Computerized algorithms work best on single-issue examinations, and worst with multi-issue or multi-faceted examinations requiring "spot" decisions.

Notes

1. Krapohl, D. and Shaw, P. (2015) The continuous display of respiration excursion. *APA Magazine*, 48(4), 95–104.
2. Gordon, N. and Cochetti, P. (1987) The horizontal scoring system. *Polygraph*, 16(2), 118–125.
3. Krapohl, D., Gordon, N., and Lombardi, C. (2008) Accuracy demonstration of the horizontal scoring system using field cases conducted with the federal zone comparison technique. *Polygraph*, 37(4).
4. Driscoll, L. and Honts, C. (1987) An evaluation of the reliability and validity of rank order and standard numerical scoring of polygraph charts. *Polygraph*, 16(4), 241–257.
5. Krapohl, D., Dutton, D., and Ryan, A. (2001) The rank order scoring system: Replication and extension with filed data. *Polygraph*, 30(3), 172–181.
6. Krapohl, D., Gordon, N., and Lombardi, C. (2008) Accuracy demonstration of the horizontal scoring system using field cases conducted with the federal zone comparison technique. *Polygraph*, 37(4), 263–268.
7. Nelson, R. et al. (2011) Using the empirical scoring system. *Polygraph*, 40(2), 67–78.
8. Grand total scores are the scores of all spots combined, or total test scores. Sub-total or cut scores are total spot (individual question) scores.

Report Writing

10

Fast is fine, but accuracy is everything.

—Wyatt Earp

There are various styles and methods to writing a report. Your report should conform to the standards of your company or agency. Having reports written in varying styles by different examiners to the same client or requestor can appear very disorganized and unprofessional.

Your report will reflect your ability and professionalism as a polygraph examiner. Be aware of the overall appearance of your report as well as your use of grammar and spelling. You want the reader of your report to understand the case as well as possible.

Many examiners will utilize the computerized instrument's report template that automatically inserts information from the polygraph file, as shown in the final report template in the Lafayette Instrument in Figure 10.1.

The Limestone Technologies' computerized system also allows the examiner to create a report using a series of optional "insert tabs" under the information headings of Personal, Medical, Polygraph, Police/Military, and Other and also allows for the creation of an invoice. This allows the examiner to easily customize the report with the exact information they want to include.

Reports should be marked "confidential" and private examiners testing for defense attorneys should have the file and report marked "Privileged and Confidential Attorney—Client Communication and/or Attorney Work Product."

The major areas of a report dealing with a specific issue examination should begin with a heading. The heading of your report should indicate the date of the report, the client's name and address, and a file number.

The examinee should be properly identified, which may include the method used for identification. Many examiners will include a picture of the examinee.

The beginning of the report should clearly indicate what the examination focuses on, often referred to as the "target issue." A statement indicating the examinee's voluntariness of the examination and the examinee's general mental and physical conditions and ability to be examined should be included. You should not be rendering any type of official psychological or physiological diagnosis unless you have the educational degree to make such a distinction. We also include a statement that the examinee knew they could stop the test and leave at any time they desired and that they remained and

Lafayette Instrument Company

Polygraph Examination Report

Personal Information

Name: <<Name>>
Date of Birth: <<DateOfBirth>>   Age: <<Age>>
Social Security: <<SSN>>
Driver' License: <<DriversLicenseNumber>>
Address: <<AddressStreet>> <<AddressApt>>
                               <<AddressCity>> <<AddressState>> <<PostalCode>>

Exam Information

Exam Location: <<Series1_$_Location>>
Exam Date: <<Series1_$_StartDate>>
Case #:   <<CaseNumber>>
Examiner: <<Examiner Name>>
Final Call: <<Series2_$_FinalCall>>

Section 1: Purpose of Examination

The main issue under consideration for the polygraph examination was whether or not the examinee was telling the truth to the pertinent questions listed under Section 3 of this report.

Section 2: Pre-Test Interview

On <<Series1_$_StartDate>>, <<Name>> arrived and voluntarily submitted to a polygraph examination. The following forms were read, completed, and voluntarily signed by the examinee:

• Polygraph Consent Form
• Polygraph Waiver Form

During the pre-test interview, <<Name>> read the forms and said he/she understood the forms and signed them agreeing to the test and waiving the rights set forth in the documents. The examiner was fully advised that the entire examination would be recorded using both audio and video. In the opinion of the examiner, <<Name>> was suitable for polygraph testing.
At the conclusion of the pre-test phase of the polygraph examination, the examiner discussed and thoroughly reviewed all the test questions with the examinee. The purpose of this detailed review is to provide the examinee an opportunity to ensure they completely understand the questions before the onset of the testing phase of the examination.

Section 3: In-Test Phase

A Lafayette computerized polygraph system, model LX4000 was used for the collection of polygraph tests (test data). This instrument makes a continuous recording of autonomic responses associated with respiration, electrodermal activity, and cardiovascular functioning. The instrument also includes sensors designed to record peripheral behavior activity and cooperation during the examination. A functionality check prior to the examination confirmed the instrument was in proper working order.
The following pertinent questions were asked during the polygraph examination.

• << Relevant Questions >>

Figure 10.1 A sample computerized instrument's report template.

(*Continued*)

Section 4: Result

It is the opinion of this examiner <<Name>> **was/was** not being truthful during testing. Global analysis of the physiological data revealed that it was of sufficient interpretable quality to complete a standardized numerical analysis of the test results. Analysis was performed using the following techniques:

Technique	Result
Empirical Scoring System	**No Deception Indicated**
OSS3	**No Deception Indicated**

Empirical Scoring System

Analysis of the polygraph tests using the Empirical Scoring System resulted in statistically significant numerical scores that support a conclusion of "**no deception indicated**" when <<Name>> was answering the above listed questions. The statistical probability that <<Name>>'s pattern of data were produced by a person belong to a deceptive distribution is less than one chance in a hundred (p-value < .01) when compared to a validation sample used to produce the normative data and considered representative of the general testing population. In other words, the likelihood that <<Name>>'s response was produced by someone lying was less than 1%.

OSS3

Analysis of <<Name>>'s test data using a computerized statistical algorithm, the Objective Scoring System, version 3, resulted in statistically significant scores indicative of **no deception** to the investigation target questions. The statistical probability that <<Name>>'s test data were produced by a deceptive person was less than 1/10th of 1 percent (p-value <.001) or about 1 chance in 1000.

Section 5: Post-Test Interview

During the post-test phase of the exam, <<Name>> was informed of the test results.

Note: The polygraph tests and allied documentation are maintained for a period of six months from the date of examination.

<<Examiner Name>>
Polygraph Examiner

Figure 10.1 (*Continued*) A sample computerized instrument's report template. (Courtesy of Lafayette Instrument Company, Lafayette, IN, www.lafayettepolygraph.com.)

completed the examination of their own free will and were treated in a fair and professional manner. Please see Figure 10.2 as an example.

Your report should indicate the test format(s) utilized, the type of examination performed, the relevant test question formulation, and the examinee's response and determinations. Test questions that do not deal with the matter under investigation, as well as unrelated information ascertained, should not be included in the report.

Polygraph determinations are based on the type of test being administered. If the examination is based on a "single issue," lying to one of the relevant questions means they are lying to all of them (same question content rephrased, such as "Did you_____?" "Regarding _____, did you_____?" "Last week, did you _____?"); our determinations will be *truthful, deceptive, inconclusive, or no opinion.*

Date of Report

Client's Name

Clients Address   *RE: File No. _____*

Dear Client's Name:

At your request we conducted a Psychophysiological Truth Verification examination on EXAMINEE'S NAME today (or on _____), concerning his/her truthfulness about <u>issue to be resolved</u>. It was determined that the examinee was physically and mentally able to submit to a polygraph examination.

Prior to the examinations the examinee signed a consent form assuring all concerned he/she was aware of his/her rights regarding the polygraph, and was taking the examinations voluntarily. He/she also signed an "Agreement of Cooperation," which stated that he/she understood the procedure required his/her full cooperation, and that only a deceptive examinee would deliberately attempt to distort the data. He/she further agreed that if he/she deliberately distorted the data the examinations conclusion would be deception. At the conclusion of the examinations he/she again signed a form assuring all concerned that he/she was well treated, and remained of his/her own free will, knowing he/she could stop the procedure and leave at any time he/she desired.

(The report should include the pre-test interview. Again, this portion will depend on what has been established at your agency or place of employment. In our office our pre-test interview is based on a Forensic Assessment)

Q: Where do you work?

A:

Q: Finish this sentence for me, this interview and polygraph examination is about?

A:

Q: Why does _____ want you to take the examination?

A:

Q: How do you feel about taking the examination?

A:

Q: Tell me in detail what your case was about and how you would explain it.

A:

Q: What are the five most important factors that created this problem?

A:

Q: Did you <u>commit the act/crime</u>?

A:

Q: If someone did do something like this, what do you think should happen to them?

A:

Q: If it was their first offense do you think they should get a second chance?

A:

Q: How do you think your polygraph test will come out today?

A:

Q: Would there be any reason evidence would turn up indicating you did do this?

A:

Q: If you had three questions to ask yourself in this test to resolve this problem, what would they be?

A:

Figure 10.2 A report sample when dealing with a specific issue. Such reports should begin with a heading that indicates the date of the report, the client's name and address, and a file number.

Truthful determinations are made where the analysis meets the numerical criteria required by the scoring system being employed to make that decision. For example, in the Utah scoring systems, total scores of a +6 or higher indicate this decision. *Deceptive* determinations are made where the analysis meets the numerical criteria required by the scoring system being employed to make that decision. For example, in the Utah scoring systems, total scores of a −6 or lower indicate this decision. Any scores in between these necessary scores, for example, a +5 to a −5, in the Utah scoring system indicate an inconclusive determination. This means the data scores did not reflect a number sufficient to make a reliable determination. The test scores may reflect numbers sufficient for a definite determination, and yet outside factors, for example, excessive movements, may indicate to the examiner that a definite decision should not be rendered and the decision will be *no opinion*.

In cases where a truthful outcome may be difficult to obtain, even if the examinee is truthful, an examiner may elect to render a *no opinion* decision even though the scores indicate deception. For example, testing a victim is a very difficult test. In some states, testing a rape victim is not allowed. In some, victims can only be tested if the accused is tested first and the outcome indicates they were truthful.

Normally, a guilty suspect has memory of the crime they committed, and an innocent person does not. With a victim, however, there is also memory of the crime, even though they are being truthful, which could elicit psychophysiological reactions. A parent who just found their child beaten to death and sexually molested is taken from the crime scene and immediately given a polygraph examination may find it difficult not to find the relevant question extremely salient. In cases, such as these, some examiners will only offer a decision of *truthful, inconclusive, or no opinion*.

If the examination is multifaceted (same crime but varying elements of the crime such as knowledge, commission, planning of the crime) or multi-issue (none of the relevant issues involve each other, such as in a screening test dealing with undetected crime, involvement with illegal drugs, theft, etc.), our determinations will be *no significant reaction, significant reaction, inconclusive reaction, or no opinion*.

This is because of anticlimactic dampening; the greatest threat or most salient questions may dampen an examinee's ability to react to other questions even though they are not being truthful. In these types of cases, a hurdle testing approach is often used, where a significant response to a relevant question will result in a second examination focusing on that question in a more accurate single issue examination.

Polygraph ethics require that the examiner, with few exceptions, give the examinee their test results at the conclusion of the examination. These exceptions include legal examinations where the examiner is instructed by the examinee's attorney not to release the result to his or her client or a test for the court where the examiner is instructed not to release results.

In cases where a test results in a deceptive outcome or significant reactions to relevant test questions, giving the results to the examinee allows him or her to offer an explanation for the reactions or to make admissions confirming the test results. The examination report should include this section of the process, indicating that the examinee was informed of their results and what they had to say concerning the outcome.

Examples are as follows: "The examinee was given his or her test results and stated _____ as an explanation for the test outcome." "At the conclusion of the examination, the examinee was given his or her test results. At this time the examinee admitted _____. He or she wrote and signed the attached statement to that effect." "At the conclusion of the examination, the examinee was given his or her test results. The examinee maintained that he or she was truthful during the pretest interview and concerning the target issue."

Recently examiners also started using the conclusion of purposeful noncooperation (PNC) to describe tests where countermeasures were believed to be employed.

Finally, your report needs a conclusion, which should always indicate that the decision is your professional opinion, for example, "The above results are my professional opinion, based on the reactions to the formulated relevant test questions." Figure 10.3 illustrates a sample report.

Our preemployment/screening reports are slightly different. Rather than the pretest interview consisting of the FAINT interview, we only include pertinent pretest admissions made by the applicant. Keep in mind that there may be laws restricting the type of information that can be reported on or whether the examination can be given.

The Americans with Disabilities Act, for example, restricts the asking or reporting of physical or mental disabilities in preconditional polygraph tests. The Employee Polygraph Protection Act eliminates the use of periodic testing and most private commercial preemployment tests, and places severe restrictions on private investigative examinations.

In certain governmental jobs, the examinee must be made aware of their rights under the Garrity Act, and in criminal cases being conducted by government examiners, the examinee must be read their Miranda warnings if it is a custodial situation.

Examinations cannot contain information concerning sex, religion, race, politics, or union matters unless those are the actual focus of the examination. Typically, in the United States, 7 years of past history is all that is considered relevant when being considered for employment in many areas, such as credit. In private examinations it is considered improper to ascertain information concerning a person's type of military discharge or arrests that did not result in a guilty finding. A sample can be found in Figure 10.4.

SAMPLE REPORT:

November 12, 2015

Detective John Fleisher
Local Police Department
40 Chestnut Street
Philadelphia, PA 19000   **File No.: 11-005-0776**

Dear Detective Fleisher:

   *At you request I conducted a Forensic Psychophysiological Truth Verification Examination today on **MS. JANE DOE**, concerning her involvement in the theft of $600.00, reported missing on November 4th from a co-worker (Kathy) at her assigned location at the Alverez Institute, located at 51 N. Elm Street, Philadelphia Pennsylvania.*

   Prior to the examination it was determined the examinee was mentally and physically capable of taking the examination, The examinee signed a consent form assuring all concerned she was aware of her rights regarding the polygraph, and was taking the examination voluntarily. She also signed an "Agreement of Cooperation," which stated that she understood the procedure required her full cooperation, and that only a deceptive examinee would deliberately attempt to distort the data. She further agreed that if she deliberately distorted the data the examination conclusion would be deception. At the conclusion of the examination she again signed a form assuring all concerned that she was well treated, and remained of her own free will, knowing she could stop the procedure and leave at any time she desired.

PRE-TEST INTERVIEW:

Q: Where do you work?

A: ASIT Records Management.

Q: How long have you worked there?

A: Roughly a year and a half.

Q: What do you do?

A: Medical records scanner. I believe the correct terminology is a MECA Scanner.

Q: How do you like working there?

A: It's a nice job. They're flexible with the hours, which is good since I have a two year old.

Q: Finish this sentence for me, this interview and polygraph examination is about, what?

A: My proving to Kathy herself, and my employer that I didn't steal money from her.

Q: Why were you asked to take this test?

A: Why was I asked? That confuses me. Money was missing from Kathy's purse apparently and I was the only one in the room that worked with her that day

Q: How do you feel about taking the test?

A: I don't feel very good about it being accused. I'm very nervous, but I'd like to clear my name here.

Q: Write in detail what this case is about and how you would explain it.

A: While working in the optomology dept at the hospital doing medical records scanning I was asked to work in a room w/ 2 hospital employees

Figure 10.3 A report with drawn conclusion included.   (Continued)

Kathy& Cindy. I was asked to work in this room because there were not enough working computers/scanners in the room provided for us. ~~On Tues~~ I worked in this room a few days a week for approximately 2 mo. On the morning of Nov 9ᵗʰ Kathy entered the room she told me that myself or anyone else from my company was not permitted to work out of this room from then on. & I asked her why and she told me the orders came from one of the dr s and I would have to ask that dr. I moved to a diff. location in the hospital's record dept when about 1.5 hrs later was found by 2 detectives and asked if I would answer some questions about a theft. This is the first I had heard about this. The detectives explained to me at the station that apparently Kathy had 12 100 dollar bills in her purse and 6 of them were missing on the 4ᵗʰ of NOV. which was a Thurs. When questioned by the detective on the following Tues I did explain I knew nothing about this missing money but apparent I am a suspect since we worked alone in the room that particular day. I was asked to take a poliograph test, which I had no problem w/ as long as my employer agreed. Which he did. So that is why I am here today. (SIC)

Q: If you had been the investigator in this case, how would you have conducted the investigation?

A: I can understand why I was a suspect. I was alone in the room. I didn't know where she kept her pocketbook until the detective told me. Just because I was the only one in the room that day does not mean that I took her money. She has a husband and children.

Q: What are the five most important factors that caused this whole situation?

A: That I was in the room alone with her. That she was missing money.
    Umm.......I'm drawing a blank.

Q: Did you ever think about doing something like this?

A: Taking money? ...No! I been called a lot of things, but never a thief. I would borrow money, never steal it. That's why it's upsetting. Kathy is a nice woman. I wouldn't steal from her.

Q: Did you take that money Kathy reported missing this month?

A: No.

Q: What do you think happened to it?

A: I don't know. It could have been misplaced, and she has a family also. I don't know who she put her personal effects down next to.

Q: When we identify the person who did this, what do you think should happen to them?

A: ....I never gave it a thought.

Q: If it was their first offense, do you think they should get a second chance

A: I don't know if you should get a second chance. Stealing is unacceptable. I don't know how to answer. I work hard for my money. I'd be very angry if someone stole from me.

Q: How do you think your polygraph test will come out today concerning whether or not you took this money?

A: .... I'm pretty sure it will turn out I am telling the truth. I am a nervous person though, I can feel my heart rate is elevated talking to you right now, so I don't know.

Figure 10.3 (Continued) A report with drawn conclusion included. (*Continued*)

Q: *Would there be any reason evidence would turn up indicating you did this*

A: *No.*

Q: *Would you be willing to chip and help pay this money back?*

A: *..On one hand I feel bad for her, on the other hand I didn't take her money so why should I have to pay for it?*

Q: *Why do you think someone would do something like this?*

A: *Desperate. They didn't think about the consequences. How it would feel if it was done to them. No conscience. Don't care if they get caught. Maybe just in their nature.*

Q: *Do you think it was stolen or lost?*

A: *I don't know, could be either, or.*

Q: *If you were the examiner about to do this test, and could ask just three questions to resolve this issue, what would you ask?*

A: *Did I take it? That's the only question that's important.*

POLYGRAPH EVALUATION:

Three charts of data using a single issue Integrated Zone Comparison Test were collected.

QUESTION FORMULATION	RESPONSE:	DETERMINATION:
1. This month, did you take Kathy's missing money?	NO	DECEPTIVE
2. Regarding Kathy's missing money, did you take it?	NO	DECEPTIVE
3. Are you the person that took Kathy's money?	NO	DECEPTIVE

REMARKS:

The Lafayette LX-4000 Computerized Polygraph System was used to collect the data. The data collected was manually scored as well as analyzed by four computerized algorithms.

POST TEST INTERVIEW;

The examinee was given her test results. She denied any involvement and left.

CONCLUSION:

*It is my professional opinion, based on the consistent significant reactions to the formulated relevant test questions, that she was **not truthful** concerning her involvement in the theft in question.*

This examination was conducted by:

_____

Nathan J. Gordon

Figure 10.3 (Continued) A report with drawn conclusion included.

SAMPLE REPORT:

KEYSTONE INTELLIGENCE NETWORK, INC.

1704 Locust Street, Philadelphia, PA 19103

October 31, 2015

Examinee: JAMES BOND   *File No. 15-05-123*

     Today, at approximately 1:00 p.m., the above examinee was given a polygraph examination in connection with his application to become a Police Officer for the City Police Department.
     The examinee signed a consent form assuring all concerned he was aware of his rights regarding the polygraph, and was taking the examination voluntarily. He also signed an "Agreement of Cooperation," which stated that he understood the procedure required his full cooperation, and that only a deceptive examinee would deliberately attempt to distort the data. He further agreed that if he deliberately distorted the data the examination conclusion would be deception. At the conclusion of the examination he again signed a form assuring all concerned that he was well treated, and remained of his own free will, knowing he could stop the procedure and leave at any time he desired.
     The purpose of the polygraph examination was to access the applicant's honesty and integrity as it relates to his suitability to become a police officer for the City Police Department. During a pre-test interview, it was determined that the examinee was physically and mentally able to submit to a polygraph examination.

PERTINENT PRE-TEST ADMISSIONS:

1. *The examinee stated he has had two full time jobs in the past 5 years, and that he has never been fired from a place of employment.*

2. *The examine stated he was late 5 times and absent 2 times in his past year of employment.*

3. *The examinee is in debt for $25,000.00 for an automobile, and $6,000.00 for a student loan.*

4. *The examinee was convicted of Disorderly Conduct in Wilmington, Delaware in 2009.*

5. *The examinee stated he would give food away while employed in High School at the ABC Deli.. He estimates it would amount to $50.00 to $100.00.*

6. *The applicant has been to a Casino once in the past year and lost $25.00 playing slots. He denies any other gambling activities.*

7. *The examinee states he tried marijuana once in 2001, and denies any other personal involvement with illegal drugs.*

POLYGRAPH EVALUATION:

     The examinee was tested regarding the following Relevant Questions, which were asked within three separate charts of an Integrated Zone Comparison Technique (IZCT) structured test using a state of the art computerized polygraph system:

Figure 10.4 Sample report for a government employee.   (Continued)

Relevant Questions:	Response:	Determinations:
Are you deliberately leaving out information you know for sure would eliminate you as a candidate?	No	No Significant Reactions
In the past 3 years, have you had any personal involvement with illegal drugs?	No	No Significant Reaction
As an adult have you committed a serious undetected crime?	No	No Significant Reactions
In the past 3 years, are the total of your thefts more than $200.00?	No	No Significant Reactions

REMARKS:

The data was analyzed manually as well as by two computerized algorithms.

A second polygraph series was then administered utilizing one chart of a Polygraph Validation Technique which verified the initial test results.

CONCLUSION:

The above results are based on our professional opinion regarding the examinee's psychophysiological reactions to the above formulated relevant questions.

This examination was conducted by:

_____

Nathan J. Gordon, Forensic Psychophysiologist

Figure 10.4 (Continued) Sample report for a government employee.

Conclusion

The examiner's report is his or her communication to others as to what took place during the examination and the test results. Our job is to ensure that the reader gets a clear understanding of what happened as if they were present in the room to witness the entire procedure. Clarity and accuracy are of the upmost important. Supervisors and clients will judge your ability and professionalism by the reports you write.

Polygraph and the Law   11

At his best, man is the noblest of all animals; separated from law and justice he is the worst.

—Aristotle

In the practice of law, there is a gap between what we know and what we can prove. Remarkable advancements in medicine, forensics, and technology have helped bridge that gap in several respects. Scientific evidence plays a role in court cases with increasing regularity, oftentimes providing decisive proof of a crucial issue in a matter before the court. The increased use of scientific methods of analyzing and presenting evidence has led to the development of a body of case and statutory law addressing its admissibility in court and its use in the workplace.

Since the development of instrumentation to detect psychophysiological changes in the body when engaging in deception, pioneers in the field have sought to utilize the tool of psychophysiological detection of deception (PDD) in investigative and employment settings. These efforts have met with limited success. Due to the variances in the reliability of polygraph examinations, there have been several landmark cases addressing the admissibility of these tests in court and laws enacted limiting their use by employers.

This chapter will discuss the history of PDD in court and its current status of admissibility in state and federal courts. The law governing employers' use of PDD will be examined, as there are professions and situations that provide for its acceptance. An analysis of the development of the law's regard for polygraph examinations will reveal a slower rate of acceptance than for other disciplines.

In 1923, the U.S. Supreme Court made its first ruling on lie detection, in *Frye v. U.S.*[1] A prominent physician in Washington, DC, was murdered. Reward money was offered for information in the case and an informant named Frye as the perpetrator. The defense hired William Marston to conduct a discontinuous blood pressure test on Frye, and Marston, quoting his 10-year accuracy rate at 95%, concluded that Frye was truthful when he denied murdering the doctor.

The prosecution argued that the discontinuous blood pressure test was not state of the art, since John Larson had developed a two-parameter instrument that measured breathing and continuous changes in cardiovascular activity in 1921.

The court ruled against the admissibility of Marston's test, stating

> Just when a scientific principle or discovery crosses the line between the experimental and demonstrable stages is difficult to define. Somewhere in the twilight zone, the evidential principle must be recognized, and while courts will go a long way in admitting expert testimony deduced from well recognized principle of discovery, the thing from which deduction is made must be sufficiently established to have gained general acceptance in the field which it belongs.
>
> We think the systolic blood pressure deception test has not gained such standing and scientific recognition among physiological and psychological authorities as would justify the courts in admitting expert testimony deduced from the discovery, development, and experiments thus far made.

The *Frye* "general acceptance" standard still keeps polygraph evidence from being admitted in courts in over half of the states in America. Even so, polygraph is relied upon by law enforcement in almost every state to focus investigations and often to obtain admissions from guilty suspects, solving crimes where there is little or no direct evidence.

After numerous cases rejecting the use of polygraph examinations in court, the Eastern District of Michigan adopted a different approach and instead set out specific conditions in order to admit a polygraph examination into evidence. In a 1972 perjury case, *U.S. v. Richard Ridling*, Ridling was charged with perjury and pleaded not guilty. As a part of his defense, he wanted to introduce testimony of one or more polygraph experts who would testify that he had told the truth when he denied perjuring himself. The court ordered a pretrial evidential hearing on the admissibility of the tests and the opinions of the polygraph experts and ruled subject to the conditions stated; the evidence will be admitted at the trial of this case.

The court has heard evidence in this case from persons who are experts in the use of polygraphs to establish the value and reliability of the results of the tests. The evidence includes the following:

1. The basic theory of the polygraph
2. The reliance on the polygraph by government agencies
3. The reliance on the polygraph by private industry
4. The comparative reliability of the polygraph and other scientific evidence such as fingerprint and ballistic evidence
5. The opinions of the experts as to whether polygraph evidence would be a valuable aid in connection with the determination of the issues such as the one facing the court in this case and in the administration of justice

In 1983, the Office of Technology Assessment (OTA) was asked by the U.S. House of Representatives to focus on the nature and application of polygraph tests, scientific controversy over polygraph testing, data from field and simulation studies, and factors that affect test validity. OTA found that the federal government's use of polygraph tests had more than tripled over the previous 10 years, with about 23,000 examinations conducted in 1982. In all federal agencies except the National Security Agency (NSA) and the Central Intelligence Agency (CIA), more than 90% of polygraph testing in 1982 was for criminal investigations. Only NSA and CIA make significant use of the polygraph for personnel security screening—preemployment, preclearance, or periodic examinations—to establish initial and continuing eligibility for access to highly classified information.

OTA concluded that the available research evidence at the time was insufficient to establish the scientific validity of the polygraph test for personnel security screening. OTA found meaningful scientific evidence of polygraph validity only in the area of investigations of specific criminal incidents and that the overall validity of specific issue polygraph examinations was about 82%.

In 1988, after years of strong lobbying by unions, the U.S. federal government passed the Employee Polygraph Protection Act (EPPA). The act basically maintains that polygraph testing does not work unless you have an important industry. If you are the CIA, polygraph works. If you own a convenience store, it does not. If you are the FBI, Secret Service, and NSA, polygraph works. If you have a clothing store or shoe store, it does not.

The act generally prevents employers from using lie detector tests, either for preemployment screening or for periodic testing of employees during the course of employment, with certain exemptions. Employers generally may not require or request any employee or job applicant to take a lie detector test or discharge, discipline, or discriminate against an employee or job applicant for refusing to take a test or for exercising other rights under the act. In addition, employers are required to display the EPPA poster in the workplace for their employees. The Employment Standards Administration's Wage and Hour Division within the U.S. Department of Labor (DOL) enforces the EPPA.

Under EPPA, employers may not use or inquire about the results of a lie detector test or discharge or discriminate against an employee or job applicant on the basis of the results of a test or for filing a complaint for participating in a proceeding under the act.

EPPA does permit preemployment polygraph tests to be administered to certain job applicants of security service firms (armored car, alarm, and guard) and of pharmaceutical manufacturers, distributors, and dispensers.

The act also permits polygraph testing of certain employees of private firms who are reasonably suspected of involvement in a workplace incident (theft, embezzlement, etc.) that resulted in specific economic loss or injury to the employer.

Where polygraph examinations are allowed, they are subject to strict standards for the conduct of the test, including the pretesting, testing, and posttesting phases. An examiner must be licensed and bonded or have professional liability coverage. The act strictly limits the disclosure of information obtained during a polygraph test.

There are specific notices that must be given to examinees. The employer is required to provide the examinee with a statement prior to the test, which fully explains the specific incident or activity being investigated and the basis for testing the particular employee. The statement must contain, at a minimum, the following information:

- An identification with particulars on the specific economic loss or injury to the business of the employer; a description of the employee's access to the property that is the subject of the investigation
- A detailed description of the basis of the employer's reasonable suspicion that the employee was involved in the incident or activity under investigation
- The signature of a person (other than the polygraph examiner) authorized to legally bind the employer

Every employer who requests an employee or prospective employee to submit to a polygraph examination, pursuant to the ongoing investigation, drug manufacturer, or security services EPPA exemptions must provide

- Reasonable written notice of the date, time, and place of the examination and the examinee's right to consult with legal counsel or an employee representative before each phase of the test
- Written notice of the nature and characteristics of the polygraph instrument and examination
- Extensive written notice explaining the examinee's rights, including a list of prohibited questions and topics, the examinee's right to terminate the examination, and the examinee's right to file a complaint with the DOL alleging violations of EPPA

Employers must also provide written notice to the examiner identifying the persons to be examined. EPPA also has recordkeeping requirements that apply to both employers and polygraph examiners. Records must be maintained for a minimum of 3 years from the date the polygraph examination is conducted (or from the date the examination is requested if no examination is conducted).

Every employer who requests an employee or prospective employee to submit to a polygraph examination pursuant to the ongoing investigation, drug manufacturer, or security services EPPA exemptions must maintain

- A copy of the written statement that sets forth the time and place of the examination and the examinee's right to consult with counsel
- A copy of the written notice provided by the employer to the examiner identifying the persons to be examined
- Copies of all opinions, reports, or other records furnished to the employer by the examiner relating to such examinations

All polygraph examiners must maintain all opinions, reports, charts, written questions, lists, and other records relating to the polygraph tests of such persons, as well as records of the number of examinations conducted during each day and the duration of each test period. The minimum time for a test is set at 90 minutes, and an examiner cannot perform more than five tests in any day.

The Secretary of Labor can bring court action to restrain violators and assess civil money penalties up to $10,000 per violation. An employer who violates the law may be liable to the employee or prospective employee for appropriate legal and equitable relief, which may include employment, reinstatement, promotion, and payment of lost wages and benefits.

The law does not preempt any provision of any state or local law or any collective bargaining agreement that is more restrictive with respect to lie detector tests. So where state or local laws are stricter than EPPA, those laws apply. Where they are weaker, EPPA applies.

In 1995, after hearing arguments concerning the admission of expert testimony, the court made a major decision overturning the 1923 *Frye* ruling in *Daubert V. Merrell Dow Pharmaceuticals, Inc.*, a Delaware corporation, defendant–appellee.

Two minors brought suit against Merrell Dow Pharmaceuticals, claiming they suffered limb reduction birth defects because their mothers had taken Bendectin, a drug prescribed for morning sickness to about 17.5 million pregnant women in the United States between 1957 and 1982. This appeal dealt with an evidentiary question whether certain expert scientific testimony is admissible to prove that Bendectin caused the plaintiffs' birth defects. Although it had nothing to do with polygraph, it had a major effect on all types of expert testimony including that of polygraph.

In an article by Matte and Kitchen,[2] they write:

United States Supreme Court in Daubert v. Merrell Dow Pharmaceuticals, 509 U.S.579 (1993) which superseded the Frye standard of general acceptance test (Frye v. U.S. 293 F. 1013 [D.C. Cir. 1923]).

The court ruled:

> The trial judge, pursuant to Rule 104(a), must make a preliminary assessment of whether the testimony's underlying reasoning or methodology is scientifically valid and properly can be applied to the facts at issue. Many considerations will bear on the inquiry, including whether the theory or technique in question can be (and has been) tested, whether it has been subjected to peer review and publications, its known or potential error rate, and the existence and maintenance of standards controlling its operation, and whether it has attracted widespread acceptance within a relevant scientific community.

The court also stated:

> Cross-examination, presentation of contrary evidence, and careful instruction on the burden of proof, rather than wholesale exclusion under an uncompromising "general acceptance" standard, is the appropriate means by which evidence based on valid principles may be challenged.

In describing the importance of peer-reviewed published studies of new scientific techniques, the court stated:

> Publication (which is but one element of peer review) is not a *sine qua non* of admissibility; it does not necessarily correlate with reliability," "and in some instances, well-grounded but innovative theories will not have been published." "But submission to the scrutiny of the scientific community is a component of *good science*, in part because it increases the likelihood that substantive flaws in methodology will be detected." "The fact of publication (or lack thereof) in a peer-reviewed journal thus will be a relevant, *though not dispositive*, consideration in assessing the scientific validity of a particular technique or methodology on which an opinion is premised. (Daubert) (italics by author).

In reducing the *Frye general acceptance* test to but one factor for admissibility, the court stated:

> "General acceptance" is not a necessary precondition to the admissibility of scientific evidence under the Federal Rules of Evidence, but the Rules of Evidence – especially Rule 702 – do assign to the trial judge the task of ensuring that an expert's testimony both rests on a reliable foundation and is relevant to the task at hand. Pertinent evidence based on scientifically valid principles will satisfy those demands.

Thus, under the *Daubert* standard, there are a number of factors that must be addressed when laying a validity foundation for potential admission of polygraph test results:

1. The specific polygraph examination technique used can be (and has been) scientifically tested.
2. With demonstrated validity and reliability.
3. Its potential error rate determined.
4. Preferably subjected to peer review and publication.
5. The existence and maintenance of standards controlling its operation.
6. Attained acceptance within a relevant scientific community.
7. The polygraph examination was properly conducted.
8. By a properly trained and competent polygraphist.
9. The entire examination was video or at a minimum audio tape recorded.

When looking at the difference between *Daubert* and *Frye*, under *Frye* the party wanting to testify concerning scientific evidence had to show that it was based on the method generally accepted in the scientific community. However, under *Daubert* the focus is on the reliability of the methodology. In *Daubert*, the court and the parties are not limited to what is generally accepted; methods accepted by a minority in the scientific community may well be sufficient.

In 1998, the Supreme Court issued its decision in the case of the *United States, Petitioner, v. Edward G. Scheffer*. This case involved the question of whether Military Rule of Evidence 707, which makes polygraph evidence inadmissible in court-martial proceedings, unconstitutionally interferes with the right of accused members of the military to present a defense. They ruled that it does not.

In March 1992, Scheffer, an airman stationed at March Air Force Base in California, volunteered to work as an informant on drug investigations for the Air Force Office of Special Investigations (OSI). His OSI supervisors advised him, from time to time during the course of his undercover work, to submit to drug testing and polygraph examinations. At some point he was asked to submit to a urine test. Shortly after providing the urine sample, but before the results of the test were known, Scheffer also agreed to take a polygraph test administered by an OSI examiner. In the opinion of the examiner, the test "indicated no deception" when the respondent denied using drugs since joining the Air Force.

When the results of the urine test concluded that he had used drugs, he was tried by a general court-martial on charges of using methamphetamine, failing to go to his appointed place of duty, wrongfully absenting himself from the base for 13 days, and, with respect to an unrelated matter, uttering 17 insufficient funds checks. He testified at trial on his own behalf, relying upon an "innocent ingestion" theory and denying that he had knowingly used drugs while working for OSI. On cross-examination, the prosecution attempted to impeach him with inconsistencies between his trial testimony and earlier statements he had made to the OSI.

Scheffer tried to introduce the polygraph evidence in support of his testimony that he did not knowingly use drugs, but the military judge denied the motion, relying on Military Rule of Evidence 707, which provides, in relevant part:

> (a) Notwithstanding any other provision of law, the results of a polygraph examination, the opinion of a polygraph examiner, or any reference to an offer to take, failure to take, or taking of a polygraph examination, shall not be admitted into evidence.

The military judge determined that Rule 707 was constitutional because "the President may, through the Rules of Evidence, determine that credibility is not an area in which a fact finder needs help, and the polygraph is not a process that has sufficient scientific acceptability to be relevant." He further reasoned that the fact finder might give undue weight to the polygraph examiner's testimony and that collateral arguments about such evidence could consume "an inordinate amount of time and expense."

Scheffer was convicted on all counts and was sentenced to a bad conduct discharge, confinement for 30 months, total forfeiture of all pay and allowances, and reduction to the lowest enlisted grade. The Air Force Court of Criminal Appeals affirmed in all material respects, explaining that Rule 707 "does not arbitrarily limit the accused's ability to present reliable evidence."

In January 2001, the National Academy of Sciences' National Research Council began project BCSS-I-00-01-A, which was a "Study to Review the Scientific Evidence on the Polygraph." The final report was published in October 2002 and titled *The Polygraph and Lie Detection*. The National Academies of Science found that in populations untrained in countermeasures, polygraph testing can discriminate lying from truth telling at rates above chance, though below perfection.

In 2007, Dr. Gordon Barland provided the following suggestions for successfully establishing the foundation for polygraph evidence into a legal proceeding:

1. Qualifications of the expert witness.
2. Scientific explanation of the polygraph.
3. Polygraph process.
4. Scientific methodology of polygraph.
5. Show that the theory or technique has been subjected to peer review and publication.
6. What is the known or potential error rate?

7. Show the established standards for conducting polygraph examinations.
8. General acceptance of polygraph by government, law enforcement, etc.
9. Show a comparison with other types of admissible evidence.
10. Cover concerns that polygraph testimony does not overwhelm juries.

Conclusion

In the Matte–Kitchen article, they quote John Henry Wigmore as saying, "If there is ever devised a psychological test for the evaluation of witnesses, the law will run to meet it." That certainly has not been the case for polygraph.

Judging the current state of the art of polygraph by the 1923 single parameter discontinuous blood pressure test administered on Frye by Marston is simply unjust. As we in the profession continue to enhance our training and validate our process, hopefully the courts will recognize polygraph's legitimate place along with other forensic evidence allowed into the courtroom to assist the trier of facts.

Notes

1. Frye v. United States 293 F. 1013 (D.C. Cir. 1923).
2. Matte, J. A. and Kitchen, D. A. (2015) Scientific validation of polygraph techniques revisits admissibility in court. *International Society of Polygraph Examiners Research Digest*, 2(6), 1–29.

Ethics and Standards 12

Ethics is knowing the difference between what you have a right to do and what is right to do.

—Potter Stewart

The following are the Code of Ethics and Standards of Practice established by the International Society of Polygraph Examiners (ISOPE).

Code of Ethics

1. Rights of Examinees
An examinee shall be treated professionally, with respect and dignity.

2. Standards for Rendering Polygraph Decisions
A member shall not render a conclusive decision without sufficient physiological data to support it. Data should be free of excessive movements and distortions. Data must meet the standards generally accepted by the profession.

3. Postexamination Notification of Results
A member shall afford each examinee a reasonable opportunity to explain physiological reactions to relevant questions in the recordings, with the following exceptions: an evidentiary examination where the court order stipulates there is to be no posttest interview, a legal examination where the examinee is represented by an attorney who instructs that the results only be released to him or her, and unusual circumstances of operational necessity.

4. Restrictions on Rendering Opinions
A member shall not provide any report or opinion that would require a medical or psychological degree concerning the mental or medical conditions of the examinee. The examiner may report information concerning the appearance or behavior of the examinee. Polygraph outcome decisions shall be based on the analyzed polygraph data.

5. Restrictions on Examinations

A member shall not conduct a polygraph examination when there is reason to believe the examination is intended to circumvent or defy the law.

6. Fees

A member shall not solicit or accept fees, gratuities, or gifts that are intended to influence his or her opinion, decision, or report. No member's fees for polygraph services can be based on the findings or results of such services, nor shall any member change his or her fee as a direct result of his or her opinion or decision of a polygraph examination.

7. Standards of Reporting

A member shall not knowingly submit, or allow employees to submit, a misleading or false polygraph examination report. Each polygraph report shall be a factual, impartial, and objective account of information developed during the examination and the examiner's professional opinion based on the analysis of the polygraph data.

8. Advertisements

A member shall not release any false or misleading statements or advertisements relating to the ISOPE or the polygraph profession. No member shall make any false representation as to their category of membership in the ISOPE. All advertisements making reference to ISOPE membership shall also list the category of membership.

9. Release of Nonrelevant Information

A member shall not disclose to any person any irrelevant personal information ascertained during a polygraph examination that has no connection to the issue to be resolved and that may embarrass or tend to embarrass the examinee, except where such disclosure is required by law.

10. Restrictions on Examination Issues

A member shall not ask questions in an examination concerning activities, affiliation, or beliefs on religion, politics, or race unless such matters are relevant to the issue under investigation.

11. ISOPE Oversight Authority

A member who administers or attempts to administer any polygraph examination in violation of the Code of Ethics or the Standards of Practice may be subject to investigation, censure, suspension, or expulsion from the society, as provided by the ISOPE Constitution.

Standards of Practice

1. Guidelines

Statement of purpose: A properly administered polygraph examination by a competent polygraph examiner using a valid testing and analysis protocol is the most accurate means known to science for determining whether a person has been truthful. To promote the highest degree of accuracy, the ISOPE establishes for its membership the following Standards of Practice. In addition, all examinations are required to be conducted in compliance with governing local, state, and federal regulations and laws.

1.1 Guidelines are the recommended practices for the preparation, conduct, analysis, documentation, and reporting of polygraph examinations based on best practices. Deviations from these guidelines are subject to review and could result in disciplinary action, including revocation of membership from the society.

2. Referenced Documents

2.1 ASTM Standards

E1954 Practice for Conduct of Research in Psychophysiological Detection of Deception

E2000 Guide for Minimum Basic Polygraph Training and Education

E2063 Calibration and Functionality Checks Used in Forensic Psychophysiological Detection of Deception (Polygraph) Examinations

E2439 Instrumentation, Sensors and Operating Software Used in Forensic Psychophysiological Detection of Deception (Polygraph) Examinations

E2229 Interpretation of Psychophysiological Detection of Deception (Polygraph) Data

E2062 PDD Examination Standards of Practice

E2031 Quality Control of Psychophysiological Detection of Deception (Polygraph) Examinations

3. Definition

3.1 Polygraph examination: A psychophysiological detection of deception interview and testing process encompassing all activities occurring between a polygraph examiner and an examinee during a series of interactions that include a proper pretest interview, recording of physiological data, analysis of test data, and the rendering of a professional opinion.

4. Location and Test Conditions

4.1 The testing environment shall be free from distractions that would interfere with the examinee's ability to appropriately focus on the issues being addressed. The examination site should be reasonably free from distractions that would interfere with the conductance of a proper examination. This is not intended to address examinations conducted for demonstration purposes.

5. Preparation

5.1 Prior to an examination the examiner should review all available information concerning the issue to be resolved.

5.2 No examination shall be conducted unless the instrument meets the manufacturer's specifications.

5.3 Where permitted by law, Evidentiary Examinations and Sex Offender Examinations should be recorded by audio or audio/visual means in its entirety. Any stops or pauses in the recording must be fully explained on the recording.

5.4 All polygraph files, data, reports and recordings shall be retained and maintained for a minimum of one year, or longer if applicable by law.

5.5 All instruments shall consist of a minimum of two separate respiratory components to record patterns in thoracic and abdominal activity, an electro-dermal component to record reflecting relative changes in the conductance or resistance of current by the epidermal tissue, a cardio component capable of recording cardiovascular activity including changes in relative blood pressure, pulse rate and pulse amplitude, and a separate data channel specifically designed to record physical body movements which would cause possible distortions. Other physiological data may also be recorded during testing, but may not be used to formulate decisions of truthfulness or deception unless validated in replicated and published research.

5.6 An examiner should not conduct more than five polygraph examinations on a calendar day.

6. Pretest Practices

6.1 The examiner shall adhere to the following practices:

6.1.1 Properly verify the correct identity of the examinee to the extent possible.

6.1.2 Properly explain to the examinee their rights concerning the examination and have the examinee sign a consent form prior to testing.

6.1.3 During the pretest phase, the examiner will ensure that the examinee is mentally and physically capable of testing to the extent legally practicable.

6.1.3.1 Mental, physical, and medical conditions of the examinee should be reviewed and documented.

6.1.3.2 If at any time the examiner believes that the examinee is not suitable for testing, the examination will be immediately terminated.

6.2 All examinations shall be conducted in compliance with the governing local, state, and federal regulations and laws.

6.3 The examiner shall treat the examinee in a professional manner and display an objective attitude.

6.4 Sufficient time shall be spent with the examinee to allow him or her to discuss the issues to be tested and to fully explain his or her position.

6.5 The examiner shall formulate all test questions and allow sufficient time to introduce each test question to the examinee in a manner that complies with the technique being used and best practices recognized.

6.6 Sufficient time shall be spent to ensure that the examinee recognizes and understands each question as well as understands the polygraph process and that total cooperation is required.

7. In-Test Practices

7.1 Examiners shall use techniques and formats that have a minimum of two published peer-reviewed research papers identifying the procedure used and accuracy of the process.

7.2 A continuous recording shall be made and maintained of the data produced during the in-test phase. All test data must be accounted for prior to rendering a professional opinion.

7.3 Questions shall be asked in a way that ensures responses are not influenced by the way the question is asked.

7.4 Question intervals shall allow for a reasonable recovery. Stimulus onset to stimulus onset should not be less than 20 seconds, nor more than 35 seconds, and timing should be consistent between questions.

8. Evaluation Practices

8.1 The examiner shall use evaluation methods for which he or she has been properly trained and that are appropriate to the testing technique being utilized.

8.1.1 Acceptable evaluation methods are those that have known error and accuracy rates established by peer-reviewed research.

8.2 The examiner shall maintain all records of test data analysis for a minimum of 1 year, or as applicable by law.

8.3 The examiner shall not disclose the results of the examination until the data obtained have been adequately and sufficiently analyzed.

8.4 Examiners shall run a sufficient number of charts and collect enough physiological data suitable for evaluation in compliance with the technique being utilized.

8.4.1 All suitable physiological data will be evaluated when formulating an opinion.

9. Posttest Practices

9.1 Following the collection and analysis of all physiological data, the examinee should be informed of his or her results unless it is otherwise mandated by a court of law or agreed otherwise by the examinee. Exception is made when the attorney representing the examinee requests that no posttest interview be conducted and the results be provided only to the attorney.

Conclusion

Conducting polygraph examinations is a position of great responsibility. Our decisions will dramatically affect the life of the examinee, whether it is a job applicant or a criminal suspect. By living a professional life of high ethics and standards, the life of a polygraph examiner becomes much easier. Always remember that getting the guilty party to be deceptive is the easy part of the position. The real art is getting the innocent to be truthful. Doing everything you can to ethically allow the examinee to pass the test not only makes for a good examiner, it also makes sleeping at night much easier.

Research

13

There are lies, damned lies and statistics.

—Mark Twain

Explorable.com states that research aims "to generate measurable and testable data, gradually adding to the accumulation of human knowledge. Science uses established research methods and standard protocols to test theories thoroughly. Scientific research, however, allows us to test hypotheses and lay solid foundations for future research and study."

Research in polygraph has generally involved three methods or types of studies: field studies, analog studies, and hybrid studies. Field studies involve actual field polygraph cases and data where intensity for the examinee is high; however, it is difficult to establish criterion of "ground truth." Therefore, selections of cases involved in these studies are somewhat selective, where only those cases resolved by confession or examinees have been found guilty in a judicial proceeding are used. Accuracy for many other cases is left out.

Analog studies are laboratory studies where *ground truth* is established and known; however, examinee intensity is low since there is no real threat of punishment for those identified as deceptive. There is no way to know how many of the participants could care less about the outcome.

Hybrid studies combine the realism of a field study with the knowledge of *ground truth* available in the analog study; however, they are very rare. Netzer Daie, a member of the Israeli Police, performed an interesting hybrid study along with polygraphists Avital Ginton and Eitan Elaad, as part of his master's thesis in 1982. Twenty-one police officers took a paper and pencil test. Later, they were given back their papers and allowed to score the tests themselves. This allowed officers to cheat if they wanted to. Unknown to them, the researchers already knew all of the original answers and could establish ground zero truth and identify officers who cheated. The group was then informed that information was leaked that some of them had cheated when they scored their tests and all of them would be required to take polygraph examinations. Hence, the study had the intensity of a real *live* field case and the establishment of ground truth present in a laboratory study. The original examiner in the study, blind to ground zero truth, correctly identified 100% of deceptive suspects and 85% of truthful suspects for an overall accuracy of 93%.

Another difficulty for the polygraph profession is researching preemployment or screening tests. Obviously in field tests, if a deceptive applicant is determined to be truthful, no one will ever know of the error. In an analog study where ground truth is established, the effects of the participant's actual life transgressions may skew the results. For example, I set up an experiment where I have a group of college students traveling from building A to building B. Some will be stopped and asked to conceal some pills in their pocket. They are informed that they will be taking a polygraph test to determine if they had any drug involvement during their travel to the building and they are to deny it. If they can *beat* the test, they receive an incentive. Other participants will have no contact and were only informed that they will take a similar test and will receive an incentive if they pass the test. A few of the truthful participants, however, smoked marijuana the day before. How will this affect their tests? It is unknown.

Obviously, whatever type of study is performed, data will be involved. The data will have to be analyzed so determinations can be made regarding its accuracy and predictability to the larger population, which is known as statistics. Statistical significance has a generally accepted rule of thumb that makes it relatively easy to determine if an event is rare enough to conclude that pure chance didn't cause it.

The probability level of the research study is influenced by the sample size and differences between groups and within group variability. There are different types of variables. Independent variables are those controlled or manipulated by the researcher and cause a change in the dependent variable (x-axis), which is the variable being measured (y-axis).

Many of the statistical studies involving polygraph involve inferential statistics, which is a method used to extrapolate from a sample to the larger population.

The accuracy for a test of truth must determine the test's sensitivity as well as its specificity. Sensitivity is how accurate the test is to detect deception. Specificity is how accurate the test is to determine truth. Obviously sensitivity and specificity must both be high for the method to be valid.

We can look at the Army MGQT that had a very high degree of sensitivity detecting about 95% of the deceptive population. Unfortunately, it had very poor specificity, incorrectly identifying almost 50% of truthful examinees as deceptive. Mean accuracy is the average of these numbers, in this case, 95 + 50 divided by 2, resulting in a mean accuracy for the Army MGQT at about 72%, which fails to meet the polygraph profession's standard requiring a minimum of 80% accuracy for investigative tests with less than a 20% inconclusive rate.

When truthful examinees are determined to be deceptive, it is classified as a false positive. When deceptive examinees are determined to be truthful, it is classified as a false negative. In the polygraph profession, the bigger problem found is generally false positives. The art of polygraph is not how to get deceptive people to be deceptive, but how to get truthful people to be determined truthful. The latter is the true art of polygraph.

Test accuracy depends on two factors: validity and reliability. All tests are designed to measure something, hopefully something specific. Whether a test is valid questions whether we are measuring what we claim to be measuring. Polygraph tests are designed to measure truth and deception. If the test does indeed measure what it is intended to measure, then we can say that the test is valid (or has validity).

Reliability refers to the extent to which a test or other instrument is consistent in its measures. Is it repeatable? If a person takes an examination, will the results be the same if another examiner tested the examinee? If another examiner evaluated the same charts as the original examiner, would he or she come to the same conclusion? These questions deal with reliability or repeatability.

A test could be reliable and yet not be valid. For example, six different voice stress analyzers may look at the same graphs and conclude deception. *There is reliability.* However, as we know based on research, the examinee may be truthful since voice stress has been shown to lack validity.

Face validity is when a test is based on the experimenter's logical analysis without proof by external standards. For example, the positive control technique appeared to measure truth and deception based on its face. As previously stated, each question was asked twice, and the examinee was instructed to answer first with a subjective lie and then when the question was repeated with their subjective truth:

Subjective lie:	Did you shoot John?	"Yes."
Subjective truth:	Did you shoot John?	"No."

Obviously one of these answers had to be true and one had to be a lie. Theoretically, the innocent examinee forced to admit to a crime they didn't do should cause greater physiological reaction, and the guilty examinee denying the crime they actually committed should result in greater physiological reaction. Positive control had excellent face validity. However, research showed it to have a high false-negative (deceptive suspects erroneously determined to be truthful) and inconclusive rate.

We are trying to measure physiological changes resulting from emotional changes due to a person's truth or deception to questions asked. We are not trying to measure changes due to other emotional changes, such as anger and shame. For a test to have *construct validity*, you must be able to define the *construct* and show its relationship in a conceptual model, primarily based on theoretical predictions of how items should interrelate or how the test should intercorrelate (*concurrent validity*) and the actual evidence. One of the arguments made against polygraph by the 1983 OTA report was that it lacked construct validity. There is no way to show that the psychophysiological changes occurring are not due to emotional changes not associated with truth or deception, nor was there any way to show what factors cause errors.

Construct validity for the polygraph procedure is subcategorized:

Psychological structure: The psychological concepts that make up the test structure must initially be in conformance with acceptable scientific principles, have face validity, and be in harmony with the theory's objectives.

Methodology: The method, verbal presentations by the examiner, etc., presented in the collection of the data.

Data analysis: How the collected data is analyzed must be consistent.

External validity refers to the extent to which the results of a study can be generalized or extended to others. For example, if a study on a drug is only conducted on white, middle-aged, overweight women with diabetes, can the results of the study be generalized to the rest of the population? Or are the results only valid to the population studied?

Researchers go to great lengths to select a group of people for the study (a sample) that is representative enough that the results can be extended to lots of people. The broader the population and settings, the more the results can be generalized to the population. Also, the more the research setting resembles the *real-life* setting, the greater the external validity.

External validity also refers to the repetition of a test or the number of charts that are administered resulting in a consistent outcome, as well as how many times the same question is asked during the examination.

Internal validity occurs when a researcher controls all extraneous variables and the only variable influencing the results of a study is the one being manipulated by the researcher. In polygraph we want to eliminate all stimuli in the room except for our questions. Therefore, we can scientifically say that the physiological reactions recorded could only be due to the questions asked. This is internal validity. A problem for polygraph is that internal validity is not easy to show when there is not a control group, which is the case with field studies.

When we consider if the test is reliable, we have to ask whether it has internal reliability. This is established in polygraph by the repetition of a core segment of a test. For example, in a single issue examination, the relevant issue is addressed with two or three questions in every chart administered; thus, scores can be combined. This demonstrates internal reliability that the outcome is based on repeatability of reactions to the same question. In a multi-issue or multifaceted test, each question may be asked only once per chart and scores cannot be combined. Therefore, these examinations have less internal reliability.

Conclusion

For the polygraph profession to become more acceptable to the scientific community, the legal community, and people in general, continued research is needed.

This research must come from both the field and the laboratory. Polygraph has become more acceptable in recent times. We currently have at least three popular television shows whose content is based almost solely on polygraph examinations.

Polygraph is becoming more acceptable within the legal and scientific communities. We still have strong detractors of our profession, as well as those who are unsure of it. Research is needed to deal with the unbelievers and to ensure the future of our profession.

Some people think that the truth can be hidden with a little cover-up and decoration. But as time goes by, what is true is revealed, and what is fake fades away.

—Ismail Haniyeh

In this chapter I will share some actual field cases—the interviews as well as charts. Names and some details have been changed to protect the actual identity of the examinees involved.

In this first reviewed case my partner at the time, Philip M. Cochetti, and I had been contacted by a District Attorney who wanted us to assist in an investigation into the death of a young baby. The baby's mother had gone out with her sister to play bingo, and his father was left watching him. His father was mildly retarded and had poor fine motor skills. He decided to feed the baby cereal for the first time. While feeding him, he kept dropping cereal on the baby and was wiping it up with a paper towel. As the paper towel became wet and slimy, the father kept folding it to get a clean area, and eventually, the father stated he accidentally dropped it into the baby's mouth. The baby died. The District Attorney wanted us to find out if the incident was accidental or deliberate, and if deliberate, was it spontaneous or planned?

The baby is Harry, and the mother is Sandy. This was the father's pretest statement to us about the event:

I would say around 2:00 p.m. Sandy left the apartment to go to her sister's. She went to Stacy's and both Sandy and Stacy walked up. They were going to play bingo that night. They go quite often. Sandy goes 4 or 5 times per week; her mother goes every day. When Sandy left she left me and the baby and my dog. The baby was asleep in the living room in a playpen. The baby slept all afternoon. When he woke up he began crying. I wanted to feed him, so I mixed up cereal and formula like it said on the box. I think it was Gerber oatmeal. I had to mix 1 or 2 tablespoons with Enfamil in a dish with warm water. I used a plastic measuring spoon to measure it. I was told by friends to feed the baby the formula and cereal. He was waking up every 15 minutes when we were feeding him by bottle, so I decided to start feeding him cereal and formula on this day. I placed the mix inside a plastic baby dish; the one that you put water inside to keep the food warm. I then took cereal into the living room. I picked up the baby and sat in my usual chair. I then got up and sat in a different chair.

The arms of the chair are higher and it was hard to feed the baby. The baby was on my lap with my left arm under his head or back of the neck. The cereal was on the right side in the arm of the chair. I began feeding the baby with my right hand. I put almost all of the food into the baby's mouth. There was 4 ounces of formula and 1 or 2 tablespoons of oatmeal in it. I think I spent about 20 minutes feeding the baby. I spilled some of the cereal onto the baby's shirt and over his mouth. That chair certainly messed me up. I never said that the chair messed me up before. I had a paper towel with me. I think that after I took the food into the living room and put it on the arm of the chair. I returned to the dining room to get a paper towel. I put the paper towel on a stand that was next to the chair. I had to keep getting the towel to wipe his face and shirt. He was crying whenever I spilled it on his mouth. The third time I dropped it on him and also the fifth time I dropped it on him. I kept cleaning him off each time I spilled it on him. He was still crying. I always kept him real clean. The towel was filling up with the cereal and it was getting wetter and wetter and got slimly and small. You have to keep moving it around to get a clean spot on the towel. He was crying as I was wiping his mouth. Somehow, while cleaning him off, I dropped the towel into his mouth. I tried to get it out with my finger, but I was pushing it further in. I probably put my finger in 4 or 5 times, but I couldn't get it out. Then I tried other stuff when I got out of the chair. I was standing up; I turned him over. I had my hand on his chest. I then hit him on his back and squeezed on his stomach a little bit. I didn't squeeze hard because he was a little baby. I couldn't get it out, so I ran downstairs with the baby. I opened the door to Sandy's mother's apartment. All of them were standing there: Mrs. Emma Jones (Sandy's mother) and Sandy's father, her brother and his girlfriend, Gloria. I think I said that the baby got a piece of paper stuck down his throat. I think I gave the baby to Sandy's mother. The baby ended up on the couch with Johnny doing whatever they told him to do. Some lady was telling us to hit the baby with the heel of the hand on the baby's back and also squeeze the baby. About 5 minutes later the ambulance people arrived. I think there were 3 or 4 ambulance people. They must have taken the baby off the couch and laid him on the table. They were ripping open packets of stuff and shining a light down his throat. They finally got it out with tweezers and set it on the dining room table. It was all bloody and messy, so I threw it into the trash can that was by the table. It was under a desk. They later showed it to me at the police station. It had cigarette ashes all over it. I didn't see anyone get it out. I just figured it was cigarette ashes because the trash can is always full of cigarette ashes. No one told me what the black stuff was on the towel, so I just figured it out. I didn't take it out of the trash can. I don't know who did it. When they were leaving I went upstairs to get my coat and came back down. I wasn't even half way down the steps when they were leaving. I could have gone with them if I wanted to, but I wanted to go get Sandy. There was nothing I could do for Harry while he was at the hospital except pray. I went back upstairs for more cigarettes for Sandy and myself. She would probably need cigarettes at the hospital. I then left and walked to the bingo hall. I asked for Sandy, but she wasn't there. I then went to Sandy's sister and asked Stacy's boyfriend where Sandy was.

He told me that she was at the bingo hall. I went back to the bingo hall and Sandy was there. I motioned for her to come to me. I told her that the baby was in the hospital. I'm not sure what she did. I don't remember whether she went back to tell Stacy or whether she got her coat.

We utilized an Integrated Zone Comparison Technique (IZCT) with the following 13 questions:

1. Is today Sunday?
2. Do you understand we will only ask the questions we told you about?
3. Are you going to answer every test question truthfully?
4. Is today Monday?
C5. During the first 28 years of your life, did you ever do anything out of anger?
R6. Did you deliberately put that towel into that baby's mouth?
7. Right now, are you in the United States?
C8 In your entire life, did you ever deliberately hurt anyone?
R9 Regarding that baby, did you deliberately put the towel into his mouth?
10. Right now, are you in Switzerland?
C11 During the first 26 years of your life, did you ever want to get even with anyone?
R12 Did you make up that story about that towel accidentally dropping into that baby's mouth?
13. Have you deliberately done anything to try and beat this test?

The examinee's charts are shown in Figure 14.1a through c. What is interesting in the examinee's statement was that he took possession of his dog (*my* dog) but not his baby (*the* baby). The term "the baby" is in the statement before and after the feeding; however, the term disappears during the feeding and time of the incident. The examinee blames the incident on "the chair." He states that he sat in his chair and then got up and sat in a different chair. Three people lived in the house: the examinee, the baby, and the mother. If he is not sitting in his chair, he is now sitting in the wife's chair, which became symbolic of the wife. The wife was always playing bingo leaving him stuck watching the baby. And, yes, he confessed.

The next case also involved the death of a baby. The examinee owned a daycare center that she operated from her house. Here is the examinee's written statement of what she says occurred:

On June 2 (Thurs) John (16 mos) arrived at daycare. As his mom handed him to me he threw a mild temper tantrum (which was unusual usually he comes right to me) He bumped his head lightly on door frame, she handed him to me,

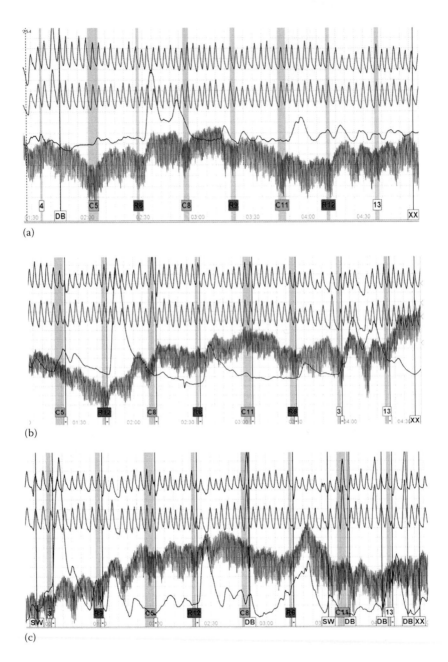

Figure 14.1 Case #1's examinee's charts. (a) Chart 1: Silent answer test. (b) Chart 2: Mixed out loud. (c) Chart 3: Mixed out loud R–G.

he continued being upset & hit me on chest. His mother stated he was tired & hadn't slept well. He settled right down as soon as I closed the door. John cuddled with me on sofa & soon he fell asleep he napped for a few hours in the morning. Nap time—Louie (baby that got hurt) was napping in his car seat. He was fussy not screaming but would wake up & fuss a bit either my husband (Ben) or me would rock him back to sleep. 3:05 my husband left to go pick up school children. I know the time because he said he was going to leave at 3:00 & I told him no reason to leave so early. I had been in on computer in adjoining room. John had been in his babyseat trying to nap. During that time I took John out of his seat & had him up on the sofa w/me playing w/toys. Baby (Louie) woke up (stirred) a few times fussed a lil & I would rock him back to sleep. Around 3:30 John was getting fussy, acting like he was ready to nap. I put him in the baby saucer to keep him safe & put up baby gate went in other room to kitchen to get his bottle ready & a lite snack & also got Louie's bottles washed out. While in the kitchen heard Louie start screaming finished washing bottle but take time to get John's bottle went in living room & John had gotten out of saucer and was near baby. Had Louie's bottle in his hand took bottle from him & put him back in saucer. Observed Louie had scratches on his face one on his nose he had a some blood on it. Unstrapped him from car seat held him to calm him, wiped his face there was a small smear of blood. Checked him he had quite a few very tiny scratches on face (baby scratches), on eyelid, forehead etc. Changed his diaper & checked his body & arms thought maybe John had bitten him (as he had bite one of the other children two days before). There were no marks on him from the neck down his face was very red with red blotches one near on left near the larger scratch. He also had a lot of red raised (rash like) spots of his forehead one on the right side. My husband came home after that w/school children told him what I thought had happened w/John scratching Louie. He said he thought he needed to get rid of John. I said he was just going through a stage. I also said I wasn't positive John had done it since I didn't see him do it. Called Louie's mom & told her that he had what looked like some kind of rash and had scratched himself badly. I should have just told her what I thought had happened but knew she would be very upset & I wasn't positive John had done it. Didn't mention it to John's mom when she picked up. Gave Louie the rest of his bottle before he got picked up & noticed a few very small drops of blood. Later when washing John up for snack noticed he also had a very small amt of blood on his fingertip. This was after Louie had left. When Louie was picked up asked the mom to call me & let me know how he was doing told her she should call his doctor was concerned about the red blotches (hives or rash exam exema) Tried to call her a few times that night to see how he was doing. At about 10:30 on Thurs. night Ben was outside working on our trailer & came in hollering up to me (was in the bathroom) that the police were there & wanted to take him in. I went downstairs & two police officers were in my living room. The detective stated she wanted to bring us in for questioning concerning what had happened at the day care that day. Tried to explain to her then about what happened or what I thought happened w/John. Thought I could clear it up right there. (SIC)

We utilized an IZCT with the following 13 questions:

1. Is today Sunday?
2. Do you understand that we will only ask the questions we reviewed?
3. Do you intend to answer every test question truthfully?
4. Is today Monday?
C5. During the first 37 years of your life, did you ever lose your temper?
R6. Did you inflict any of those injuries that resulted in that baby's death?
7. Right now, are you in the United States?
C8 In your entire life, did you ever wish harm on anyone?
R9 Regarding that baby, did you inflict any of those injuries that resulted in his death?
10. Right now, are you in Switzerland?
C11. During the first 37 years of your life, did you ever deliberately hurt anyone?
R12. Were you the person that inflicted those injuries on that baby?
13. Have you deliberately done anything to try and beat this test?

The examinee's IZCT charts are shown in Figure 14.2a through c, and her polygraph validation test (PVT) is shown in Figure 14.3. What is interesting to observe in the PVT is that the examinee distorted almost every question except the relevant question at R5.

In this last case, we have a police applicant who was given a reexamination using an evidence statement test. In her initial test, she was asked four relevant questions concerning (1) deliberately omitting information she knew for sure would eliminate her as an applicant, (2) personal involvement with illegal drugs, (3) committing serious undetected crimes, and (4) thefts in excess of $200.00 in the past 3 years.

She showed significant reactions to the question concerning illegal drug involvement and was given a more accurate single issue examination on that issue. Since she knew she had failed that question in her original test, we felt the question would probably be stigmatized. Therefore, we used an "evidence statement test."

On a pad we wrote:

Evidence Statement of *name*
Date

As an adult have you had any personal involvement with illegal drugs?

She answered the question by writing "no," signed the sheet and then read it out loud.

1. Is today Sunday?
2. Do you understand that we will only ask the questions we reviewed?

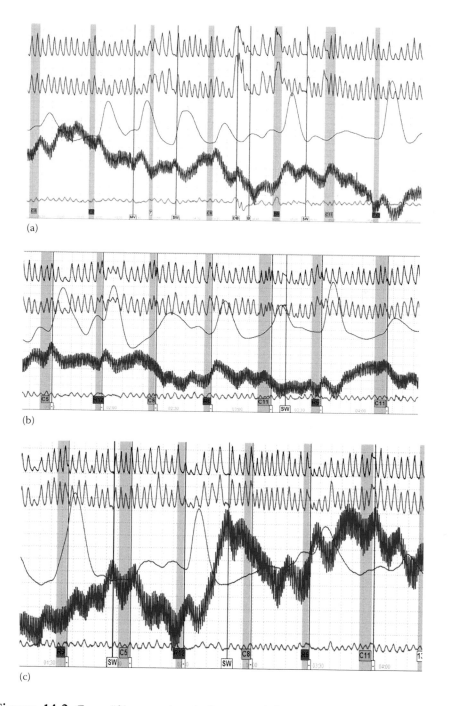

(a)

(b)

(c)

Figure 14.2 Case #2's examinee's Integrated Zone Comparison Technique charts. (a) Chart 1: Silent answer test. (b) Chart 2: Mix out loud. (c) Mixed–Relevant/comparison sequence.

PVT

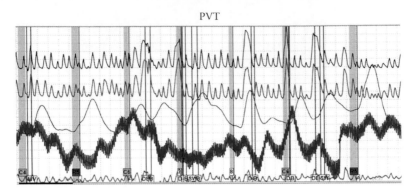

Figure 14.3 Case #2 PVT.

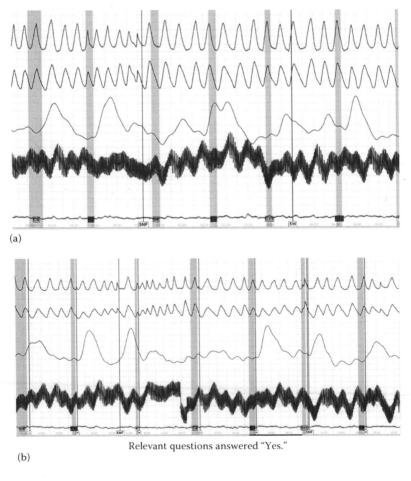

(a)

Relevant questions answered "Yes."

(b)

Figure 14.4 Case #3 examinee's charts. (a) Evidence statement preemployment—Chart 1: Silent answer test. (b) Evidence statement preemployment—Chart 2: Mixed out loud test.   (*Continued*)

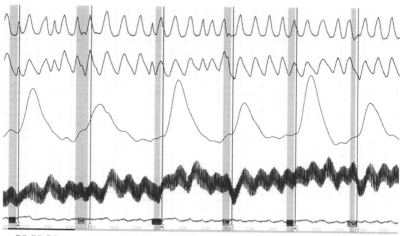

RS (Y) RE: your Evidence Statement today, did you answer that question truthfully?

(c)

Figure 14.4 (*Continued*) Case #3 examinee's charts. (c) Evidence statement pre-employment—Chart 3: Mixed out loud R–G test.

3. Do you intend to answer every test question truthfully?
4. Is today Friday?
C5. During the first 21 years of your life, did you ever lie to avoid responsibility for something you did?
R6. Today, did you answer that question truthfully on your evidence statement?
7. Right now, are you in the United States?
C8. In your entire life, did you ever lie to someone who trusted you?
R9. Regarding your evidence statement today, did you answer that question truthfully?
10. Right now, are you in Switzerland?
C11. During the first 21 years of your life, can you remember telling an important lie?
R12. Was your answer on your evidence statement today true?
13. Have you deliberately done anything to try and beat this test?

The examinee's charts are shown in Figure 14.4a through c.

Conclusion

The cases reviewed in this chapter hopefully gave you some insight into actual field cases that were successfully resolved by the use of polygraph.

There is enormous pressure on the polygraph examiner to make the correct determinations in the cases they perform. The goal of the examiner should be to conduct every test as if it was going to be reviewed and critiqued by the world. Conduct every examination in a professional manner, giving every examinee the best possibility of a truthful outcome. If they still fail, as the deceptive will do, you can believe in your data.

Future

15

Change is inevitable in life, for stillness is death. If we are not moving forward, enhancing our profession, then we and what we practice are falling
behind. So, where will the search for truth lead us in the years to come?

Polygraph, as we know it today, is without question the "gold standard"
for truth verification. I do not believe there will be a new instrument that
unto itself will have higher validity and reliability than that of the polygraph in the hands of a competent examiner today. I do believe that we will
see additional instrumentation to be added to our current instrumentation,
collecting additional physiological phenomena and by doing so increasing
our accuracy.

There has been a renewed interest in several areas that were researched
in the past. The plethysmograph, which collects cardiovascular blood volume
changes from the finger, is being touted as a possible additional component
to the traditional polygraph. In the 1800s both Mosso and Lombrosso were
interested in devices using concepts to monitor blood volume changes. In the
1970s we have seen finger devices such as the cardio activity monitor from
the Stoelting Instrument Company and the thumb cuff from the Lafayette
Instrument Company introduced. Today's device utilizes a photosensitive
cell to measure light reflected or passed through the tissue segment of the finger where the monitor is placed. The light source used produces a light in the
infrared range creating a cardio tracing. During sympathetic arousal there is
a decrease of blood flow to the extremities. It is this same phenomenon that
creates the "ghost white" facial appearance displayed by many people when
experiencing fear. By traveling in deeper vessels, there is less chance that during an emergency if cut, you will bleed to death. This decrease in blood at the
finger results in a decrease in the tracing size of the plethysmograph as can
be seen in Figure 15.1. Hopefully, due to improvements in the component, it
may offer important additional data in the future.

There is a long history of interest in changes in pupil size. During sympathetic arousal the pupils dilate. Like the electrodermal response, the pupil

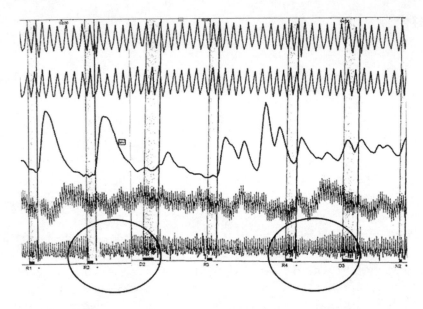

Figure 15.1 A decrease in blood at the finger results in a decrease in the tracing size of the plethysmograph. Reaction in the plethysmograph is illustrated when the tracing size becomes smaller.

only has sympathetic innervation. A number of oculomotor tests have surfaced showing these changes, so one would expect similar accuracy from pupil dilation as is achieved with the EDR. Studies have shown pupil dilation in detection of deception to range from mid 70% to 80% accuracy.[1] The Lafayette Instrument Company now offers an instrument that detects deception based on pupil changes and eye blinking, which researched by its developers indicates accuracy at the mid 80% level.

While lecturing in Moscow, I was made aware of testing based on eye focus. An item, such as a cell phone, was stolen in a mock theft at the university. As truthful and deceptive suspects were brought into an interview room and questioned, their eye gaze was monitored to see how much time the suspect focused on a similar cell phone left out in the room. I was told that using this method they were able to achieve accuracy in detecting the deceptive suspects over 80% of the time.

Another area of research involving the eyes is blinking activity. Under threat there is believed to be an increase in blinking activity, perhaps to lessen the possibility of injury to the open eye during times of hostility. Research has shown overall accuracy of this method of detecting deception to be at about 75%.[2] In this study, changes in blink count during and immediately following individual questions, total number of blinks, and maximum blink time length differentiated those with false intent from truthful intent participants.

In the 1960s the U.S. Army was interested in developing a covert system for detecting deception. They selected a research team consisting of Colonel Mc Quiston, a federally trained polygraph examiner; Colonel Bell, a researcher; and Captain Ford, an electrician. They considered three possibilities: smell, lasers, and voice.

It is a known fact that animals can sense fear in humans through their sense of smell, so that was a possibility. There were rumors that invisible lasers could detect physiological changes in humans and that there was already a device that could monitor a person's breathing from a distance without their knowledge. However, the team decided on developing an instrument that could detect stress from changes in the voice; they are identified as microtremors.

In 1964, the House Government Operations Subcommittee conducted hearings into the use of polygraphs, or lie detectors by federal agencies, chaired by John Moss, of California. According to the study, almost 20,000 polygraph tests were given by 19 government agencies in 1963, excluding those administered by the Central Intelligence and National Security Agencies, which said they could not reveal their figures for security reasons. These 19 agencies owned 512 polygraphs, according to the study, acquired at a cost of $428,000. The study said that the 639 federal employees authorized to conduct the tests in 1963 were paid $4.3 million in government salaries that year. The House Government Operations Committee on March 22, 1965, released a report (H.Rept 198), based on the 1964 hearings, entitled "Use of Polygraphs As 'Lie Detectors' by the Federal Government." The finding was very negative toward the government's overt use of polygraph, and as a result, the Army decided to end their research into covert lie detection.

Bell, Mc Quiston, and Ford retired from the military and opened Dektor Counterintelligence and Security, a private company in Virginia, and introduced the Psychological Stress Evaluator (PSE) in 1969. A former polygraph examiner, Michael Kradz, was brought in as an instructor, and Dektor offered the PSE for sale with a 5-day training course. There was a falling out among the principles, and Mc Quiston left for Florida where he later developed the first computerized voice stress system.

Over the years many voice stress systems have appeared, including the computerized voice stress analysis (CVSA); the Truster; Mark I, II, III, and IV; instruments; and layered voice stress analysis.

The CVSA has been marketed by Charles Humble, while CEO of NITV Federal Services, a private company offering training in voice stress and manufacturing the CVSA instrument. The U.S. government was using the equipment in both Iraq and Afghanistan until research showed its accuracy rate to detect deception somewhere between 0% and 65%. On national television, ABC News Primetime Webcast, Dr. Humble was interviewed by

Brian Ross. Humble admits during the interview that there is not a single scientific study showing that the CVSA was accurate in detecting deception. Instead, he states that it is being used by many law enforcement agencies who will attest to its accuracy based on the amount of additional information they have been able to obtain in interviews and the amount of confessions taken since employing the instrument. As stated earlier, tests for truth can serve a utility purpose as well as a scientifically valid purpose. Humble refers only to the CVSA's as utility value. If suspects believe they are about to take a "lie detector" test, they will give more information, and if they are told they failed the test, they are more likely to confess. Making decisions about a suspect's guilt or innocence using the device, or an applicant's suitability for a sensitive position, however, is a grave miscarriage of justice. ABC News Primetime investigators discovered that Dr. Humble received his doctorate degree in Psychology from a bible college, Indiana Christian University, which was located in a strip mall where Humble also had a business, after taking 6 hours of bible classes.

In an exhaustive 2006 study out of the University of Florida into voice stress technology, including the computerized voice stress analyzer (CVSA) and layered voice analyzer (LVA), Dr. Harry Hollien and his team concluded that neither the CVSA nor LVA showed any sensitivity to the presence of deception or stress.

In a 2007 study for the U.S. Department of Justice by Kelly Damphouse et al., they compared the accuracy of CVSA and LVA in detecting truth and deception with confirmed urinalysis drug results. They found little support for either the CVSA or LVA to detect deception. The CVSA detected deception 8% of the time and the LVA 21% of the time.

The U.S. Forces in Iraq and Afghanistan were employing the use of the CVSA until 2008; the Department of Defense issued the following policy memorandum:

By Policy Memorandum 08–11, dated June 16, 2008, Adm. Eric T. Olson, Commanding Officer of the U.S. Special Operations Command (SOCOM), has prohibited the use of Computer Voice Stress Analysis (CVSA) as a credibility assessment tool throughout his command.

In 2008, Admiral Eric T. Olsen, Commanding Officer of the U.S. Special Operations Command (SOCOM), issued a memorandum prohibiting the use of the CVSA as a tool for credibility assessment throughout his command. The polygraph and PCASS became the only instruments allowed for credibility assessment in the Department of Defense.

"Pursuant to USD(I) policy, however, research and improvements on other potential credibility assessment tools continue to be a priority for DOD."

The United States replaced the CVSA with a new device, the Preliminary Credibility Assessment Screening System (PCASS), which is a handheld computer or personal digital assistant that attempts to measure stress primarily by measuring changes in the electrodermal activity and blood volume changes monitored with a plethysmograph. The physiological data are interpreted by an algorithm designed by the Johns Hopkins University Advanced Physics Laboratory[3] that displays the word "Green" if the person is thought to be telling the truth, "Red" for deceptive, and "Yellow" for inconclusive. A PCASS examiner gets 1 week of training, either in the field or at the Defense Academy for Credibility Assessment (DACA) where the instrument was developed, and is now known as the National Center for Credibility Assessment (NCCA). The PCASS is manufactured by Lafayette Instrument Co. of Lafayette, Indiana, which also sells polygraph equipment. The cost is approximately $7526 apiece, plus about $600 per year for maintenance and technical support. The Army initially bought 94, and CIFA/DACA/NCCA bought 40 for testing and training. Accuracy for the PCASS system including inconclusives is between 63% and 79%, and it appears to be very susceptible to simple countermeasures.

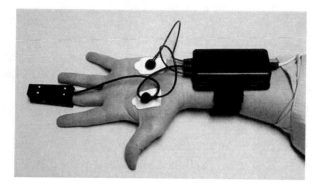

After 9/11 there was also interest generated in thermal imaging. The thermal imaging camera captures variations in facial temperature that can be monitored during questioning. The periorbital areas around the eye are highly sensitive to increases in temperature due to increases in mental activity. Accuracy for the device in a research study at an airport where 51 subjects were interviewed and screened showed 64% accuracy for truth tellers and 69% accuracy for deception.[4] Interviewers in the research study actually did better than the cameras, properly identifying 72% of the truthful and 77% of the liars. Since nervousness is a common factor for just about anyone being questioned by a customs agent in an airport, which in itself would cause facial temperature changes, actual use of the device may have an even higher false-positive rate.

The search for truth seems to be focusing more on the brain and its activity during truth and deception. It seems like lying should result in much more mental activity than telling the truth. The truth teller merely recalls facts. The liar has make the decision to lie, decide what to say, question if it will contradict something already stated, wonder if it can be investigated and proved to be false, and worry about what will happen if caught.

Lawrence Farwell, PhD, developed a process for detecting deception, which he named brain fingerprinting in the early 1990s. He maintained it was a scientific way to connect information of the crime with the memory of it stored in the brain of the perpetrator by monitoring brain waves. During the process, electroencephalograph signals are recorded noninvasively from the scalp. If a subject recognizes something, only the perpetrator would know, the brain emits an "Aha!" response, resulting in a specific and identifiable pattern known as a P300-MERMER, which indicates that the examinee possesses relevant knowledge of the crime that a truthful person would not be aware of.

There are limitations to the process. For example, it would not be applicable to screening testing of applicants. It could not be utilized if the suspect would have knowledge, even though innocent of the crime under investigation. For example, if a house was burglarized and the suspect had been in the house before, there may not be any aspect of the crime that would be unique to only the guilty party. A parent accused of molesting their child, or a victim of a crime, would have memories not associated necessarily with guilt or deception.

In 2005, I was contacted by Dr. Scott Faro, a radiologist, who was interested in setting up an experiment that compared the accuracy of functional magnetic resonance imaging (fMRI) technology to detect deception as compared to the accuracy of polygraph. There had already been research performed on fMRI in detecting deception at the University of Pennsylvania; however, the research used simple tasks, versus applying it to an actual mock crime, as Faro wanted to do, and no one had tested it against the polygraph.

I met with Dr. Faro and his team: Dr. Feroze Mohamed, a radiologist; Dr. Steven Platek and Dr. J. Michael Williams, neuropsychologists; and graduate medical student Harris Ahmad. They explained to me that the fMRI (Figure 15.2) stood for functional magnetic resonance imaging, which is a noninvasive medical test using a powerful magnetic field, radio-frequency pulses, and a computer to produce detailed pictures of organs, soft tissues, bone, and virtually all other internal body structures. fMRI is a relatively new procedure that uses MRI to measure the tiny metabolic changes that take place in an active part of the brain.

I was tasked with coming up with a mock crime. I wanted a scenario that would be memorable to the perpetrators and would involve as many of the senses as possible and decided on having them fire a gun. The participants

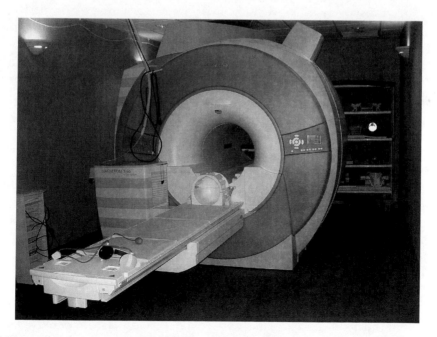

Figure 15.2 Functional magnetic resonance imaging is a relatively new procedure that uses MRI to measure the tiny metabolic changes that take place in an active part of the brain.

would be medical students, and firing a gun for most, if not all of them, would be a first time experience—handling a gun, pulling the trigger, hearing the explosion, seeing the flame and smoke, and smelling the burnt gunpowder. I also wanted everyone to be motivated to pass the tests. In real life everyone wants to come out truthful, both the innocent and guilty. All participants received a monetary amount for participating and an additional amount if they were determined to be truthful.

Dr. Faro met individually with each participant. Some were told that someone fired a gun in the hospital and they would be taking tests to determine their involvement. They were instructed to be cooperative and tell the truth. Others were told to fire the gun and deny the act. Faro was the only one who knew the difference between the two groups, and a gun was fired prior to each of the participants being interviewed or tested.

The rest of the team was blind and asked to differentiate between the shooters and innocent participants based on the fMRI findings versus the polygraph findings.[5]

We theorized a model of what happens in the brain and the areas that would be activated between truthful and deceptive people (Figure 15.3), which clearly showed that truthful individuals would have much less activation than those who lied.

Initially, we were going to perform both tests at the same time; however, we quickly discovered that when the fMRI was activated, it totally destroyed EDR data, and additionally, when a person is lying on their back, respiration is affected.

All participants were first interviewed using the Forensic Assessment Interview Technique. This actually resulted in one of the guilty participants confessing and being eliminated from the study. Following the interview, half of the participants were given fMRI tests followed by polygraph examinations and the other half polygraphs followed by fMRI.

Since brain activation required a great deal of data, the fMRI sequence was as follows: First, they listened to the same Integrated Zone Comparison Test (IZCT) questions that would be used throughout the testing. Then they were told to answer each question truthfully.[6] They then were instructed to lie to every test question.[7] The fourth test was administered like a positive control examination where each question was asked twice, with the participant instructed to lie to the question first and then tell the truth when it was repeated, and the last test reversed the order to tell the truth first and then lie when the question was repeated.

The polygraph examination was administered as an IZCT with the first chart administered as a silent answer test, the second chart answered out loud truthfully with the relevant test question order rotated, and the third chart again answered out loud with the relevant questions again rotated and the relevant questions now asked prior to the comparison questions. Polygraph

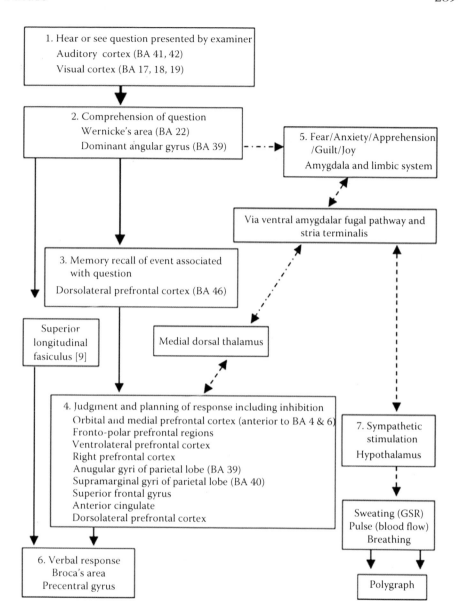

Figure 15.3 Diagram shows hypothetical model of deception. (Reprinted from Mohamed, F.B. et al., *Radiology*, 238, 679, 2006. With permission from Radiological Society of North America.)

data were collected using a Lafayette Computerized LX4000 System and scored by three algorithms: ASIT PolySuite, PolyScore, and OSS II.[8]

The fMRI showed brain activity for deceptive participants (Figure 15.4) to be almost twice as much as for truthful participants (Figure 15.5) and resulted in accuracy in the mid 80%. The accuracy with inconclusives

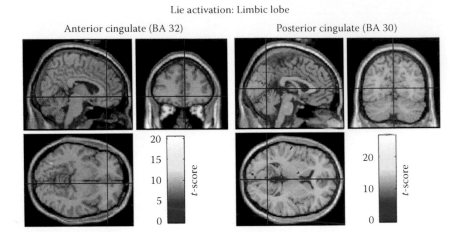

Figure 15.4 Functional magnetic resonance imaging deception activation.

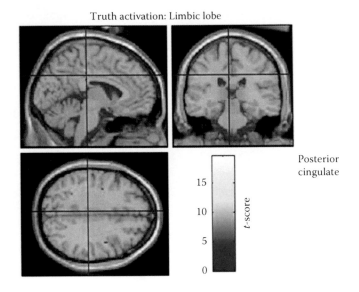

Figure 15.5 Functional magnetic resonance imaging truth activation.

counted as errors for ASIT PolySuite was 90%, while for PolyScore and OSS II, both were 72%. When inconclusives were excluded, all three algorithms had 100% accuracy.

When the fMRI data were included with the polygraph data, allowing for each parameter to have equal input and increasing the total score required for truth or deception from $a \pm 13$ to $a \pm 18$, the polygraph had 100% accuracy and no inconclusive results with ASIT PolySuite. When the fMRI data were merged with the scores generated from the polygraph, the outcome for

PolyScore and OSS II accuracy was 90%. The synergy of the data increased the accuracy of the outcome. The creation of an even more sophisticated brain imaging technique is called magnetic particle imaging. The future will see what that means to the search for truth.

We do not know where technology in the search for truth will take us in the future; however, we do know that the need to accurately determine credibility will always be needed. Additional physiological components will definitely be added, and perhaps someday these physiological data will be monitored and collected without having to attach anything to the examinee's body. Regardless of the technology examiners will still be needed to conduct proper interviews, prepare the examinees for the test, to develop the test questions, and to conduct focused interviews after examinations that indicate deception or significant reactions to test questions.

Always remember that the art of truth verification is eliminating false/positives. Ensuring that truthful examinees, are in fact determined to be truthful. This is the real "art" of polygraph.

Notes

1. Webb, A. et al. (2009). Eye movements and pupil size reveal deception in computer administered questionnaires, *Foundations of Augmented Cognition. Neuroergonomics and Operational Neuroscience*, Springer Berlin Heidelberg, pp. 553–562.
2. Marchak, F. Detecting false intent using eye blink measurements. Original research article *Frontiers in Psychology*, 4, 736. Available at http://dx.doi.org/10.3389/fpsyg.2013.00736 (accessed October 11, 2013).
3. The Johns Hopkins University Advanced Physics Laboratory is also the developers of the polygraph algorithm PolyScore.
4. Warmeling, L. et al. (2011) Thermal imaging as a lie detection tool at airports. *Law and Human Behavior*, 35(1), 40–48.
5. Mohamed, F. B. et al. (2006) Brain mapping of deception and truth telling about an ecologically valid situation. *Radiology*, 238(2), 679–688.
6. Innocent participants would be telling the truth to the Irrelevant and Relevant questions, while lying to the Comparison questions, and guilty participants would be telling the truth to the Irrelevant questions and lying to the Comparison and Relevant test questions.
7. Innocent participants would be telling the truth to Comparison questions and lying to the Irrelevant and Relevant test questions, while guilty participants would be telling the truth to Relevant questions and lying to all other questions.
8. Gordon, N. J. et al. (2006) Integrated zone comparison polygraph technique accuracy with scoring algorithms. *Physiology and Behavior*, 87, 251–254.

Appendix

Medical Release Waiver for Polygraph Examination

PATIENT'S Name: _____ Date of Birth: _____ Age: _____

Address: _____City:_____

State: _____ Zip/Postal Code: _____Email Address: _____

Home Phone: _____ Cell: _____

Pre-existing Medical Conditions (include allergy and prescription information):

_____

_____

_____

_____

Prescribed Medication:

_____

_____

_____

_____

I, the undersigned physician of the individual named above, do hereby agree that it is my professional medical opinion that it is safe for the individual to participate in the aforementioned polygraph examination for the purpose of:

_____

_____

and authorize the polygraph examiner of _____,
representing their client _____
_____ to perform said examination.

_____   _____

Physician's Signature   Date

Physician's Name Printed _____Phone #_____

It is understood that as in any test procedure, participation involves a certain element of risk. Understanding this I request the examination be administered, and hereby release the polygraph examiner, the polygraph firm, the requesting agency/company, and all of their employees, executives, and heirs, both present and future, from all and any liability resulting from this polygraph examination.

_____   _____

Examinee's Signature   Date

Agreement of Cooperation

Keystone Intelligence Network, Inc.

1704 Locust Street, Philadelphia, PA 19103, www.keystone-intelligence.com, 215–545–1111.

Agreement of Cooperation

- I understand and agree that the polygraph procedure requires my total cooperation.
- I agree that a truthful person would offer full cooperation to the procedure and that a person who is lying would be uncooperative.
- I further agree that as in any scientific procedure, deliberate attempts to defeat the purpose of the assessment are counterproductive and in itself a sign of deception.
- Therefore I accept that any lack of full cooperation on my part will be considered to be the behavior of a deceptive individual and the grounds for the examiner to report the results as same.

_____   _____

Signed by Examinee   Date

_____   _____

Witnessed by Examiner   Date

Sample Polygraph Form with Faint

Keystone Intelligence Network, Inc.

1704 Locust Street, Philadelphia, PA 19103, (215) 545-1111; Fax (215) 454-1773

Name: _____   File No.: _____

Address: _____   Date of Interview: _____

_____   Client: _____

_____   Telephone No.: _____

Telephone No.: _____   Requested By: _____

Interviewee Arrived: _____   Oral Report To: _____

Interview Started: _____   Location of Interview:_____

Interview Ended: _____   _____

Interviewee Left: _____   _____

Interviewer: _____   Investigator Present?: ☐ YES ☐ NO

Verified By: _____   Name: _____

CONSENT FORM

I, _____, have been advised, before submitting myself to a
Polygraph Examination, on this the _____ day of _____,
20_____, that I cannot be forced to submit myself to take a Polygraph
Examination for any reason. Furthermore, I have the absolute right to refuse
such interview. With full knowledge of these rights and without duress, coer-
cion, force, intimidation, or promises of immunity or reward, I do hereby
request a Periodic Assessment Interview be given to me by an Interviewer of
Keystone Intelligence Network, Inc., for the mutual benefit of myself and ___

_____.

I also authorize the Interviewer of Keystone Intelligence Network, Inc., to
disclose both orally and/or in writing, all information, results, conclusions, and/
or opinions arising from said interview, to _____,
for whatever uses they may determine. I further authorize Keystone
Intelligence Network, Inc., to electronically record this interview for the purposes of review, reporting, research, or training. I understand fully that I can
terminate this interview anytime I so desire. Intending to be legally bound,
I remise, release, waive, and forever discharge all and each of the above cor-
porations, firms, and/or individuals from any and all actions or causes of

action, claims or demands, liability, or legal action which I may have now or may ever have resulting directly or indirectly, or remotely both by my taking said interview and/or oral or written information, results, conclusions, and/ or opinions, rendered because of said Polygraph Examination.

In Witness Whereof, I Have Hereunto Set My Hand and Seal

_____   _____
WITNESS   DATE   (SEAL) Signature of Interviewee   DATE

This interview was concluded at _____, on the above date. Having submitted myself freely to the interview, I hereby reaffirm my agreement as expressed above. I swear that during said interview, I was well treated and remained of my own free will, knowing that I could leave anytime I so desired. I also swear and certify there were no threats, and/or harm done to me, or any promises made to me during the entire time that I have been here, either in connection with the interview or the signing of this form.

_____   _____
WITNESS   DATE   (SEAL) Signature of Interviewee   DATE

PERSONAL DATA:

Age: _____ DOB: _____ Married: ☐ Single ☐ Separated ☐ Divorced

Children: _____ Driver's License/ID: _____ Ever Arrested?: ☐ YES ☐ NO

If yes, explain: _____

_____

When asked to do interview?: _____ By Whom: _____

How far did you go in school?: 1 2 3 4 5 6 7 8 9 10 11 12 Did you graduate?: YES ☐ NO ☐

College: _____ Years Attended: _____ Degree: _____

Military Service: _____ Years: _____ Type Discharge: _____

MEDICAL DATA:

Have you been hospitalized in the last 5 years?: YES ☐ NO ☐
If yes explain: _____

Under the care of a physician at this time?: YES ☐ NO ☐
If yes explain: _____

Taking any medication at this time?: YES ☐ NO ☐
If yes explain: _____

Do you have any pain or discomfort at this time?: YES ☐ NO ☐
If yes explain: _____

Ever have problems with: Heart_____Asthma_____
Epilepsy_____Hypertension_____
Hearing_____ Orthopedic_____ Optical_____ Are you
pregnant_____

Do you know of any mental or physical reason why you could not take a polygraph examination?: YES ☐ NO ☐

If yes explain: _____

MISCELLANEOUS:

How many hours sleep did you get last night?: _____ Norm _____
Sleep soundly? YES ☐ NO ☐

If no explain: _____

In the past 24 hours have you had any alcohol/used any illegal substances?:
YES ☐ NO ☐

If yes explain: _____

Do you need to go to the bathroom: _____ Left:_____
Returned:_____

POSTURE/DEMEANOR (+1 Truthful/0 Inconclusive/−1 Deceptive)
Score: (+) (0) (−)

ELICITED VERBAL RESPONSES
1a. Where do you work?

_____

_____

1b. How long have you worked there/here?

_____

_____

2. What do you do?

_____

_____

3. How do you like working there/here?

_____

_____

(Positive Answer/No Hesitation-Adaptors-Coding) **Score: (+3) (0)**

4. What is this interview and investigation about?

_____

_____

(Strong Language: Steal/Theft/Rape) **Score: (+2) (−2)**

5. Why were you selected to be interviewed?

_____

_____

(Includes Self as Suspect) **Score: (+1) (0)**

6. How do you feel about being interviewed?

_____

(Positive Answer with No Hesitation/No Adaptors) **Score: (+2) (0)**

7. Please write/tell me in detail what you know about this and how you would explain it.

_____

(Explains Crime with Strong Language/Proper Use of Pronouns)
Score: (+1) (−2)

8. If you were the investigator, how would you conduct the investigation?

_____

_____

Score: (+1) (0) (−1)

9. What are the five most important causes that would have created this situation?

_____

_____

Score: (+1) (0) (−1)

10. Did you ever think about doing something like this?

_____

_____

(No Hesitation—Adaptors) **Score: (+1) (−1)**

11. (Comparison) During the first ___ years of your life did you ever

_____

_____

12. Did you

_____

_____

Score: (+1) (0) (−1)

13. (Comparison) In your entire life, did you ever

_____

_____

14. Who would you suspect?

_____

_____

Score: (+3) (0)

15. Who would you vouch for?

_____

_____

Score: (+2) (0)

16. When the person who did this is caught, what do you think should happen to them?

_____

_____

(Strong Punishment: Fired/Prosecution) **Score: (+2) (−1)**

17. Would you give them a second chance?

_____

_____

("No" without Any Hesitation) **Score: (+2) (−1)**

18. We will be doing a thorough investigation. We will interview everyone and conduct forensic tests. How do you think the investigation will come out concerning you, and whether or not you did this?

_____

_____

(Positive Answer) **Score: (+2) (−1)**

19. Would there be any reason evidence would turn up indicating you did this?

_____

_____

("No" without Any Hesitation—Hedges) **Score: (+2) (−1)**

20. Would you be willing to chip in to pay for _____?
_____

_____

Score: (+3) (−1)

21. Why do you think someone would do something like this?
_____

_____

(Negative/Condescending/I Don't Know) **Score: (+1) (0)**

22. Do you think it was done deliberately, or could it have been accidental?
_____

_____

Score: (+3) (0)

23. Do you know for sure who did this?
_____

_____

("No," with No Hesitations or Adaptors) **Score: (+2) (0)**

24. In your entire life, did you ever tell a lie to get out of trouble?
_____

_____

25. Did you lie about whether or not you did this?
_____

_____

Score: (+) (0) (−)

26. If you had been the interviewer, and had three questions to ask to resolve this problem, what would you have asked?
_____

_____

(Asks a strong relevant question: "Did I do it?") **Score: (+1) (0)**

27. If we need to speak with you again, would you be willing to return?
_____

AFTER INTERVIEW

How do you feel now that the interview is over? _____

Should I believe your answers? *(Note: Must answer "Yes" here to be considered for a +3)*

_____

If yes, give me one reason why.

_____

What would you say if the investigation proves you did this?

_____

What were your emotions during the interview?

_____

Were you afraid?_____

If you were asked to pay, how much would you be willing to pay?

_____

                                                           Score: (+3) (0)

Note: To receive a +3: must answer Question #2 "Yes," and then say: "I did not lie," "I told the truth," "I did not do the crime" as part of their answer to any other question.

Employee Polygraph Protection Act (EPPA)

29 USC Chapter 22—Employee Polygraph Protection

TITLE 29 - LABOR

CHAPTER 22 - EMPLOYEE POLYGRAPH PROTECTION

Sec.
2001. Definitions.
2002. Prohibitions on lie detector use.
2003. Notice of protection.
2004. Authority of Secretary.
2005. Enforcement provisions.
2006. Exemptions.
2007. Restrictions on use of exemptions.
2008. Disclosure of information.
2009. Effect on other law and agreements.

Sec. 2001. Definitions

As used in this chapter:

(1) *Commerce*: The term "commerce" has the meaning provided by section 203(b) of this title.
(2) *Employer*: The term "employer" includes any person acting directly or indirectly in the interest of an employer in relation to an employee or prospective employee.
(3) *Lie detector*: The term "lie detector" includes a polygraph, deceptograph, voice stress analyzer, psychological stress evaluator, or any other similar device (whether mechanical or electrical) that is used, or the results of which are used, for the purpose of rendering a diagnostic opinion regarding the honesty or dishonesty of an individual.
(4) *Polygraph*: The term "polygraph" means an instrument that
　(A) records continuously, visually, permanently, and simultaneously changes in cardiovascular, respiratory, and electrodermal patterns as minimum instrumentation standards; and
　(B) is used, or the results of which are used, for the purpose of rendering a diagnostic opinion regarding the honesty or dishonesty of an individual.
(5) *Secretary*: The term "Secretary" means the Secretary of Labor.

Sec. 2002. Prohibitions on lie detector use

Except as provided in sections 2006 and 2007 of this title, it shall be unlawful for any employer engaged in or affecting commerce or in the production of goods for commerce -

   (1) directly or indirectly, to require, request, suggest, or cause any employee or prospective employee to take or submit to any lie detector test;

   (2) to use, accept, refer to, or inquire concerning the results of any lie detector test of any employee or prospective employee;

   (3) to discharge, discipline, discriminate against in any manner, or deny employment or promotion to, or threaten to take any such action against -

      (A) any employee or prospective employee who refuses, declines, or fails to take or submit to any lie detector test, or

      (B) any employee or prospective employee on the basis of the results of any lie detector test; or

   (4) to discharge, discipline, discriminate against in any manner, or deny employment or promotion to, or threaten to take any such action against, any employee or prospective employee because

      (A) such employee or prospective employee has filed any complaint or instituted or caused to be instituted any proceeding under or related to this chapter,

      (B) such employee or prospective employee has testified or is about to testify in any such proceeding, or

      (C) of the exercise by such employee or prospective employee, on behalf of such employee or another person, of any right afforded by this chapter.

Sec. 2003. Notice of protection

The Secretary shall prepare, have printed, and distribute a notice setting forth excerpts from, or summaries of, the pertinent provisions of this chapter. Each employer shall post and maintain such notice in conspicuous places on its premises where notices to employees and applicants to employment are customarily posted.

Sec. 2004. Authority of Secretary

  (a) In general

     The Secretary shall -

     (1) issue such rules and regulations as may be necessary or appropriate to carry out this chapter;

(2) cooperate with regional, State, local, and other agencies, and cooperate with and furnish technical assistance to employers, labor organizations, and employment agencies to aid in effectuating the purposes of this chapter; and

(3) make investigations and inspections and require the keeping of records necessary or appropriate for the administration of this chapter.

(b) Subpoena authority

For the purpose of any hearing or investigation under this chapter, the Secretary shall have the authority contained in sections 49 and 50 of title 15.

Sec. 2005. Enforcement provisions

(a) Civil penalties

(1) In general

Subject to paragraph (2), any employer who violates any provision of this chapter may be assessed a civil penalty of not more than $10,000.

(2) Determination of amount

In determining the amount of any penalty under paragraph (1), the Secretary shall take into account the previous record of the person in terms of compliance with this chapter and the gravity of the violation.

(3) Collection

Any civil penalty assessed under this subsection shall be collected in the same manner as is required by subsections (b) through (e) of section 1853 of this title with respect to civil penalties assessed under subsection (a) of such section.

(b) Injunctive actions by Secretary

The Secretary may bring an action under this section to restrain violations of this chapter. The Solicitor of Labor may appear for and represent the Secretary in any litigation brought under this chapter. In any action brought under this section, the district courts of the United States shall have jurisdiction, for cause shown, to issue temporary or permanent restraining orders and injunctions to require compliance with this chapter, including such legal or equitable relief incident thereto as may be appropriate, including, but not limited to, employment, reinstatement, promotion, and the payment of lost wages and benefits.

(c) Private civil actions
  (1) Liability
      An employer who violates this chapter shall be liable to the
      employee or prospective employee affected by such violation. Such
      employer shall be liable for such legal or equitable relief as may be
      appropriate, including, but not limited to, employment, reinstate-
      ment, promotion, and the payment of lost wages and benefits.
  (2) Court
      An action to recover the liability prescribed in paragraph (1) may
      be maintained against the employer in any Federal or State court
      of competent jurisdiction by an employee or prospective employee
      for or on behalf of such employee, prospective employee, and
      other employees or prospective employees similarly situated. No
      such action may be commenced more than 3 years after the date
      of the alleged violation.
  (3) Costs
      The court, in its discretion, may allow the prevailing party (other
      than the United States) reasonable costs, including attorney's
      fees.
(d) Waiver of rights prohibited
    The rights and procedures provided by this chapter may not be
    waived by contract or otherwise, unless such waiver is part of a writ-
    ten settlement agreed to and signed by the parties to the pending
    action or complaint under this chapter.

Sec. 2006. Exemptions

(a) No application to governmental employers. This chapter shall not
    apply with respect to the United States Government, any State or
    local government, or any political subdivision of a State or local
    government.
(b) National defense and security exemption
  (1) National defense
      Nothing in this chapter shall be construed to prohibit the admin-
      istration, by the Federal Government, in the performance of any
      counterintelligence function, of any lie detector test to -
    (A) any expert or consultant under contract to the Department of
        Defense or any employee of any contractor of such Department;
        or
    (B) any expert or consultant under contract with the Department of
        Energy in connection with the atomic energy defense activities
        of such Department or any employee of any contractor of such
        Department in connection with such activities.

(2) Security

Nothing in this chapter shall be construed to prohibit the administration, by the Federal Government, in the performance of any intelligence or counterintelligence function, of any lie detector test to -

(A)

   (i)   any individual employed by, assigned to, or detailed to, the National Security Agency, the Defense Intelligence Agency, the National Geospatial-Intelligence Agency, or the Central Intelligence Agency,

  (ii)   any expert or consultant under contract to any such agency,

 (iii)   any employee of a contractor to any such agency,

 (iv)   any individual applying for a position in any such agency, or

  (v)   any individual assigned to a space where sensitive cryptologic information is produced, processed, or stored for any such agency; or

(B) any expert, or consultant (or employee of such expert or consultant) under contract with any Federal Government department, agency, or program whose duties involve access to information that has been classified at the level of top secret or designated as being within a special access program under section 4.2(a) of Executive Order 12356 (or a successor Executive order).

(c) FBI contractors exemption

Nothing in this chapter shall be construed to prohibit the administration, by the Federal Government, in the performance of any counterintelligence function, of any lie detector test to an employee of a contractor of the Federal Bureau of Investigation of the Department of Justice who is engaged in the performance of any work under the contract with such Bureau.

(d) Limited exemption for ongoing investigations

Subject to sections 2007 and 2009 of this title, this chapter shall not prohibit an employer from requesting an employee to submit to a polygraph test if -

(1) the test is administered in connection with an ongoing investigation involving economic loss or injury to the employer's business, such as theft, embezzlement, misappropriation, or an act of unlawful industrial espionage or sabotage;

(2) the employee had access to the property that is the subject of the investigation;

(3) the employer has a reasonable suspicion that the employee was involved in the incident or activity under investigation; and

(4) the employer executes a statement, provided to the examinee before the test, that -
    (A) sets forth with particularity the specific incident or activity being investigated and the basis for testing particular employees,
    (B) is signed by a person (other than a polygraph examiner) authorized to legally bind the employer,
    (C) is retained by the employer for at least 3 years, and
    (D) contains at a minimum -
        (i)   an identification of the specific economic loss or injury to the business of the employer,
        (ii) a statement indicating that the employee had access to the property that is the subject of the investigation, and
        (iii) a statement describing the basis of the employer's reasonable suspicion that the employee was involved in the incident or activity under investigation.
(e) Exemption for security services
    (1) In general
        Subject to paragraph (2) and sections 2007 and 2009 of this title, this chapter shall not prohibit the use of polygraph tests on prospective employees by any private employer whose primary business purpose consists of providing armored car personnel, personnel engaged in the design, installation, and maintenance of security alarm systems, or other uniformed or plainclothes security personnel and whose function includes protection of -
    (A) facilities, materials, or operations having a significant impact on the health or safety of any State or political subdivision thereof, or the national security of the United States, as determined under rules and regulations issued by the Secretary within 90 days after June 27, 1988, including -
        (i)   facilities engaged in the production, transmission, or distribution of electric or nuclear power,
        (ii) public water supply facilities,
        (iii) shipments or storage of radioactive or other toxic waste materials, and
        (iv) public transportation, or
    (B) currency, negotiable securities, precious commodities or instruments, or proprietary information.
    (2) Access
        The exemption provided under this subsection shall not apply if the test is administered to a prospective employee who would not be employed to protect facilities, materials, operations, or assets referred to in paragraph (1).

(f) Exemption for drug security, drug theft, or drug diversion investigations
  (1) In general
      Subject to paragraph (2) and sections 2007 and 2009 of this title, this chapter shall not prohibit the use of a polygraph test by any employer authorized to manufacture, distribute, or dispense a controlled substance listed in schedule I, II, III, or IV of section 812 of title 21.
  (2) Access
      The exemption provided under this subsection shall apply -
      (A) if the test is administered to a prospective employee who would have direct access to the manufacture, storage, distribution, or sale of any such controlled substance; or
      (B) in the case of a test administered to a current employee, if -
          (i) the test is administered in connection with an ongoing investigation of criminal or other misconduct involving, or potentially involving, loss or injury to the manufacture, distribution, or dispensing of any such controlled substance by such employer, and
          (ii) the employee had access to the person or property that is the subject of the investigation.

Sec. 2007. Restrictions on use of exemptions

(a) Test as basis for adverse employment action
  (1) Under ongoing investigations exemption
      Except as provided in paragraph (2), the exemption under subsection (d) of section 2006 of this title shall not apply if an employee is discharged, disciplined, denied employment or promotion, or otherwise discriminated against in any manner on the basis of the analysis of a polygraph test chart or the refusal to take a polygraph test, without additional supporting evidence. The evidence required by such subsection may serve as additional supporting evidence.
  (2) Under other exemptions
      In the case of an exemption described in subsection (e) or (f) of such section, the exemption shall not apply if the results of an analysis of a polygraph test chart are used, or the refusal to take a polygraph test is used, as the sole basis upon which an adverse employment action described in paragraph (1) is taken against an employee or prospective employee.
(b) Rights of examinee

The exemptions provided under subsections (d), (e), and (f) of section 2006 of this title shall not apply unless the requirements described in the following paragraphs are met:

(1) All phases
   Throughout all phases of the test -
   (A) the examinee shall be permitted to terminate the test at any time;
   (B) the examinee is not asked questions in a manner designed to degrade, or needlessly intrude on, such examinee;
   (C) the examinee is not asked any question concerning -
       (i)   religious beliefs or affiliations,
       (ii)   beliefs or opinions regarding racial matters,
       (iii) political beliefs or affiliations,
       (iv)   any matter relating to sexual behavior; and
       (v)   beliefs, affiliations, opinions, or lawful activities regarding unions or labor organizations; and
   (D) the examiner does not conduct the test if there is sufficient written evidence by a physician that the examinee is suffering from a medical or psychological condition or undergoing treatment that might cause abnormal responses during the actual testing phase.
(2) Pretest phase
   During the pretest phase, the prospective examinee -
   (A) is provided with reasonable written notice of the date, time, and location of the test, and of such examinee's right to obtain and consult with legal counsel or an employee representative before each phase of the test;
   (B) is informed in writing of the nature and characteristics of the tests and of the instruments involved;
   (C) is informed, in writing -
       (i)   whether the testing area contains a two-way mirror, a camera, or any other device through which the test can be observed,
       (ii)   whether any other device, including any device for recording or monitoring the test, will be used, or
       (iii) that the employer or the examinee may (with mutual knowledge) make a recording of the test;
   (D) is read and signs a written notice informing such examinee -
       (i)   that the examinee cannot be required to take the test as a condition of employment,
       (ii)   that any statement made during the test may constitute additional supporting evidence for the purposes of an adverse employment action described in subsection (a) of this section,
       (iii) of the limitations imposed under this section,

          (iv) of the legal rights and remedies available to the examinee if the polygraph test is not conducted in accordance with this chapter, and

          (v) of the legal rights and remedies of the employer under this chapter (including the rights of the employer under section 2008(c)(2) of this title); and

    (E) is provided an opportunity to review all questions to be asked during the test and is informed of the right to terminate the test at any time.

(3) Actual testing phase

During the actual testing phase, the examiner does not ask such examinee any question relevant during the test that was not presented in writing for review to such examinee before the test.

(4) Post-test phase

Before any adverse employment action, the employer shall -

    (A) further interview the examinee on the basis of the results of the test; and

    (B) provide the examinee with -

          (i) a written copy of any opinion or conclusion rendered as a result of the test, and

          (ii) a copy of the questions asked during the test along with the corresponding charted responses.

(5) Maximum number and minimum duration of tests

The examiner shall not conduct and complete more than five polygraph tests on a calendar day on which the test is given, and shall not conduct any such test for less than a 90-minute duration.

(c) Qualifications and requirements of examiners

The exemptions provided under subsections (d), (e), and (f) of section 2006 of this title shall not apply unless the individual who conducts the polygraph test satisfies the requirements under the following paragraphs:

(1) Qualifications

The examiner -

    (A) has a valid and current license granted by licensing and regulatory authorities in the State in which the test is to be conducted, if so required by the State; and

    (B) maintains a minimum of a $50,000 bond or an equivalent amount of professional liability coverage.

(2) Requirements

The examiner -

(A) renders any opinion or conclusion regarding the test -

    (i)   in writing and solely on the basis of an analysis of polygraph test charts,

   (ii)   that does not contain information other than admissions, information, case facts, and interpretation of the charts relevant to the purpose and stated objectives of the test, and

  (iii)   that does not include any recommendation concerning the employment of the examinee; and

(B) maintains all opinions, reports, charts, written questions, lists, and other records relating to the test for a minimum period of 3 years after administration of the test.

Sec. 2008. Disclosure of information

(a) In general

A person, other than the examinee, may not disclose information obtained during a polygraph test, except as provided in this section.

(b) Permitted disclosures

A polygraph examiner may disclose information acquired from a polygraph test only to -

(1) the examinee or any other person specifically designated in writing by the examinee;

(2) the employer that requested the test; or

(3) any court, governmental agency, arbitrator, or mediator, in accordance with due process of law, pursuant to an order from a court of competent jurisdiction.

(c) Disclosure by employer

An employer (other than an employer described in subsection (a), (b), or (c) of section 2006 of this title) for whom a polygraph test is conducted may disclose information from the test only to -

(1) a person in accordance with subsection (b) of this section; or

(2) a governmental agency, but only insofar as the disclosed information is an admission of criminal conduct.

Sec. 2009. Effect on other law and agreements

Except as provided in subsections (a), (b), and (c) of section 2006 of this title, this chapter shall not preempt any provision of any State or local law or of any negotiated collective bargaining agreement that prohibits lie detector tests or is more restrictive with respect to lie detector tests than any provision of this chapter.

Sample EPPA Notice of Ongoing Investigation

Notice of Ongoing Investigation

To Employee:

Investigation Concerning: _____

We respectfully request your cooperation to help resolve the above mentioned (**Economic Loss**) by taking a forensic psychophysiological truth verification/polygraph examination as part of an ongoing investigation. (This is a scientific instrument which permanently records cardiovascular, pulmonary and electro-dermal responses of the person being examined.)

Please be advised that you have the right to consult with legal counsel or an employee representative before each phase of the examination. However, your attorney or employee representative may be excluded from the room where the examination is administered during the actual testing phase.

To wit: The above employee had reasonable access to the property that is subject to the investigation and as a result of this ongoing investigation there is reasonable suspicion for the following reasons to request this examination of the above employee:

    ____ **Conflict in Statements/Records**
    ____ **Sole Access**
    ____ **Unusual Behavior**

The instrument to be used in this examination is a _____

The employee has been given at least 48 hours' notice prior to the actual examination which is to be conducted at KEYSTONE INTELLIGENCE NETWORK, INC.
1704 Locust Street, Philadelphia, PA 19103, 215–545–1111

Date:_____ Time:_____

Issued by:_____
    (Company Name)   _____
                                  Date

Received by:_____
    Employee's Signature   _____
                              Date/Time

To be **RETAINED BY EMPLOYER FOR 3 YEARS**
with copies to employee & Keystone Intelligence Network, Inc.

EPPA Pre-employment 48 Hour Waiver

USE EMPLOYER'S LETTERHEAD

MODEL LETTER
from
EMPLOYER TO APPLICANT
To Be Polygraphed

TO: <u>Name and Address of APPLICANT</u>   Date:_____

You are herewith being offered a job at this company contingent upon your satisfactorily meeting all of the job requisites and standards based on you verified completed job application and employer interview. You are hereby requested to submit to a pre-employment polygraph examination on _____, 20_____ at _____ (am) (pm) with Keystone Intelligence Network, Inc., 1704 Locust Street, 2nd Floor, Philadelphia, PA 19103, (215)545–1111.

Please be advised that you have 48 hours, excluding weekend days and holidays, in which to consult with an attorney or an employee representative before the scheduled examination. You also have the right to consult with legal counsel or an employee representative before each phase of the polygraph examination. However, your attorney or employee representative may be excluded from the room where the examination is administrated during the actual testing phase. You may at your sole option give written consent to the administration of the polygraph test within 48 hours but no earlier than 24 hours after receipt of this notice.

(I DO) (DO NOT) WAIVE THE 48 HOURS REQUIREMENTS _____
                                                    (Signature of Applicant)

_____   _____

(Singed by Job Applicant)   (Must be signed by any person other than
                             polygraphist who is legally authorized to bind
                             employer)

_____

(Time and Date of Receipt of this
Letter by Applicant)

(FAX executed copy to Keystone Intelligence Network, Inc., at 215–545–1773)

EPPA Rights of the Examinee

Keystone Intelligence Network, Inc.
1704 Locust Street, Second Floor, Philadelphia, PA 19103, (215) 545–1111;
Fax (215) 545-1773

Your Polygraph Examination Rights

NOTICE TO POLYGRAPH EXAMINEE

Section 8(b) of the Employee Polygraph Protection Act, and the U.S. Department of Labor regulations (29 CFR 801.22) require that you be given the following information before taking a polygraph examination:

1.
   a. The polygraph examination room (does) (does not) contain a camera, or other device by which you may be observed.
   b. Another device, such as those used in monitoring conversation, or recording the same, (will) will not) be used during the examination.
   c. Both you and the employer have the right, with the other's knowledge, to electronically record the entire examination.
2.
   a. You have the right to end the test anytime.
   b. You have the right, and will be given the opportunity, to review all questions to be asked during the test.
   c. You may not be asked questions in a way that degrades or needlessly intrudes.
   d. You may not be asked any questions concerning: Religious beliefs or opinions; beliefs regarding racial matters; political beliefs or affiliations; matters relating to sexual behavior; beliefs, affiliation, opinions, or lawful activities regarding unions or labor organization.
   e. The test may not be conducted if there is sufficient written evidence by a physician that you are suffering from a medical or psychological condition or undergoing treatment that may cause abnormal responses during the examination.
3.
   a. The test is not and cannot be required as a condition of employment.
   b. The employer may not discharge, dismiss, discipline, deny employment or promotion, or other discriminations against you based on the analysis of a polygraph test, or based on your refusal to take such a test without additional evidence that would support the action.
   c.
      (1) In connection with an ongoing investigation, the additional evidence required for an employer to take adverse action against you, including termination, may be (A) evidence that you had access to

the property that is the subject of the investigation, together with (B) the evidence supporting the employer's reasonable suspicion that you were involved in the incident or activity under investigation.

(2) Any statement made by you before or during the test may serve as additional supporting evidence for an adverse employment action described in 3 (b) above, and any admission of criminal conduct by you may be transmitted to an appropriate government law enforcement agency.

4.

  a. Information acquired from a polygraph examination may be disclosed by the examiner or by the employer only;

  (1) to you or any other person specifically designated in writing by you to receive such information;

  (2) to the employer that requested the test;

  (3) to a court, governmental agency, arbitrator, or mediator that obtains a court order;

  (4) to a U.S. Department of Labor official when specifically designated in writing by you to receive such information.

  b. Information acquired from a polygraph test may be disclosed by the employer to an appropriate governmental agency without a court order where, and only insofar as the information disclosed is an admission of criminal conduct.

5. If any of your rights or protections under the law are violated, you have the right to file a complaint with the Wage and Hour Division of the U.S. Department of Labor, or take action in court against the employer. Employers who violate this law are liable to the affected examinee, who may recover such legal or equitable relief as may be appropriate, including employment, reinstatement, and promotion, payment of lost wages and benefits, and reasonable costs, including attorneys' fees. The Secretary of Labor may also bring action to restrain violations of the act, or may assess civil money penalties against the employer.

6. Your rights under the Act may not be waived, either voluntarily or involuntarily, by contract or otherwise, except as part of a written settlement to a pending action or complaint under the Act, and agreed to and signed by the parties.

I acknowledge that I have received a copy of the above notice, and that it has been read to me.

_____   _____
Date   Examinee Signature

_____   _____
Witness   Please print your name here

EPPA How the Polygraph Works

The Nature and Characteristics of the Polygraph Instrument/Examination

What Is a Polygraph?

The polygraph instrument is a scientific instrument, consisting of at least three sub-parts that allow the polygraph examiner to monitor and record some of your physiological (bodily) functions. These functions include cardiovascular (heart) activity sweat gland activity and body movements.

How Does a Polygraph Test Work?

All people have an emergency, or survival system, commonly known as the "fight or flight" system. Any time your brain thinks you are in danger, this system is automatically turned on, causing sudden changes to take place within you to better prepare you to meet the threat. Before the polygraph examination, the examiner will review all of the test questions with you. So, you will know exactly what you are going to be asked during the test. If, during the test, you are asked a question you have decided to lie to, your brain will perceive this question as a threat and turn on your body's emergency system. You will experience sudden changes taking place within your body, and simultaneously the polygraph instrument will permanently record them. For your protection, the examiner will run more than one test (asking the questions more than once). This is to ensure that any changes taking place in your body are due to your fear of detection caused by lying to a specific question, and is not just some accidental change occurring.

I acknowledge that the nature and characteristics of the polygraph instrument and examination have been explained to me, that I have had the opportunity to ask questions and feel satisfied with the explanations. I have received a copy of this document.

_____   _____
Date   Examinee Signature

_____   _____
Witness   Please print your name here

EPPA Checklist for Examiners

Polygraph Examination Checklist

T F 1. I hereby consent to be examined by means of the polygraph technique.

T F 2. I have received a statement setting forth the specific reason for the examination.

T F 3. I have received a statement setting forth the information that I had access to and the reason for this examination.

T F 4. I have received a statement setting forth the reason why they believe I am involved in the incident or activity for which this test is being conducted.

T F 5. I have received a statement setting forth the date, time and location of this examination.

T F 6. I have received a statement setting forth my rights to legal counsel or an employee representative before each phase of the test.

T F 7. I have received a statement setting forth the full nature of the test and type instrument being used.

T F 8. I have received a statement setting forth whether or not the testing area contains any means whatsoever through which the test can be observed.

T F 9. I have received a statement setting forth the fact whether or not the testing area contains any device for recording or monitoring the test and whether or not it will be used.

My answers to the above questions are true and correct.

Date

Examinee Signature

Witness

Please print your name here

Note: The polygraph is an instrument that records continuously, visually, permanently, and simultaneously, changes in cardiovascular, respiratory, and electrodermal patterns as minimum instrumentation standards and is used, or the test results of which are used, for rendering a diagnostic opinion regarding the honesty or dishonesty of an individual.

Glossary

3-Point scale: A simplified version of Backster's 7-point scale for data analysis where scores of a +1, 0, or −1 are assigned to relevant questions based on their comparison to adjacent comparison questions.

7-Point scale: Backster's numerical scoring system where scores ranging from a +3 to a −3 are assigned to relevant questions based on their comparison to adjacent comparison questions. Three major systems use variations of this based on how they select the comparison questions that will be used to generate a score for the relevant question: Backster, Federal Government, and Utah 7-point scoring systems.

Acetylcholine: A neurotransmitter produced by neurons referred to as cholinergic neurons. In the peripheral nervous system, acetylcholine plays a role in skeletal muscle movement, as well as in the regulation of smooth muscle and cardiac muscle. In the central nervous system, acetylcholine is believed to be involved in learning, memory, and mood.

Acquaintance test: A polygraph test, designed to familiarize the examinee with the polygraph, allows the examiner to gain some insight into the examinee's reactions capability and assists in identifying possible examinee countermeasures or augmentations.

Activity monitor: A sensor that detects movements in an examinee that would create an artifact in the physiological data. These sensors can monitor movement when an examinee is seated on it and can also be used to detect foot or arm movements.

Adrenal glands: Two endocrine glands located on top of the kidneys that release hormones such as adrenaline and noradrenaline that can have an effect on a wide variety of body processes and can influence behavior and innervate the sympathetic nervous system.

Adrenaline: A hormone secreted by the adrenal glands, especially in conditions of stress, which increases rates of blood circulation, breathing, and carbohydrate metabolism and prepares muscles for exertion.

Afferent: An anatomical term describing something that conducts or conducts inward or toward something.

Afferent neuron: Sensory nerves that take messages from the environment to the brain.

Air Force Modified General Question Technique (AFMGQT): A test that utilizes 4 relevant questions originally taken from the Army/Reid

269

technique and placed in a Zone format: Irrelevant – Sacrifice Relevant – C – R – C – R – C – R – C – R. Some have modified it using 3 comparison questions with 4 relevant questions: I – SR – C – R – R –C – R – R – C, which still needs additional research for validation.

Alarm reaction: The first body reaction to stress according to Hans Selye's theory of general adaptation syndrome where the body responds to the distress signal sent to the hypothalamus with a burst of energy to help deal with the stressor.

Algorithm: A computerized scoring system that uses formulas for analyzing data.

All Relevant Test (ART): Polygraph test using all relevant questions, which then uses a hurdle approach to follow up major responses with single issue zone comparison tests.

Alveoli: Tiny sacs within our lungs that allow oxygen and carbon dioxide to move between the lungs and bloodstream.

Amygdala: A primitive part of the brain that is the integrative center for emotions, emotional behavior, and motivation.

Analog polygraph instrument: Mechanical and electrical instrumentation before the advent of computerized polygraph systems.

Analog study: A laboratory study using mock crimes, where "ground truth" is known and controlled by the researcher.

Anatomy: The branch of science concerned with the bodily structure of humans, animals, and other living organisms, especially as revealed by dissection and the separation of parts.

Anticlimactic dampening: A Backster theory that states the greatest threat or most salient questions in a test will dampen an examinee's ability to react to questions of lesser threat or importance.

Aorta: The main artery of the body, supplying oxygenated blood in the systemic circulatory system from the heart pumped from the left ventricle.

Aortic semilunar valve: The semilunar valve separating the aorta from the left ventricle that prevents blood from flowing back into the left ventricle. The pumped blood rebounding off the closing of this valve creates the dicrotic notch in the cardio tracing.

Apnea: The temporary stoppage of breathing.

Army Modified General Question Technique (AMGQT): Modified polygraph technique based on Reid's New General Question Technique but using exclusive comparison questions that resulted in a high false-negative rate.

Arousal: An emotional or physiological reaction or response.

Arterioles: Tiny branches of arteries that lead to capillaries that are under the control of the sympathetic nervous system and constrict and dilate to regulate blood flow.

Artery: Muscular-walled tubes forming part of the circulation system by which blood is transported from the heart to all parts of the body.

Arther known lie test: A modified polygraph technique based on Reid's Original General Question Test, where extra irrelevant questions were removed and the concept of a specialized "known truth" comparison question was employed.

Augmentation: Deliberate distortions created by truthful examinees feeling the need to assist the examiner in arriving at the correct determination due to distrust in the procedure or disbelief in the competency of the examiner.

Automatic mode: An electrodermal option of recording that cancels the basil or nominal skin resistance creating a constant baseline showing only the quick changing galvanic resistance or conductance.

Autonomic: Involuntary or unconscious; relating to the autonomic nervous system.

Autonomic nervous system: The part of the nervous system consisting of the parasympathetic and sympathetic nervous systems responsible for control of the bodily functions not normally under conscious control, such as breathing, the heartbeat, and digestive processes.

Axon: The sending part of the neuron that conducts an electrical impulse away from the cell toward the synapse.

Backster's exploratory technique: A multi-issue zone comparison technique allowing four relevant questions to be employed.

Backster's S-K-Y technique: A multifaceted zone comparison technique where a specialized comparison question concerning "suspicion" is used in comparison with a question concerning actual "knowledge."

Backster's "You Phase" technique: A single issue zone comparison technique where all relevant questions deal with the exact same issue and lying to any one of them means lying to all.

Backster's zone comparison techniques: Three tests that employed the theories of Backster: the single issue "You Phase," the multifaceted S-K-Y test, and the multi-issue "exploratory." These techniques were the first formats that placed the comparison questions before the relevant questions and incorporated his psychological concepts of super dampening, anticlimactic dampening, and spot analysis, giving birth to all other zone techniques, including the Federal Zone, Utah Zone, AFMGQT, Matte Quadri-Track, and Integrated Zone Comparison Technique.

Baseline: Tonic level or homeostatic physiological norm.

Baseline arousal: A term used to identify an upward baseline change of the respiration tracing that is supported by research to be indicative of physiological arousal.

Basic emotional factor: A person's day-to-day emotional norm that is part of Backster's theory leading to his belief for "spot analysis."

Behavioral Assessment Interview (BAI): An early forensic interviewing technique developed by Dr. Frank Horvath while associated with John Reid to assess a person's veracity based on verbal and nonverbal behavior.

Black zone: Color code Backster assigned to symptomatic questions.

Blocking: A term in polygraph that indicates involuntary stoppage of breathing.

Blood pressure: The pressure the blood in the circulatory system exerts on the walls of the vessels it travels in, often measured in millimeters for diagnosis since it is closely related to the force and rate of the heartbeat and the diameter and elasticity of the arterial walls. Increases in blood pressure are indicative of physiological arousal.

Blood volume: Is the volume of blood in the circulatory system of any individual affected by cardiac output as well as vasoconstriction and dilation, which is one of the factors effecting blood pressure.

Brachial artery: A major blood vessel located in the upper arm and is the main supplier of blood to the arm and hand. This is usually the preferred location for placement of the blood pressure cuff during a polygraph examination.

Brain: The brain is an organ that serves as the center of the nervous system in all vertebrate, including humans. Its function is to exert centralized control over the other organs of the body by generating patterns of muscle activity and by driving the secretion of chemicals called hormones. This centralized control allows rapid and coordinated responses to changes in the environment.

Brain fingerprinting: A forensic science technique that uses electroencephalography (EEG) to determine whether specific information is stored in a subject's brain.

Brain stem: The brainstem is the region of the brain that connects the cerebrum with the spinal cord. It consists of the midbrain, medulla oblongata, and the pons. Motor and sensory neurons travel through the brainstem allowing for the relay of signals between the brain and the spinal cord. The brainstem coordinates motor control signals sent from the brain to the body. The brainstem also controls life supporting autonomic functions of the peripheral nervous system.

Bronchi: Bronchi are the main passageway into the lungs. When someone takes a breath through their nose or mouth, the air travels into the larynx. The next step is through the trachea, which carries the air to the left and right bronchus.

Buffer question: A type of question containing incorrect information in a peak of tension test format.

Capillary: Tiny hair like blood vessels that connect the smallest arteries (arterioles) to the smallest veins (venules). Capillaries form a network throughout the body for the exchange of oxygen, metabolic waste products, and carbon dioxide between blood and tissue cells.

Cardiac cycle: A complete heartbeat from its generation to the beginning of the next beat, including the diastole, the systole, and the intervening pause.

Cardiac output: The volume of blood pumped per minute by each ventricle of the heart. Cardiac output is affected by stroke volume (the amount of blood pumped from a ventricle in a single heartbeat) and minute volume (heartbeats per minute).

Cardio Activity Monitor (CAM): An electrical device using a transducer to monitor blood volume changes and heart rate when attached to the thumb.

Cardio component: The polygraph component used to monitor cardiovascular activity such as changes in mean blood pressure, blood volume, and heart rate.

Case intensity factor: A concept that Backster used to aid in determining the reliability of a polygraph examination based on the degree of punishment a person could receive for their crime and ranked from greatest to least by life, liberty, security, and reputation.

Cell: The smallest structural and basic functional unit of an organism, typically microscopic and consisting of cytoplasm and a nucleus enclosed in a membrane. Microscopic organisms typically consist of a single cell, which is either eukaryotic or prokaryotic.

Central Nervous System (CNS): The part of the nervous system that in humans consists of the brain and spinal cord, to which sensory impulses are transmitted and from which motor impulses pass out, and that coordinates the activity of the entire nervous system.

Chart: The recording of the physiological data collected by the polygraph instrumentation.

Chart analysis: The interpretation of physiological data collected during a polygraph examination manually and/or by computerized algorithms.

Circulatory system: The circulatory system, also known as the cardiovascular system or vascular system, is an organ system that permits blood to circulate and transport nutrients and oxygen to the cells in the body and remove carbon dioxide and wastes from it.

Classical conditioning: The classical conditioning (also known as Pavlovian conditioning) is a learning process in which a neutral stimulus takes on the properties of an unconditioned stimulus and can elicit the unconditioned response by itself.

Cognitive dissonance: The state of having inconsistent thoughts, beliefs, or attitudes, especially as relating to behavioral decisions and attitude change.

Comparative response question: The original name given by John Reid to a polygraph question that is now identified as a comparison question.

Comparison question: A polygraph question used to compare to a relevant test question. They include both probable lie questions (PLC) and specialized comparison questions, which may be technique specific such as suspicion (Backster and IZCT), known truth (Arther), known lie (Marcy), and the directed lie (DLC).

Comparison question technique: A polygraph format that utilizes physiological reactions to comparison questions to compare to physiological reactions in relevant questions in analyzing the data and making polygraph question and or test determinations.

Compensation: The process of making amends for something. Physiological compensation is the automatic changes in systems or organs in the body to make up for losses in those systems or organs in an attempt to maintain balance and return to a homeostatic norm.

Computerized Voice Stress Analyzer (CVSA): Technology with no scientific research said to record psychophysiological stress responses identified as microtremors that are allegedly present in the human voice when a person experiences psychological distress in response to a stimulus, such as a question.

Concealed Information Test (CIT): A series of peak of tension tests where each chart contains a different aspect of a crime and critical key question. While the questions are reviewed, the examinee never knows the actual question order and the position of the key question changes in each chart. Data analysis is performed based solely on electrodermal activity.

Conductance: The degree to which an object conducts electricity.

Conductivity: A measure of a material's ability to conduct an electrical current.

Confirmatory test: A polygraph test used to confirm the statement of an examinee that could be a suspect, witness, and in some occasions a victim.

Construct validity: The appropriateness of inferences made on the basis of observations or measurements, specifically whether a test measures the intended construct.

Containment team: In postconviction situations the containment team consists of members from law enforcement (parole or probation), therapy, and polygraphy responsible for protecting the community and society by attempting to ensure against recidivism.

Control question: Earlier term in polygraph evolution to describe a comparison question.

Control question technique: Earlier term in polygraph evolution to describe a comparison question technique.

Countermeasures: Deliberate distortions created by a nontruthful polygraph examinee in hopes of causing a false-negative or inconclusive outcome.

Credibility assessment: The use of multiple disciplines to determine the veracity of a person or statement that may include forensic statement analysis, psychological projective tests, response time, verbal behavior, nonverbal behavior, and psychophysiological data.

Dampening effect: Anything that reduces an examinees nervousness, fears, or anxieties done deliberately by the examiner or due to examiner error and includes Backster's theories of anticlimactic dampening and super dampening.

Data analysis: The interpretation of physiological data collected during a polygraph examination manually and/or by computerized algorithms.

Deception Indicated (DI): A polygraph conclusion that an examinee was not truthful in a single issue examination based on a validated method of analysis.

Deliberate distortion: Changes in physiology from homeostatic norm deliberately created by the examinee as a countermeasure or augmentation, and not due to autonomic arousal or compensation.

Demonstration test: A polygraph test designed to familiarize the examinee with the polygraph, allow the examiner to gain some insight into the examinee's reactions capability, and assist in identifying possible examinee countermeasures or augmentations.

Dendrite: The receiving part of a neuron.

Dermis: The inner layer of the two main layers of the skin. The dermis has connective tissue, blood vessels, oil and sweat glands, nerves, hair follicles, and other structures. It is made up of a thin upper layer called the papillary dermis, and a thick lower layer called the reticular dermis.

Diaphragm: A sheet of internal skeletal muscle that separates the thorax, or chest, from the abdomen and is the major muscle involved in breathing.

Diastole: The part of the cardiac cycle when the chambers of the heart are filling; often described as the heart relaxing, and creating the downward stroke of the cardiac cycle created on the polygraph chart.

Dicrotic notch: An upward movement in the diastolic stroke of the cardio tracing due to blood that was pumped rebounding off of the closing aortic semilunar valve.

Differential salience: A description to replace the traditional definition of "psychological set," which described examinees focusing on those questions of greatest immediate threat, to the varied degrees of importance an examinee places on various questions in an examination based on the degree of intensity emitted to different questions in a polygraph test.

Directed Lie Comparison (DLC) question: A question where the examiner instructs the examinee to answer a question, such as "Have you ever broken a traffic law?" with a lie ("No") so he could use the response to compare it with the response emitted to the relevant question. While some in the profession perceive this as a politically correct way to develop a question for comparison to the relevant questions and eliminates the skill necessary for a professional examiner to develop and introduce a probable lie comparison question, others in the profession believe this creates false-negative outcomes.

Distortion: Changes in polygraph data being collected not caused due to physiological arousal or relief.

DodPi bi-spot zone comparison technique: A federal single issue zone utilizing just two relevant questions, as originally taught by Backster and often incorrectly described as a Bi-Zone.

DodPi zone comparison technique: More commonly now referred to as the Federal Zone Comparison Technique, since DodPi has undergone name changes. The test employs three relevant test questions, often with the third relevant question dealing with a secondary issue, such as knowledge.

Duration: The entire length of time a reaction takes, from start to finish.

Dyspnea: Difficult or labored breathing.

Earlier in life control question: Term that has been replaced with comparison question.

Eccrine sweat gland: The major sweat glands of the human body, found in virtually all skin, with the highest density in palms and soles, then on the head, but much less on the trunk and the extremities.

Efferent neurons: Generally used to describe motor neurons taking messages from the brain and spinal cord to the various muscles and organs of the body.

Ego defense mechanisms: Ego coping techniques described by Freud that reduces anxiety arising from satisfying the wants of the id while not offending the moralistic character of the superego.

Electrodermal Activity (EDA): The property of the human body that causes continuous variation in the electrical characteristics of the skin.

Electrodermal Response (EDR): Electrical changes in the skin measured by skin resistance, conductance, or potential.

Embarrassing Personal Question (EPQ): A question, usually of a sexual nature, used to determine an examinee's potential to react early in the development of polygraph.

Empirical Scoring System (ESS): Simplified numerical scoring system that doubles the value of the EDR over that of the other components, regardless of the examinee's overall reaction capability to the various physiological indices being collected.

Epidermis: The upper or outer layer of the two main layers of cells that make up the skin.

Epinephrine: More commonly known as adrenaline that is a hormone secreted by the medulla of the adrenal glands. Strong emotions such as fear or anger cause epinephrine to be released into the bloodstream, which causes an increase in heart rate, muscle strength, blood pressure, and sugar metabolism. This reaction, known as the "flight or fight response," prepares the body for strenuous activity.

EPPA: Employee Polygraph Protection Act of 1988, which severely limited the use of polygraph testing to the private sector.

Eupnoea: Normal breathing.

Evidence statement test: A testing technique introduced by Dr. Stanley Abrams to be utilized in very emotional tests or test requiring very emotional language.

Evidentiary examination: Polygraph examination requiring accuracy above 90%, with less than a 20% inconclusive rate, since it is being performed to be presented as evidence in a judicial proceeding.

Examination: The entire process of a polygraph test from the examinee's arrival to the collection and analysis of collected data.

Exclusive comparison question: Probable lie comparison question introduced by Backster that excludes the time period of the commission of the crime.

Exhaustion: The final stage of Hans Selye's general adaptation syndrome theory, where the body's energy is depleted; corresponds to the "waning effect" in Backster's basic emotionality factor and his argument for "spot analysis."

Exploratory test: A multi-issue polygraph test that can be used for screening tests or exploring different levels of possible criminal involvement.

External reliability: External reliability refers to the extent to which a measure varies from one use to another. In polygraph it refers to the consistency in data collected by a number of charts.

External respiration: The exchange of gases inhaled into the lungs (oxygen and nutrients) for carbon dioxide and wastes from the blood to be exhaled.

External validity: The extent to which the results of a study can be generalized to other situations and to other people.

Extrasystole: A premature contraction of the heart that is independent of the normal rhythm of the heart and that arises in response to an impulse in some part of the heart other than the normal impulse from the sinoatrial (SA) node.

Face validity: The degree to which a procedure, especially a psychological test or assessment, appears effective in terms of its stated aims.

False negative: A deceptive examinee incorrectly determined to be truthful.

False positive: A truthful examinee incorrectly determined to be deceptive.

Federal Rules of Evidence 702: The Supreme Court in the 1998 case of *William Daubert v. Merrell Dow Pharmaceuticals* replaced the Frye standard of "general acceptance," with the Federal Rules of Evidence as the standard for expert testimony. *A witness who is qualified as an expert by knowledge, skill, experience, training, or education may testify in the form of an opinion or otherwise if: (a) the expert's scientific, technical, or other specialized knowledge will help the trier of fact to understand the evidence or to determine a fact in issue; (b) the testimony is based on sufficient facts or data; (c) the testimony is the product of reliable principles and methods; and (d) the expert has reliably applied the principles and methods to the facts of the case.*

Federal zone comparison test: A zone comparison test employing three comparison questions and three relevant test questions, often with the third relevant question dealing with a secondary issue, such as knowledge.

Field research: Polygraph research studies utilizing actual field examinations for data. These examinations have greater intensity than analog studies, but lack "ground truth."

Fight-flight freeze response: The "fight-flight response" is now being identified as the "fight, flight or freeze response," in deference to the fact that instead of fighting or fleeing, we often tend to freeze (like a deer in the headlights) in traumatic situations. Backster, in 1979 at an APA seminar, stated that what we see as reactions on a polygraph test are rarely what we would expect from "fight or flight," but more likely due to the examinee "holding and hoping," his way of describing "freezing."

fMRI: Functional magnetic resonance imaging or functional MRI (fMRI) is a functional neuroimaging procedure using MRI technology that measures brain activity by detecting changes associated with blood flow. This technique relies on the fact that cerebral blood flow and neuronal activation are coupled.

Focused interview: Analogous to posttest interview or interrogation.

Forebrain: The anterior part of the brain, including the cerebral hemispheres, the thalamus, and the hypothalamus.

Forensic Assessment Interview Technique (FAINT): Pretest interview format used to analyze nonverbal behavior, projective analysis of unwitting verbal cues, and forensic statement analysis.

Forensic psychophysiologist: Polygraph examiner.

Forensic psychophysiology: Polygraph.

Format: The actual rules involving the selection and order of questions used in a polygraph test.

Frye standard: The first Supreme Court ruling on polygraph that denied expert testimony in the 1923 case of *Frye v. United States* based on the "general acceptance" rule. Frye was prosecuted and found guilty of murder, and William Marston's "discontinuous blood pressure test" for the defense was not admitted.

Galvanic Skin Conductance (GSC): Changes in the conductance of an electrical current by the skin.

Galvanic Skin Response (GSR): The property of the human body that causes continuous variation in the electrical characteristics of the skin. Historically, electrodermal activity (EDA) has also been known as skin conductance, galvanic skin response (GSR), electrodermal response (EDR), psychogalvanic reflex (PGR), skin conductance response (SCR), and skin conductance level (SCL). The long history of research into the active and passive electrical properties of the skin by a variety of disciplines has resulted in an excess of names, now standardized to electrodermal activity (EDA). The traditional theory of EDA holds that skin resistance varies with the state of sweat glands in the skin. Sweating is controlled by the sympathetic nervous system, and skin conductance is an indication of psychological or physiological arousal. If the sympathetic branch of the autonomic nervous system is highly aroused, then sweat gland activity also increases, which in turn increases skin conductance. In this way, skin conductance can be a measure of emotional and sympathetic responses.

Gland: An organ in the human body that secretes particular chemical substances for use in the body.

Global analysis or evaluation: Analyzing the polygraph data as a whole, rather than in segments of reactions at question "spots." A very early method of data analysis that is still employed by some and appears to be more valuable in assessing data from peak of tension tests and relevant–irrelevant tests.

Greater circulatory system: Also known as the systemic circulatory system that is the circulation of the blood to all parts of the body except the lungs. Systemic circulation transports oxygenated blood away from the heart through the aorta from the left ventricle where the blood has been previously deposited from the pulmonary circulatory system.

Green zone: Color code designated to the comparison question by Backster.

Ground truth: A term used in various fields to refer to information provided by direct observation as opposed to information provided by inference. In polygraph research analog/laboratory studies have "ground truth," meaning that those participants in an experiment who are telling the truth and not telling the truth are known.

Guilt: An internalized message we learn from our parents that teaches us when we do wrong we are unlovable; a message we then use to mentally punish ourselves when we compromise our own standards of conduct or have violated a moral standard and feel significant responsibility for that violation.

Guilt complex: An early theory in polygraph that there may be some individuals who would react to any accusatory question.

Guilt complex question: A question dealing with a fictitious crime, described in a way that the examinee knows it is a crime they did not commit. Reid used it in his technique when an examinee emitted large reactions to both comparison and relevant questions to try and determine if the examinee was a guilt complex reactor. Arther at one time used the question in nonemployee crimes as a specialized comparison question.

Guilt complex test: A test in the Reid technique where questions about a fictitious crime are mixed with actual crime questions under investigation when a person showed strong reactions to both the comparison and relevant questions in previous charts. If the examinee still reacts strongly to the actual crime questions but does not show significant reactions to the guilt complex questions, it is an indication of deception.

Guilty Knowledge Test (GKT): A peak of tension researched by Dr. David Lykken where the question order and changing position of the "key" question are never known to the examinee.

Habituation: The diminishing of a physiological or emotional response due to a frequently repeated stimulus or question.

Heart: A muscular organ in humans, which pumps blood through the blood vessels of the circulatory system.

Herring–Bruer reflex: Named for Josef Breuer and Ewald Hering, it is a reflex triggered to prevent overinflation of the lung. Pulmonary stretch receptors present in the smooth muscle of the airways respond to excessive stretching of the lung during large inspirations.

Hindbrain: The lower part of the brainstem, comprising the cerebellum, pons, and medulla oblongata.

Hippocampus: The elongated ridges on the floor of each lateral ventricle of the brain, thought to be the center of emotion, memory, and the autonomic nervous system.

Holding: Term used to describe an examinee who deliberately stops breathing as an attempt to distort the data.

Homeostasis: The tendency of a system, especially the physiological system of higher animals, to maintain internal stability, owing to the coordinated response of its parts to any situation or stimulus that would tend to disturb its normal condition or function. Homeostasis is the property of a system in which variables are regulated so that internal conditions remain stable and relatively constant.

Horizontal Scoring System (HSS): Scoring system innovated in 1984 by Gordon and Cochetti and published in 1987 where all reactions in a parameter were ranked from greatest to least, resulting in less subjectivity in data analysis.

Hormone: A regulatory substance produced in an organism and transported in tissue fluids such as blood to stimulate specific cells or tissues into action.

Hypothalamus: A portion of the brain that contains a number of small nuclei with a variety of functions. One of the most important functions of the hypothalamus is to link the nervous system to the endocrine system via the pituitary gland. The hypothalamus controls body temperature, hunger, important aspects of parenting and attachment behaviors, thirst, fatigue, sleep, and circadian rhythms.

Inconclusive: A determination in a polygraph examination when a decision of truth or deception cannot be made usually because of numerical values that do not meet the criteria necessary for a scientifically accurate decision.

Inhalation: The action of inhaling.

Inhalation exhalation ratio (I/E Ratio): A ratio of the time in a cycle of breathing involved in inhaling versus exhaling; reported in 1914 by Dr. Benussi who found that when breathing went from a normal I/E ratio (3:5) to a shortened time of inhalation and longer time of exhalation (2:6), it was a reliable indication of deception.

Inside issue: Matte theory that false-negative outcomes may be due to an innocent examinee's fear of error. Therefore, he uses a set of specialized questions where he compares the comparison question "fear of error" with the relevant question "hope of error."

Instant offense investigative test: PCSOT examination where additional information or behaviors in context with the crime of conviction seem necessary even though there are no allegations covering information about the number of times acts were performed, whether there were hands-on acts or force used. These examinations are administered as multifaceted or multi-issue type of examinations using a hurdle approach, or series of single issue exams.

Instant offense tests: Also referred to as "index tests," which are polygraph examinations utilized in PCSOT testing when the offender is in denial of their crime of conviction, or key aspects of the crime. This test may confirm the offender's innocence or assist in breaking through a guilty offender's denial to assist the therapist in optimizing treatment. Ideal format used is a single issue zone, where the frame of reference is preconviction information such as case facts, victim statements, and police reports and the time of reference for polygraph questions is the time of the crime.

Integrated Zone Comparison Technique (IZCT): A flexible zone comparison technique with crucial modifications that can be used in any type of examination.

Intercostal muscles: A group of muscles that run between the ribs, and help form and move the chest wall. The intercostal muscles are mainly involved in the mechanical aspect of breathing. These muscles help expand and shrink the size of the chest cavity to facilitate breathing.

Internal respiration: Occurs in the metabolizing tissues, where oxygen diffuses out of the blood and carbon dioxide diffuses out of the cells.

Interrogation: A focused interview with the goal of obtaining an admission or confession.

Investigative examination: Defined by the APA as a polygraph examination for which the examination is intended to supplement and assist an investigation and for which the examiner has not been informed and does not reasonably believe that the results of the examination will be tendered for admission as evidence in a court of record. Types of investigative examinations can include applicant testing, counterintelligence screening, and postconviction sex offender testing, as well as routine multiple-issue or multiple-facet criminal testing. Investigative examinations are required to be conducted with a testing and analysis technique that has been validated through published and replicated research.

Irrelevant question: A question used in the beginning of most polygraph formats to establish a normal physiological baseline in the test or reestablish a norm due to a distortion or other interruption during the collection of data. These questions have nothing to do with the matter under investigation, and are often background type questions that should not evoke physiological arousal.

Key question: The correct information that only the guilty person would know in a peak of tension test.

Known Solution Peak of Tension (KSPOT) test: A peak of tension test where only the examiner and guilty examinee would know the "key question."

Kymograph: The chart drive mechanism of an analog polygraph instrument.

Latency: The delay between the beginning of the examiner's question and the examinee's response to it.

Layered Voice Analysis (LVA): A voice stress device that alleges to identify various types of stress levels, cognitive processes, and emotional reactions that are reflected in the properties of the voice.

Lesser circulatory system: Also known as the pulmonary circulatory system that is the portion of the cardiovascular system that carries deoxygenated blood away from the heart to the lungs and returns oxygenated blood back to the heart.

Limbic system: A complex system of nerves and networks in the brain, involving several areas near the edge of the cortex concerned with instinct and mood. It controls the basic emotions of fear, pleasure, anger as well as basic drives like hunger, sex, dominance, and parenting.

Lykken scoring: A scoring system utilized in the Concealed Information Test (CIT) where only the electrodermal activity is scored. The greatest electrodermal activity receives a 2, and the next greatest a 1. After all of the charts are administered, if the "key questions" have a total score equal to, or greater than, the number of charts administered, the determination would be that there was "recognition," indicating the examinee has knowledge and/or involvement in the crime.

Maintenance Examination (ME): A PCSOT examination given periodically to an offender to assure he is in compliance with his conditions of treatment and parole/probation.

Marcy technique: A polygraph technique heavily geared at identifying countermeasures using a format influenced by both Reid and Backster.

Matte Quadri-track zone comparison technique: A traditional Backster's Zone Comparison Test where the third comparison–relevant set of questions involves the "fear of error" versus the "hope of error."

Medium relevant question: A relevant question dealing with secondary involvement in a crime, such as knowledge and conspiracy, which was color coded by Backster as red over yellow.

Medulla oblongata: The continuation of the spinal cord within the skull, forming the lowest part of the brainstem and containing control centers for the heart and lungs.

Mental countermeasures: Mental attempts to alter the reactions in a polygraph test.

Midbrain: A portion of the central nervous system associated with vision, hearing, motor control, sleep/wake, arousal (alertness), and temperature regulation.

Minute volume: The amount of cardiac output in a minute.

Monitor examination: A PCSOT examination involving whether an offender has reoffended since their release or last polygraph examination or a single issue test performed on an issue previously found to have significant reactions in a maintenance examination. It is also referred to as a sexual offender monitor examination (SOME).

Motor nerve: Generally used to describe efferent neurons taking messages from the brain and spinal cord to the various muscles and organs of the body.

Multifaceted test: A polygraph examination with various degrees of possible involvement in the same crime, for example, "Did you plan?" "Do you know who?" "Did you?"

Multi-issue test: A polygraph examination where the relevant questions have anything to do with each other, such as a preemployment screening tests where you may have relevant questions dealing with illegal drug use, undetected serious crime, theft, loyalty, etc.

Myelination: A term in anatomy that is defined as the process of forming a myelin sheath around a nerve to allow nerve impulses to move more quickly.

Nerve: Fibers that transmit impulses of sensation to the brain or spinal cord and impulses from the brain or spinal cord to the muscles and organs of the body.

Nerve impulse: An electrical signal that travels along an axon due to a sudden change in the voltage across the membrane of the axon.

Neuron: Cells of the nervous system, called nerve cells or neurons, are specialized to carry "messages" through an electrochemical process.

Neurosis: A relatively mild mental illness that is not caused by organic disease, involving symptoms of stress (depression, anxiety, obsessive behavior, hypochondria) but not a radical loss of touch with reality.

Neurotransmitter: A chemical substance that is released at the end of a nerve fiber by the arrival of a nerve impulse and, by diffusing across the synapse or junction, causes the transfer of the impulse to another nerve fiber, a muscle fiber, or some other structure.

Neutral question: See *Irrelevant Question*.

No call: A polygraph determination where the examiner is unwilling to make a final call even though the analysis supports it due to other influences the examiner perceives could have affected the data.

No Deception Indicated (NDI): A polygraph conclusion that an examinee was truthful in a single issue examination based on a validated method of analysis.

No Significant Reactions (NSR): A polygraph conclusion that an examinee did not show any consistent strong reactions to relevant questions in a multi-issue or multifaceted examination based on a validated method of analysis.

Node of Ranvier: Also known as myelin sheath gaps, are periodic gaps in the insulating myelin sheaths of myelinated axons where the axonal membrane is exposed to the extracellular space, which facilitates the rapid conduction of the impulse.

Numerical analysis: The assignment of numbers to the observable differences of physiological reactions to questions in a polygraph test to assist in a more objective and scientifically reliable determination.

Onset: The beginning of something, in polygraph generally identifying when a physiological reaction occurs.

Operant conditioning: The expectation of receiving a reward or punishment for an act based on previous experiences.

Organ: A part of an organism that is typically self-contained and has a specific vital function, such as the heart or liver in humans.

Orienting response: Also called "orienting reflex," is an organism's immediate response to a change in its environment; a reaction to a novel or significant stimuli. Researchers have found a number of physiological mechanisms associated with OR, including changes in phasic and tonic skin conductance response (SCR) and heart rate. These observations all occur within seconds of stimulus introduction.

Outside issue: Refers to symptomatic questions that are designed to ensure issues outside the test are not interfering with an examinee's ability to focus on the questions within the test format.

Outside issue question: Traditional Backster's questions to ensure "super dampening" did not affect the examination, such as "Do you believe me when I promise not to ask a question in this test I have not gone over word for word?" and "Even though I promised I would not, are you afraid I will ask a question in this test I have not gone over word for word?" In the IZCT the question has been simplified to "Do you understand I will only ask the questions I reviewed?"

Padding question: Another name for "buffer questions" used in peak of tension tests.

Parasympathetic nervous system: Part of the autonomic nervous system, sometimes called the rest and digest system, or housekeeper, since the parasympathetic system conserves energy as it slows the heart rate and thoracic activity, as it increases abdominal activity and relaxes sphincter muscles in the gastrointestinal tract.

PDD: An alternate name for polygraph: psychophysiological detection of deception.

Peak of Tension (POT) test: POT was developed by Keeler and characterized as a "recognition test" used in criminal investigations. The POT test uses a set of five to nine questions asking if the examinee knows about a particular detail related to a crime, one of which (key) only the guilty person would know. The questions and the sequence in which they are asked are reviewed with the subject in the pretest interview. The key question with the true detail is usually presented in the middle of the sequence, so that the examinee's physiological reactions will increase up to the key question, where they will reach a peak, hence the name, and fall back down again.

Pedophile: A person who is sexually attracted to children.

Peripheral nervous system: The nervous system outside the brain and spinal cord.

Personal coding: The redefining of the crime under investigation by a guilty person so it is no longer the crime under investigation by the examiner.

Phasic response: A physiological response from homeostatic norm due to a stimulus.

Photoplethysmograph (PPG): A devise usually attached to the finger that monitors the change in blood volume from the skin caused by the pressure pulse by illuminating the skin with a light from a light-emitting diode (LED) and then measuring the amount of light either transmitted or reflected to a photodiode.

Phrenic nerve: A nerve that originates in the neck (C3–C5) and passes down between the lung and heart to reach the diaphragm. It is important for breathing, as it passes motor information to the diaphragm and receives sensory information from it.

Physiology: The branch of biology that deals with the normal functions of living organisms and their parts.

Plethysmograph: A plethysmograph is an instrument for measuring changes in volume within an organ or whole body (usually resulting from fluctuations in the amount of blood or air it contains).

Pneumograph: The component in the polygraph instrument that measures breathing activity by monitoring upper body movements of the chest and stomach.

Polygraph: The modern definition is an instrument that simultaneously records respiration, electrodermal activity, cardiovascular activity, and body movements

Polygraph Sensitivity Test (PST): A simple demonstration or stimulation test by Arther utilizing three colored cards.

Polygraph Validation Test (PVT): Also referred to as a polygraph verification test, which was introduced to identify possible false-positive results in an initial comparison question polygraph examination or assist in overcoming a guilty examinee's denials and in identifying countermeasures.

Polygraphist: A person that conducts polygraph examinations; also referred to as a "polygraph examiner" or a "forensic psychophysiologist."

Pons: The part of the brainstem that links the medulla oblongata and the thalamus. The pons serves as a message station. It helps relay messages from the cortex and the cerebellum. Without the pons, the brain would not be able to function because messages would not be able to be transmitted or passed along. It also plays a key role in sleep and dreaming.

Positive control technique: A variation by Sylvestro Reali of the Morton Sinks Yes–No Technique where each test question is asked twice, once with the examinee's subjective truth and then with their subjective lie. The technique can be applied to any test format; however, it has a high false-negative rate and inconclusive rate. It is used as an anticountermeasure test in the IZCT technique.

Postconviction Sexual Offender Testing (PCSOT): Polygraph examinations used to assist parole/probation and therapists in dealing with the treatment and containment of sexual offenders while on parole or probation.

Posttest interview: A focused interview after a polygraph examination has been completed to inform an examinee of their test results and allow them the opportunity to explain any significant reactions or a deceptive test outcome.

Preemployment test: A screening examination to attempt to select the best applicants by predicting their future behavior based on their past behavior and integrity.

Preliminary Credibility Assessment Screening System (PCASS): The Preliminary Credibility Assessment Screening System is a handheld computer or personal digital assistant utilized by the U.S. government that attempts to measure stress to decide if a subject is telling the truth by monitoring electrodermal activity and cardio activity via a plethysmograph. Initially the "p" stood for "portable," but it became "preliminary" to emphasize the idea that the device shouldn't be used to make final decisions of truth or deception.

Premature Ventricular Contraction (PVC): Premature ventricular contractions (PVCs) are premature heartbeats originating from the ventricles of the heart. PVCs are premature because they occur before the regular heartbeat.

Preparatory question: The initial part of the buffer and key questions in a peak of tension test that is common to all of the questions. For example, "Regarding that man that lost his life last week, …?"

Pretest interview: The interview prior to the collection of physiological data in a polygraph test. This will include explaining an examinee's rights concerning the test, ascertaining the examinee's consent to take the test, reviewing the examinee's background including medical and psychological information to ensure they are fit to take the test, and reviewing the details of the case and issues to be resolved.

Prior Allegation Evaluation Test (PAE): A PCSOT polygraph examination used to assist parole/probation and therapist in better understanding an offender's actual actions in their crime of conviction where many of the victim's allegations were dropped as part of the judicial proceedings.

Probable Lie Comparison (PLC) question: Questions credited to John Reid that are broad in scope and deal with issues similar but less threatening than the relevant issue to be resolved. They are questions one would expect everyone to truthfully answer, "Yes." In reality, they create a threat to innocent examinees, making them feel as if they must lie.

Psychological set: Backster's theory that an examinee will focus his mind on those questions in a polygraph test that holds the greatest immediate threat to his or her general well-being. (In 1980, Gordon added: "or greatest interest.")

Psychological stress evaluator: The first instrument purported to measure and to portray graphically differential levels of distress in human speech due to microtremors that can be used to detect deception.

Psychological veracity examination: Another name given for polygraph.

Psychology: The scientific study of the human mind and its functions, especially those affecting behavior in a given context.

Psychopath: Also referred to as psychopathy, was traditionally defined as a personality disorder characterized by enduring antisocial behavior, diminished empathy and remorse, and disinhibited or bold behavior. It may also be defined as a continuous aspect of personality, representing scores on different personality dimensions found throughout the population in varying combinations. The definition of psychopathy has varied significantly throughout the history of the concept; different definitions continue to be used that are only partly overlapping and sometimes appear contradictory.

Psychosis: Psychosis is a symptom or feature of mental illness typically characterized by radical changes in personality, impaired functioning, and a distorted or nonexistent sense of objective reality.

Pulmonary Circulatory System: The portion of the cardiovascular system that carries deoxygenated blood away from the heart to the lungs and returns oxygenated blood back to the heart.

Purposeful Noncooperation (PNC): A polygraph determination that the data cannot be reliably interpreted due to an examinee's deliberate noncooperation and distortions of the data.

Rank Order Scoring System (ROSS): The Horizontal Scoring System using "Kircher rules" of what constitutes greatest to least reactions.

Rationalization: A defense mechanism in which controversial behaviors or feelings are justified and explained in a seemingly rational or logical manner to avoid the true explanation.

Red zone: Color code assigned by Backster to relevant test questions. Solid red indicated a strong and direct relevant question; red over yellow, a secondary relevant question; and yellow over red, a weak relevant question that sounded important; however, it was not used to determine an examinee's veracity.

Reid general question technique: The inclusion of comparison questions into the R/I technique by Reid. A typical format consisted of four irrelevant, four relevant, and two comparison questions (I, I, R, R, C, I, I, R, R, C).

Relevant–Irrelevant Technique (R/I): A noncomparison question polygraph technique credited to Keeler and Larson as the first polygraph format consisting of only irrelevant and relevant questions. When currently used today, it is done in the area of preemployment screening.

Relevant Issue Gravity (RIG): A theory of Avital Ginton that the difference between truthful and deceptive suspects is the strength by which the suspect's attention is directed, which is dependent on the internal state of mind that the examinee holds.

Relief: A term used in polygraph to indicate physiological compensation to return the body to a homeostatic norm after a reaction.

Resistance stage: The second stage of Hams Selye's theory of how the body deals with stress where the body attempts to resist or adapt to the stressor.

Respiration: Respiration is defined as the movement of oxygen from the outside air to the cells within tissues, and the transport of carbon dioxide in the opposite direction.

Respiration Line Length (RLL): A simple measurement of the length of the respiration line for a fixed period of time. The greater the reaction the shorter the line.

Respiratory blood volume fluctuations: Fluctuations in heart rate and arterial blood pressure induced by respiration, frequently caused by controlled breathing.

Response Onset Window (ROW): The expected time for a valid reaction to occur when a stimulus (question) is presented.

Sacrifice relevant question: Classified by Backster as a weak relevant question usually asked in the very beginning of a format. It is not used in the determination of truth or deception, but employed to avoid potential errors by scoring the first relevant question the examinee hears in the test, which may result for reasons other than deception.

Salience: The state or condition of being prominent. The Oxford English Dictionary defines salience as "most noticeable or important." In polygraph, it is used to explain that examinees react to those questions they perceive as most important to them.

Screening test: Usually a multi-issue preemployment examination, although other areas of investigation may be classified as a screening test.

Searching peak of tension test: A peak of tension test where only the guilty suspect would know the correct answer and the examiner is searching or probing for possible solutions. This was often used in employee theft cases to determine a guilty examinee's total amount of thefts from their company and could also be used to locate stolen goods, a body, or a bomb.

Semilunar valve: The semilunar valves are pocket-like structures attached at the point at which the pulmonary artery and the aorta leave the ventricles. The pulmonary valve guards the orifice between the right ventricle and the pulmonary artery. The aortic valve protects the orifice between the left ventricle and the aorta.

Semirelevant question: See *Sacrifice Relevant*.

Sensitivity: True positive rate; in polygraph it refers to the accuracy of finding deceptive examinees deceptive.

Sensory nerve: A nerve that carries sensory information toward the central nervous system (CNS).

Senter rules: A secondary or two-stage rule introduced by Dr. Stuart Senter for single issue tests to try and reduce inconclusive outcomes.

Sexual History Evaluation I (SHE I): PCSOT therapeutic test focusing on an offender's lifetime history of victimization focused on his or her crime of conviction, to include victim selection, victim access, and the number of victims.

Sexual History Evaluation II (SHE II): PCSOT therapeutic test focusing on an offender's various types of lifetime sexual deviancy.

Silent Answer Test (SAT): A polygraph examination where the examinee is instructed not to answer questions out loud.

Single issue test: A polygraph examination where all of the relevant questions deal specifically on the same thing. Lying to one means the answers to all have to be lies. For example, "Did you shoot John?" "Regarding John, did you shoot him?" "Were the person that shot John?"

Somatic nervous system: Part of the peripheral nervous system associated with skeletal muscle and voluntary control of body movements.

Specificity: True negative rate, in polygraph it refers to the accuracy of finding truthful examinees truthful.

Sphincter: A circular muscle that normally maintains constriction of a natural body passage or orifice and that relaxes as required by normal physiological functioning.

Sphygmomanometer: An instrument for measuring blood pressure, typically consisting of an inflatable rubber cuff that is usually applied to the upper arm of the examinee over the brachial artery to monitor cardiovascular activity.

Spinal cord: The cylindrical bundle of nerve fibers and associated tissue that is enclosed in the spine and connects nearly all parts of the body to the brain. Along with the brain it forms the central nervous system.

Spot: The specific assignment of a relevant test question in a zone as defined by Backster.

Spot analysis: The numerical evaluation of a relevant spot by comparing it to a comparison question located immediately before or after it.

Stimulation test: See *Acquaintance or Demonstration Test.*

Stimulus onset: The initial introduction of a stimulus, such as the asking of a question.

Stroke volume: The amount of blood pumped out of the heart (from the left ventricle to the body) during each contraction measured in mL/beat (milliliters per beat).

Successive hurdle approach: The administration of a more accurate single issue test after an examinee has shown significant reactions to a relevant question in a multi-issue or multifaceted test.

Super dampening effect: Backster's concept that if an examinee has a greater concern about being asked surprise questions about an issue outside of the scope of the test, it may dampen their ability to react to relevant or comparison questions within the test.

Suppression: A reference in polygraph to an examinee taking smaller breaths than normal, thereby receiving less air, which is one of the primary reactions in breathing.

Symptomatic nervous system: A part of the nervous system that serves to accelerate the heart rate, constricts blood vessels, and raises blood pressure. The sympathetic nervous system and the parasympathetic nervous system make up the autonomic nervous system.

Symptomatic question: Traditional Backster's questions to ensure "super dampening" did not affect the examination, such as "Do you believe me when I promise not to ask a question in this test I have not gone over word for word?" and "Even though I promised I would not, are you afraid I will ask a question in this test I have not gone over word for word?" In the IZCT the question has been simplified to "Do you understand I will only ask the questions I reviewed?"

Synapse: A junction between two nerve cells, consisting of a minute gap across which impulses pass by diffusion of a neurotransmitter.

Systemic system: Systemic circulation transports oxygenated blood away from the heart through the aorta from the left ventricle where the blood has been previously deposited from the pulmonary circulatory system.

Systole: The phase of the heartbeat when the heart muscle contracts and pumps blood from the chambers into the arteries. This results in the upward stroke of the cardio tracing in a polygraph examination.

Technique: Everything said and done in a polygraph test from the examinee's arrival to the analysis of the collected data.

Test for Espionage and Sabotage (TES): A multiple-issue test used for screening by the U.S. government.

Thalamus: Two masses of gray matter lying between the cerebral hemispheres on either side of the third ventricle, relaying sensory information, and acting as a center for pain perception.

Time bar: Wording that creates an exclusive comparison question by separating the question from the time period of the relevant issue, such as "Between the ages of 21 and 25...?" and "During the first 25 years of your life...?" (Suspect's age was 28 at the time crime was committed.)

Tissue: An aggregation of morphologically similar cells and associated intercellular matter acting together to perform specific functions in the body.

Tonic level: An examinee's homeostatic norm.

Tonic response: A physiological change indicative of a reaction.

Total test minutes: A Backster's theory that each component in a polygraph examination became more productive during various time periods of the test.

Two-stage rules: See *Senter Rules*.

Utah zone comparison technique: A variation of Backster's ZCT that inserted irrelevant questions between each set of comparison and relevant questions (I, C, R, I, C, R, I, C, R).

Vagus nerve: The tenth cranial nerve, and interfaces with parasympathetic control of the heart and digestive tract. The vagus nerves are paired; however, they are normally referred to in the singular.

Validity: Validity is the extent to which a concept, conclusion, or measurement is well-founded and corresponds accurately to the real world. The validity of a measurement tool (e.g., a polygraph test) is considered to be the degree to which the tool measures what it claims to measure; in this case, the validity is an equivalent to accuracy.

Vasoconstriction: The narrowing of the blood vessels resulting from contraction of the muscular wall of the vessels, in particular the large arteries and small arterioles. The process is particularly important in preventing hemorrhaging and acute blood loss. When blood vessels constrict, the flow of blood is restricted or decreased, thus retaining body heat or increasing vascular resistance. This makes the skin turn paler because less blood reaches the surface, reducing the radiation of heat. On a larger level, vasoconstriction is one mechanism by which the body regulates and maintains mean arterial pressure.

Vasodilation: The widening of blood vessels resulting from relaxation of smooth muscle cells within the vessel walls, in particular in the large veins, large arteries, and smaller arterioles. In essence, the process is the opposite of vasoconstriction, which is the narrowing of blood vessels. The primary function of vasodilation is to increase blood flow in the body to tissues that need it most.

Vein: Vessels that carry blood from the capillaries toward the heart.

Wheatstone bridge: The monitoring of an unknown current coming from the examinee's body by introducing a known current from the polygraph instrumentation, allowing for the monitoring of electrodermal activity.

Window of evaluation: The default time window, which is defined as a measurement of time from response onset to response end. *Not necessarily from stimulus onset.*

Zone: Backster described a polygraph test as a procedure that monitors an examinee's flow of psychological set: the red zone (relevant questions) was to draw the focus of the deceptive, the green zone (comparison questions) to draw the focus of the truthful, and the black zone (symptomatic questions) to ensure the examinee had the ability to focus on the test questions that held the greatest importance or threat to his or her immediate general well-being. Thus, he called his techniques "Tri-Zones."

Zone comparison test: The family of test formats derived from Backster's techniques and theories to include the Air Force MGQT, Federal Zone Comparison Technique, Integrated Zone Comparison Technique, Matte Quadri-Track Zone Comparison Technique, and Utah Zone Comparison Technique.

Index

A

Academy for Scientific Interrogation, 22–23
Academy for Scientific Investigative
    Training, 23–24, 95, 113, 182
Acquaintance test, 82–83, 88, 98–99, 162
Adrenal glands, 66
Afferent neurons, 59
Agreement of cooperation, 98, 190, 193, 245
Air Force Court of Criminal Appeals, 206
Air Force Modified General Question
    Technique (AFMGQT), 94–95
All relevant test (ART), 143
Alveoli, 65
Ambassador, 36–37
American Academy for Polygraph
    Examiners, 23
American Polygraph Association (APA), 1,
    109, 112, 118, 153, 182
Americans with Disabilities Act, 192
AMGQT, *see* Army Mixed General
    Question Technique
Ampere, Andre, 7
Ampere's principle, 11
Analog polygraph instrument
    community inking, 36, 38
    individual/captive inking system, 38
    kymograph, 38–39
    Lafayette Ambassador, 36–37
    mechanical analog instrument
        cardio component, 32–33
        GSR component, 33–35
        pneumo component, 29–32
    multifunction components, 36
    Ultrascribe, 36–37
Analog study, 215
Animal electricity, 7
Anticlimactic dampening, 46, 73–74, 191
Aortic semilunar valve, 64
APA, *see* American Polygraph Association
Apnea, 168–169
Approach–approach conflict, 72

Approach–avoidance conflict, 73
Area under the curve (AUC), 117
Army Mixed General Question Technique
    (AMGQT), 23, 86–87
ART, *see* All relevant test
Artery, 6–7, 63–64
Arther known lie test, 23, 50–51, 86–89
Arther, Richard O., 23
ASIT PolySuite, 113–114, 120, 123, 239–240
ASTM Standards, 211
Autonomic nervous system
    motor nerves, 59
    parasympathetic system, 59–60
    sympathetic system, 59, 61
Avoidance–avoidance conflict, 72
Axciton Computerized System, 39–40

B

Backster, Cleve, Jr., 27
    anticlimactic dampening, 73–74
    basic emotionality factor, 75–76
    case intensity factor, 74
    individual reaction capability, 74
    7-point scale, 177–180
    polygraph technique formatting,
        changes to, 89–90
    psychological set, 70–71, 89
    spot analysis, 75–76
    super dampening, 54, 89
    symptomatic questions, 52, 54, 89
    zone comparison test, 23
        Either-Or Rule, 118
        exploratory, 91–92
        S-K-Y test, 91
        You Phase, 25, 90–92
Barefoot, J. Kirk, 23–24
Baseline arousal, 168, 170–171
Basic emotionality factor (BEF), 70, 75–76
Benussi, Vittorio, 13–14
Blood pressure, 7, 14, 176
Blood pressure cuff, 175